REPRESENTING THE MALE

Gender Studies in Wales
Astudiaethau Rhywedd yng Nghymru

Series Editors
Dawn Mannay, Cardiff University
Rhiannon Marks, Cardiff University
Diana Wallace, University of South Wales
Stephanie Ward, Cardiff University
Sian Rhiannon Williams, Cardiff Metropolitan University

Series Advisory Board
Jane Aaron, University of South Wales
Deirdre Beddoe, Emeritus Professor
Paul Chaney, Cardiff University
Mihangel Morgan, Aberystwyth University
Paul O'Leary, Aberystwyth University
Teresa Rees, Cardiff University

The aim of this series is to fill a current gap in knowledge. As a number of historians, sociologists and literary critics have for some time been pointing out, there is a dearth of published research on the characteristics and effects of gender difference in Wales, both as it affected lives in the past and as it continues to shape present-day experience. Socially constructed concepts of masculine and feminine difference influence every aspect of individuals' lives; experiences in employment, in education, in culture and politics, as well as in personal relationships, are all shaped by them. Ethnic identities are also gendered; a country's history affects its concepts of gender difference so that what is seen as appropriately 'masculine' or 'feminine' varies within different cultures. What is needed in the Welsh context is more detailed research on the ways in which gender difference has operated and continues to operate within Welsh societies. Accordingly, this interdisciplinary and bilingual series of volumes on Gender Studies in Wales, authored by academics who are leaders in their particular fields of study, is designed to explore the diverse aspects of male and female identities in Wales, past and present. The series is bilingual, in the sense that some of its intended volumes will be in Welsh and some in English.

REPRESENTING THE MALE

Masculinity, Genre and Social Context
in Six South Wales Novels

John Perrott Jenkins

UNIVERSITY OF WALES PRESS
CARDIFF
2021

© John Perrott Jenkins, 2021

All rights reserved. No part of this book may be reproduced in any material form (including photocopying or storing it in any medium by electronic means and whether or not transiently or incidentally to some other use of this publication) without the written permission of the copyright owner except in accordance with the provisions of the Copyright, Designs and Patents Act. Applications for the copyright owner's written permission to reproduce any part of this publication should be addressed to the University of Wales Press, University of Wales Registry, King Edward VII Avenue, Cardiff CF10 3NS.

www.uwp.co.uk

British Library Cataloguing-in-Publication Data
A catalogue record for this book is available from the British Library.

ISBN   9781786837783
e-ISBN 9781786837790

The right of John Perrott Jenkins to be identified as author of this work has been asserted in accordance with sections 77 and 79 of the Copyright, Designs and Patents Act 1988.

The publisher acknowledges the financial support of the Books Council of Wales.

Typeset by Mark Heslington Ltd, Scarborough, North Yorkshire
Printed by CPI Antony Rowe, Melksham, United Kingdom

For Steph
and in memory of my mother and father

Contents

Acknowledgements ix

Introduction 1

1 Dominant, Residual, Emergent: Forms and Formations of
   Male Identity in Gwyn Jones's *Times Like These* (1936) 13

2 Genre and the Tribulations of Masculinity in Lewis Jones's
   Cwmardy (1937) 44

3 Investigating Genre and Gender in Menna Gallie's *Strike
   for a Kingdom* (1959) 73

4 Reading Hector Bebb: Masculinity and Mythic Paradigms
   in *So Long, Hector Bebb* (1970) 99

5 Patriarchy, Power and Politics: Masculinities in *Dark
   Edge* (1997) and *Until Our Blood is Dry* (2014) 120

Conclusion 156

Notes 162

Bibliography 189

Index 207

Acknowledgements

I am indebted to Professor Diana Wallace for suggesting that I write this book; to Dr Rob Gossedge who guided it through as a doctoral thesis, on which it is based; to Dr Marina Williamson for being a critical but constructive reader and adviser from the start of this project; to Professor Angela V. John for generously providing background information on Menna Gallie; to Dr Aidan Byrne who so kindly offered me access to his research at an early stage of my own into anglophone Welsh writing, and for friendship thereafter; to Professors Katie Gramich and Jane Aaron for their help and support; and to Lesley Berry for her gift of a copy of an unpublished essay by her father.

I should like to thank Lawrence and Wishart for permission to quote from Lewis Jones's *Cwmardy* (1937); Honno from Menna Gallie's *Strike for a Kingdom* (1959); Parthian from Ron Berry's *So Long, Hector Bebb* (1970) and Kit Habianic's *Until Our Blood is Dry* (2014); and Seren from Roger Granelli's *Dark Edge* (1997). All efforts have been made, without success, to locate the copyright holders of Gwyn Jones's *Times Like These*, and I encourage them to contact me.

I am enormously grateful to the staff at the National Library of Wales, Aberystwyth, for their patience, efficiency and kindness during my work there on the archives of Gwyn Jones and Menna Gallie, and to the staff at both the University of Swansea Library and the Miners' Library for their help in gaining quick access to the Ron Berry archive and invaluable material on Lewis Jones respectively.

Further thanks are due to Sian Rhiannon Williams, and to Llion Wigley, Bethan Phillips, Siân Chapman, Dafydd Jones and Bronwen Swain at the University of Wales Press, whose guidance, help, patience and advice have been truly invaluable. I am also grateful to UWP for permission to include chapters on *So Long, Hector Bebb* and *Strike for a Kingdom* that have appeared in shorter forms in *Fight and Flight: Essays on Ron Berry*, ed. Georgia Burdett and Sarah Morse (Cardiff:

Acknowledgements

University of Wales Press, 2020), and the *International Journal of Welsh Writing in English* (vol. 7. Issue 1. 2020) respectively.

Sarah Chase found the time to read the chapter on *So Long, Hector Bebb* with her usual perspicacity, and suggested several improvements to style. Caitlin Abbey's close reading of an early draft of the Introduction drew attention to those areas needing attention. Anne and John Phillips, and Bridget Baker were instrumental in making the front cover available for reproduction, and Kate Abbey was always there with sound editorial advice. Grateful thanks to them.

And Steph. What can I say? Thanks and thanks again don't begin to cover it.

Cultures which exult in the belief in the intrinsic maleness of such values as control, indifference to feelings and a ruthless pursuit of power produce a psychopathic masculinity from which not merely women but many men turn away.

(Anthony Clare, *On Men: Masculinity in Crisis*)

[F]orms and genres may have long and fascinating histories, not as static and separate but entwined, interacting, conflicting, contesting, playing off against each other, mixing in unpredictable combinations, protean in energy, moving quickly between extremes from pathos to farce, intensity to burlesque, endlessly fertile as narrative, theatricality, and performance.

(John Docker, *Postmodernism and Popular Culture: A Cultural History*)

The creative liberty of writers from peripheral countries is not given to them straight away: they earn it as the result of struggles whose reality is denied in the name of literary universality and equality of all writers as creative artists, by inventing complex strategies that profoundly alter the universe of literary possibilities.

(Pascale Casanova, *The World Republic of Letters*, trans. M. B. Devoise)

Introduction

Masculinity was once regarded as a settled state of being, a nexus of attributes supposedly present in Men that made them different from Women.[1] It was taken to be an arrangement 'Ordained by Nature'.[2] 'Real' men, those engaged in physically taxing and dangerous activities like miners, boxers and soldiers, brought the frisson of danger, strength and an edgy presence to burnish further the allure of masculinity and justify its claim to power. Within the structural arrangement of patriarchal capitalism and its consequent gender asymmetry such as operated in the industrial south Wales Valleys, men dominated public space, and created and organised the means of production, distribution and exchange, while women managed the household economy and brought up the children. It was, as the philosopher and gender theorist Rosi Braidotti states, a 'falsely universalistic model, which results in reducing "difference" to pejoration, disqualification and exclusion'.[3] The historian Deirdre Beddoe had already observed in 1986 that such 'differences' made Welsh women 'culturally invisible'.[4] Welsh men, however, suffered no such handicap. Beddoe records that there was, given their different gender practices from women, a specific image of Welsh men – or, rather, Welshmen, for they appeared to be indistinguishable from each other. Collectivised into one homogeneous group, they were coal miners, rugby players and male voice choristers, instantly identifiable as 'male and mass, [and ...] macho'.[5] They were patriarchal figures exhibiting an unqualified masculine presence. Post-structural feminism and post-industrial decline in Wales have made more visible the hitherto marginalised female presence, but reappraisals of Valleys' fiction challenging this universalistic image of patriarchal empowerment have been less forthcoming.[6] This book subjects six Valleys' novels – *Times Like These* (1936), *Cwmardy* (1937), *Strike for a Kingdom* (1959), *So Long, Hector Bebb* (1970), *Dark Edge* (1997) and *Until Our Blood is Dry* (2014) – to gender-specific reading to argue that within the prevailing assumptions of 'masculinity', it was not only women who were subjected to 'pejoration, disqualification and exclusion'.

The expressive nature of fiction offers an ideal route into examining how cultural influences shaped the representation of male characters in these novels. Focusing on the complex interaction between individual subjects and their phenomenological context, fiction offers an arena where the cultural practices and the individual consequences of performing what is considered normative masculinity can be identified, inspected and discussed from a variety of theoretical perspectives. As I propose to demonstrate, when examined through a gender-specific prism, these novels challenge the image that the coordinates of Valleys' masculinity were uniform and comprehensive, while acknowledging that such coordinates had enormous signifying power during the Valleys' industrial century. When subjected to individual, gender-specific examination, the universal image of 'corporate ranks' of Welshmen,[7] stable in their identity, hegemonic in their patriarchy, and collectively coded by their male-voice choir blazers and rugby-club kit breaks ranks and retreats. The image of the 'heroic' miner served the material demands of patriarchal industrial capitalism and gave the miner in return the small compensation of status, but the image of a transcendent masculinity, generated and promoted by this cultural system, was as unrepresentative of the individual self as it was of the mythic homogenised group. Collectively, the structure of Valleys' industrial capitalism consigned men to labour as expendable wage-slaves, and women to lives of domestic drudgery. Individually, the stable, dominant masculinity expected of the model patriarch imposed an array of desirable but rarely achievable or even consistently identifiable masculine signifiers. In the words of Stephen Whitehead, they often led to the 'pathological and emotionally damaging consequence of striving to live out [an] unattainable masculine behaviour'.[8]

Among the gender theorists whose ideas have greatly influenced the chapters that follow, the work of two, R. W. Connell and Judith Butler, requires some explanation. As a historian whose work melded with the sociology of gender, R. W. Connell was intrigued by how hierarchical power systems such as patriarchy come into being and are sustained through practice. It was from his study of Antonio Gramsci, an Italian Marxist imprisoned by Mussolini for his political sympathies, that Connell evolved his influential theory of the power structures that enabled gender asymmetry. In his *Prison Notebooks*, Gramsci observed that a power system, a hegemony, comes into being when a perfect formulation of directives is matched by a perfect arrangement of the organisms of execution and verification, and by a perfect preparation of the 'spontaneous' consent of the masses who must 'live' those directives, modifying their own habits, their own will, their own convictions to conform with those directives and with the objects which they propose to achieve.[9]

Adapting Gramsci's theory that patriarchal capitalism is an instrument of political control to his own theory that power structures, not nature, determine gendered identity, Connell postulated a form of gendering in *Gender and Power* (1987) that he called 'hegemonic masculinity'. Hegemonic masculinity, he argued, is the most privileged form of masculinity within a patriarchal system, and is always constructed 'in relation to various subordinated masculinities as well as in relation to women'.[10] Because it is a 'perfect formulation of directives' it acquires what Connell describes as 'a social ascendancy achieved in a play of social forces that extends beyond contests of brute power into the organisation of private life and cultural processes'.[11] Further developing Gramsci's arguments into how a power model like patriarchy maintains control, Connell argued that, while this model was not posited on the practice of violence to sustain order, it legalised it as a tactic whenever it was considered necessary – as industrial conflict in these novels clearly verifies. Six years after *Gender and Power*, Connell's landmark *Masculinities* (1993), with its provocatively pluralised title, further defined hegemonic masculinity as 'the accepted answer to the problem of the legitimacy of patriarchy which guarantees (or is taken to guarantee) the dominant position of men and the subordination of women'.[12]

The practices and problematics that emerge from this conjunction of patriarchy and hegemonic masculinity are evident in each of the novels examined. Their mutually beneficial relationship has led to their being sometimes regarded as synonyms for the practice of male power. However, in these novels they may be read as having a symbiotic relationship that facilitated a power structure, rather than being alternative expressions of the same thing. Stephen Whitehead, for instance, suggests that while hegemonic masculinity lubricates the functioning of patriarchy, it differs from its institutional practice 'in that there is less of an essentialist assumption about the outcome'.[13] Patriarchy, Whitehead observes, operates as a structural mode of social organisation posited on gender binaries, where, broadly speaking, men are defined as instrumental, rational and competitive, and females as expressive, emotional and nurturing. Given patriarchy's structural gender asymmetry, it is a monolithic model that leaves relatively little room for diversity. Hegemonic masculinity, by contrast, is more diffusely defined. It is no more than the 'currently accepted strategy' of dominant masculinity,[14] and works by excluding those men whose masculinity falls short because it deviates from whatever the established norm is. The value of hegemonic masculinity to patriarchy consists in its flexibility, so that it may modify over time and be expressed in different forms and in different contexts, from the presence in these novels of a Machiavellian Adam Smith-Tudor in the boardroom to the boxer Hector Bebb in the ring.[15] Hegemonic masculinity, then, is evident in performance while it also eludes simple exposition; it is empty of clarity but simultaneously vibrant with significance. Through its protean nature, it at once demotes those men who do not or cannot conform to its ineffable presence at the same time that it offers a conceptual justification of the patriarchal male as the privileged gender.

Judith Butler's *Gender Trouble* (1990) further developed and underlined the non-essentialist, power-influenced nature of gendered identities in her argument that gender categories emerge through performativity. For Butler, identity is constructed through a series of performances so that the gendered self 'has no ontological status apart from the various acts which constitute its reality'.[16] Given the narrow paradigms of acceptable male definition in Valleys mining culture, the series of performances available was necessarily limited. In the novels I examine, the tensions, both individually and socially, generated by these prescribed roles are externalised by social upheaval in the form of strikes, and internalised in the damaged formation of miners' subjectivity. Miners in these novels are required to perform, negotiate, resist or strive to reconcile the irreconcilable demands of a hierarchical power system where, within a model of industrial capitalism, they are accorded subordinate status at work, while in theory they are patriarchally sanctioned principals at home. Ideologically subservient, and 'feminised', in one context, they are ideologically dominant and 'masculinised' in another. When represented in fiction, and read from a gender-focused perspective, rather than standing as exemplars of a stable patriarchy, figures like Jim and Len Roberts in *Cwmardy* (1937), D. J. Williams in *Strike for a Kingdom* (1959) and Gwyn Pritchard in *Until Our Blood is Dry* (2014) become divided selves, unable to achieve an experiential reconciliation between the personal and public roles they are committed to by the power systems that seek to shape them.

Introduction

One development arising from the growth of gender studies is that masculinity, as John Tosh states, can no longer 'confidently be located in specifically "masculine" contexts of work, family and homosocial networks. Its discursive traces are found in every area of culture and society.'[17] However, it is principally through these three channels – work, family and homosocial bonding – that mining masculinity is exhibited in these novels as conforming to or diverging from certain culturally formulated norms. Individually and collectively they reveal how a model of masculinity satisfying the requirements of industrial capital was imposed on the Valleys and acquired a self-generating momentum. Within this model, the ideals of machismo were nurtured, disseminated and mythologised as the ideal. Illustrated principally through bodily practice requiring strength, courage, skill and endurance, mining masculinity was recognisable in Wales through a range of associated signifiers such as contact sport, especially boxing and rugby, homosocial bonding and dominance of public space.[18] In Gramscian terms, so deeply internalised do such cultural processes become that they acquire the status of normalised standards of behaviour and value to which men should aspire.

The story of the Valleys, of their literature and masculinities is a story of a hybrid industrial society subjected to immense cultural upheaval,[19] and discontinuous with the more settled *gwerin* culture of rural mid-Wales.[20] As M. Wynn Thomas explains, the Valleys are 'a unique society', producing a literature connecting 'the writers' common experience [...] of belonging to a place apart', neither recognisably English nor traditionally Welsh.[21] It is out of this 'unique society' that certain practices and forms of gender definition become distinctive to this particular culture, so that as a consequence 'different types of men and women and different types of masculinity and femininity emerge. There is the possibility of considerable variation depending on people's local circumstances and the way these interact with national and global movements'.[22] Topographically separated from each other, culturally discontinuous from the rest of Wales but united by a single and dangerous industry, socially hybridised but strongly communal, rich in coal but economically exploited, the Valleys therefore constitute a fascinating site, a crucible for examining through its literature the effect which a socio-economic model – patriarchal industrial capitalism[23] – predicated on the concept of the fixed identity of the hegemonic male, has had upon masculinity as a culturally defined construct. As Steffan Courtney-Morgan observes, within the parameters of Valleys' masculinity, 'the experience of emotionality and passivity, nurturing and intimacy was made problematic because of their association with essentially feminine characteristics.'[24] Writing of the restrictions such a structure imposes on the possibilities of autonomous selfhood, and locating it within a system of socio-economic practice, Rosi Braidotti points out that:

> no freedom is possible within capitalism because the axiom of money and profit knows no limit. The system functions axiomatically, which means [...] that it refuses to provide definitions of the terms it works with, but prefers to order certain domains into existence with the addition or subtraction of certain norms or commands.[25]

It is through a 'domain' of industrial capitalism that a 'norm' of masculinity as an expression of power in whatever context shaped the representation of male characters in the six novels comprising this study.[26]

Four chapters of this book subject a single novel, and the fifth chapter two related novels, to a careful gender-specific scrutiny of its male characters. The first chapter examines masculine representation in Gwyn Jones's *Times Like These* (1936), a text that has not fared well when read as an industrial novel, perhaps because Lewis Jones's more dynamic *Cwmardy* was published just a year later. *Times Like These* has enjoyed frequent but brief appearances in surveys of the Welsh industrial novel, but it has never been published in Wales, and although Raymond Williams and Glyn Jones were enthusiasts,[27] critical comment has been more cautious in its judgements. James A. Davies gives credit where he feels it is due, but is perhaps more direct than most in feeling that Gwyn Jones has not 'worked out in fictional terms a coherent relationship with what is, for him, emotionally charged material'.[28] My chapter does not read *Times Like These* principally as an industrial novel focusing on labour relations and industrial conflict, but as a study of masculinities performing within and attempting to accommodate differing tranches of social and cultural process. From this different perspective it becomes a novel where Stephen Knight's guardedly critical comment that Jones's apparently dispassionate approach to his subject is 'sympathetic but crucially distant' becomes less a critique of its emotional detachment than a comment on its evaluative method.[29] Accepting that Gwyn Jones, as the middle-class university lecturer son of a working-class striking miner, is himself personally implicated in the social dynamics the novel studies, I suggest that his novel's imaginative thrust emerges from what Raymond Williams calls 'the complex interrelations between movements and tendencies both within and beyond a specific and effective dominance'.[30] More specifically, the chapter locates masculinity in the novel within the frame of three broad categories of social process that Williams calls the 'dominant', the 'residual' and the 'emergent'. Williams argues that the last two 'in any real process, and at any moment in the process, are significant both in themselves and in what they reveal of the characteristics of the "dominant"'.[31] The chapter focuses principally on four representations of masculinity, each of which is drawn from a differing cultural repository, three of which take the novel outside an industrial context. The 'dominant' masculinity is practised through a repertoire of performative patriarchal rituals in which the mine owner, Sir Hugh Thomas, is a perversion of the Victorian 'man of character', and his henchmen Webber and Henshaw expose how their form of capitalism provides the opportunity for the systemic degradation of the miners they employ. Two 'residual' forms of masculinity, that is masculinities 'formed in the past, but [...] still active in the cultural process',[32] are represented collectively and singly in the pastoral practices of the miners whose values interfuse with recognisable elements of eighteenth-century neo-Augustan communal civility represented through the figure of Denis Shelton. Through them, the grasping forms of industrial capitalism embodied in the dominant characters are critiqued through juxtaposition with the communal pastoral activities of the miners and the more genteel form of patriarchy embodied in Shelton. In the culturally liminal figure of Broddam, an upwardly mobile businessman, the novel constructs a figure engaged in the 'emergent' reformulation and gentrification of his identity. Broddam embodies a figure that recurs in varying forms throughout Valleys' fiction, and through him *Times Like These* examines the challenges of identity facing the ambitious Anglo-Welshman. In his 'process of becoming' within a class-based and capitalist schema,[33] Broddam is anxious to acquire the signifiers of the English 'gentleman', but is equally anxious to avoid humiliating *faux pas*. His Monmouthshire background is significant here for, like Gwyn Jones, he was born in what Katie Gramich describes as, 'a notoriously ambivalent county',[34] neither Welsh nor English at the time. The chapter argues that in Broddam the novel addresses the problematic of the hybridised self, a figure who runs the risk of emerging as a form of colonised 'mimic-man', a shadow figure lacking the substance of an interior landscape.[35] Broddam is not read as a fictionalised *doppelgänger* of Jones, but he arguably represents a study of the possible trajectory and problematics facing a cultural and class hybrid, of which Jones himself was an example. Lewis Jones's *Cwmardy* and *We Live* (1937 and 1939) have been read together as 'a major Marxist contribution from Britain to international industrial fiction'.[36] Chapter 2 approaches *Cwmardy* as generically different from *We Live*, which tells 'the larger story' of 'community radicalisation'.[37] When read less as a doctrinaire text, and with the focus on the gendering of its two principal characters, I argue that the extraordinary achievement of *Cwmardy* lies in its powerfully humanistic critique of how Len and Jim Roberts are, to borrow Rosi Braidotti's graphic terms, 'stuck with the burden of self-perpetuating Being'.[38] Locked into the restrictive patterns of male behaviour required of industrial capitalism – where Jim is confined to self-expression through his 'magnificent body' (*Cwmardy*, p. 11), and the temperamentally passive Len is divided between two incompatible roles – they are offered no possibility of creative self-development but simply a reiterative enactment of limiting, predetermined roles. Through their construction, the novel reveals the paradox of a capitalist system posited on individual autonomy when, in truth, it reduces them to mere functionality.[39] Doctrinally, *Cwmardy* charts the *Bildung* figure Len Roberts from youth to stabilised political activist, rather as Zola does with Étienne Lantier in *Germinal* (published in English in 1894). I argue that the generic form of *Cwmardy* lies in its subversion of the doctrinal *Bildungsroman* with its fabled teleological progression of the protagonist towards a unified political self, to show how Len remains 'a queer lad for his age' (*Cwmardy*, p. 14) whatever his age.

When subjected to a gender-focused reading, Menna Gallie's seemingly innocuous 'whodunnit', *Strike for a Kingdom* (1959), reveals a subversive strategy that may be called 'Sly civility'.[40] Set in the pit village of Cilhendre during the 1926 strike,[41] the novel offers opportunities for bifocal reading in which it encodes a trenchantly anti-patriarchal industrial narrative through seeming acquiescence in the implicit social reassurances expected of the whodunnit. Referencing both Gallie's archive and Gayle Rubin's argument that 'men and women are closer to each other than either is to anything else',[42] the chapter analyses the text's incorporation of Cilhendre male characters into a gender triad with women and children so that subjectively they are barely distinguishable from each other. Indigenous Cilhendre culture is presented in the novel as 'a whole way of life',[43] poorly understood and barely acknowledged by those whose power structures are predicated on a different form of socio-cultural practice. Detaching Welsh miners from ideological socialism and from representations of combative gender acquisition, the novel accommodates them in the seemingly uncontroversial whodunnit genre, whose readership was accustomed to a divertingly transgressive act progressing towards the re-establishment of a stable social order.[44] The novel therefore not only challenges the generic conventions of the whodunnit, but allows its female narrative voice to distinguish representations of Welsh miners from earlier portrayals in Welsh fiction that acknowledged commonly accepted, though not necessarily indigenous, models of masculinity.

As the eponymous Hector Bebb is a boxer for part of the novel, *So Long, Hector Bebb* (1970) is generally placed within the genre of sporting fiction as a novel about a boxer, a genre which, like that of Menna Gallie's whodunnit, presupposes a certain kind of reader reading a generic novel in certain kind of way. Chapter 4 offers a different perspective: that it is both a celebration and a critical inspection of hypertrophic, competitive masculinity for which, at the outset, the elemental and brutal nature of boxing provides a frame of reference. As a figure embodying the characteristics of legendary combative masculinity, Hector Bebb did not spring fully formed like some Platonic conception from Berry's head. Rather, he evolved through several draft narratives in which he is, at various points, an unhappily married patriarch, a promising boxer, father of a disabled son, and a minor criminal, to his final incarnation as an essentialised, mythopoeic figure. Constructed finally through an intertextual collage of classical, English and American mythic archetypes, and representing a strict gender dimorphism, Hector Bebb offers a provocative response to 1960s second-wave feminism. (The coincidental publication of Berry's novel, with its hypertrophic protagonist, and Germaine Greer's *The Female Eunuch* in 1970 is one of literature's less acknowledged ironies.) Unlike the passive striking miners in *Strike for a Kingdom*, Hector Bebb is defined by his somatic agency. In his doomed trajectory from champion boxer to fugitive farm hand, then to wild man living on the moors and his tragic though inevitable early death, the novel addresses the problematic interaction in the elite, 'authentic' male of the civilised and the primitive, the passive and the active, the instinctive and the cerebral. In a text whose narrative fragmentation replicates the existential isolation of the characters and the mutual incompatibility of men and women, inter-gender relationships are presented as unfulfilling, and marriage at best as an invitation to muted domestic discord.

In Roger Granelli's *Dark Edge* (1997) and Kit Habianic's *Until Our Blood is Dry* (2014), the 1984–5 miners' strike is not represented as a temporary rupture in industrial relations but an overture to the virtual disappearance of deep mining in the Valleys, and its consequent effects on masculinity in a post-industrial, impoverished arena.[45] Each novel pairs masculinities connected by a common thread to examine their differences of gender definition through implicit counter-discourses. Focusing its narrative on the divergent trajectories of two half-brothers, Edwin and Elliott Bowles, *Dark Edge* places them on opposing sides of the strike and constructs their narratives through two differing generic forms. Elliott's narrative is examined as a *roman à thèse*, a form 'at once novelistic and demonstrative, narrative and doctrinaire [that] uses fiction in order to impose (or attempt to impose) a "truth" and possibly a mode of being or an action on the reader'.[46] By such means, Elliott's construction as a somatically powerful, thuggish policeman is presented as a study in psychotic patriarchal narcissism endemic in neoliberal consumerism. The striking miner, Edwin, is investigated as an adaptation of a Bakhtinian *Bildung*, and I argue that Edwin progresses through his *chronotopic*,[47] quasi-religious communion with Welsh landscape, quickened by his developing affection for the Englishwoman Kathryn Peters, towards the possibility of a fulfilled, hybridised future.

Until our Blood is Dry is positioned in the tradition of the realistic novel although it also employs a similar antithetical pairing strategy where Gwyn Pritchard and Iwan Jones, connected through the marriage of their children, are diverging representations of patriarchal masculinity, Gwyn's pathologically controlling, Iwan's expressing inter-gender respect and expressive affection. The power struggle between the government and the miners is illustrated discursively through the contrast between Adam Smith-Tudor's powerfully unified, charismatic masculinity representing the ruthless coherence of management, and the political equivocation and grubby lubriciousness of the Labour MP, Harry Cross. And the novel's representation of an unambiguously presented gay relationship, among the first in Welsh mining fiction, portrays the formative impact of employment on gender identification, where the stabilised identity of the gay hairdresser Siggy differs from the crisis of gender definition his partner Matthew Price experiences as a gay miner.

A glance again at the outlines of the novels given above illustrates the generic diversity through which their narratives are transmitted. The theorist John Docker, writing of postmodernism as a liberating force in cultural production, observed that 'Genres are open fields of possibility, not closed books of fixed discursive meaning'.[48] To position the novels in this book within a genre of industrial narrative, and sporting fiction in the case of *So Long, Hector Bebb*, serves a primary purpose of identification, but it does not acknowledge or celebrate their formal invention and hybridity. Docker's point that genres are not 'static and separate, but entwined, interacting, conflicting, contesting, playing off each other' is amply justified:[49] a moment's thought reveals how *Cwmardy* subverts the *Bildungsroman*, *Strike for a Kingdom* manipulates conservative conventions of the whodunnit, and *Dark Edge* adapts two different generic forms to tell two different stories.

Through such hybridised forms, these six novels illustrate how industrial patriarchy in south Wales absorbed the individual person into a manufactured prescription of desirable masculinity to satisfy the demands of a particular socio-economic order. Embedded in the discourses of the novels examined are the consequences of this institutionalising of masculinity. The collapse of heavy industry in south Wales has, M. Wynn Thomas suggests, effected a sundering that is different from, but as radical as, the earlier discontinuity between rural and industrial Wales: where writers now feel a 'sense of being separated from the history of their own community' as they engage with Wales's post-industrial trauma.[50] Yet this is only partially the case. Katy Shaw writes that 'history is not only open to confrontation and revision but is incremental',[51] and there are indications of an incremental literary engagement with, rather than separation from, south Wales's industrial history and the identities its form of patriarchal capitalism imposed. Keith, in Christopher Meredith's *Shifts* (1988), set in a distressed former Welsh steel town, for instance, comes to understand his present circumstances through studying the history of his region. To consolidate his identity, and perhaps forge a new one, he begins to learn Welsh.[52] Dai Smith's kaleidoscopic novel *Dream On* (2013)[53] considers south Wales's history through what he describes as 'the lens of the last century's time-capsule'.[54] Nigel Jarrett's volume of poetry and photographs, *Miners at the Quarry Pool* (2013), draws on his grandparents' lives in their mining community.[55] Owen Sheers's mesmerising dramatic poem for voices, *The Green Hollow* (2016), commemorates the fiftieth anniversary of the Aberfan disaster and gives voices to those who suffered and those who suffer still.[56] Louise Walsh's novel *Black River* (2016) centres on the aftermath of the Aberfan disaster in 1966, and the intrusive presence of London-based reporters as the first anniversary approaches.[57] And in an audacious *tour de force* where history dissolves into fiction and fiction into history, Dai Smith's *The Crossing* (2020) incorporates verbatim much of *Dream On* into a larger story of the coal magnate D. A. Thomas, to connect Wales with America, and its mining past with its uncertain future.[58] As these works illustrate, the Valleys' troubled history, together with the disenfranchised people it engendered, continues to nag its writers into engagement with its recent past, and the tensions of its history. In focusing attention on Valleys' masculinities, this book studies one aspect of it.

1

Dominant, Residual, Emergent: Forms and Formations of Male Identity in Gwyn Jones's Times Like These *(1936)*[1]

Clustered amid other anglophone Welsh novels written within the generic sphere of industrial fiction in the 1930s, *Times Like These* has attracted brief critical comment and predominantly guarded acknowledgement.[2] Perhaps this is the reason for Gwyn Jones's own modest assessment of the novel in 1987, as 'a quiet and honest story about quiet and honest people living their quiet and honest lives in a South Wales mining valley'.[3] Set in a period between 1924 and 1931, and written by a young academic on his return to Wales from England rather than by a politically active figure like Lewis Jones, the novel's perceived lack of passion and absence of ideological centrality have led fellow academics to formulate judgements as non-committal in their phrasing as they believe the text to be in its ideology. Stephen Knight, for instance, regards it as 'judiciously cautious in its judgements',[4] but compared to the 'dynamic hybridised quality' of Gwyn Thomas's fiction, he finds it 'a sombre and somewhat passive account'.[5] For Dai Smith, it is 'scrupulously weighted',[6] while Katie Gramich regards it as a 'well-known south Wales industrial novel'.[7] James A. Davies is less guarded. In an article devoted principally to Gwyn Thomas, he comments that the book is 'marred by a tonal uncertainty pointing to a failure of vision' because Gwyn Jones 'did not wish or was unable to remain in the world of his upbringing'.[8] Scholars on one side see intellectual restraint as the novel's distinguishing feature, and on the other regard the narrative as emotionally incoherent.

When read alongside Lewis Jones's *Cwmardy*, as a dramatic novel of industrial conflict, psychological torment, immiseration, brutality and struggle, *Times Like These* is always likely to be found wanting. But read as a novel examining the performance of differing forms of masculinity working through social, cultural and historical process – including the industrial capitalist process – it has very real value both as a work of fiction and as a product of its times. Raymond Williams, who admired the novel, offers a helpful paradigm for this kind of approach. Writing generally of the intricate layering of historical process, he observes:

> the 'dominant' culture can be judged only alongside the 'residual' and the 'emergent', which in any real process, and at any moment in the process, are significant both in themselves and what they reveal of the characteristics of the 'dominant'.[9]

The values of a 'residual' culture for Williams have been 'effectively formed in the past, but they are still active in the cultural process, not only and often not at all as an element of the past, but as an effective element of the present'.[10] The 'emergent' culture occupies a more liminal position, one in which 'new meanings and values, new practices, new relationships and kinds of relationships are continually being created', although it necessarily seeks to accommodate 'earlier social formations and phases of the cultural process'.[11] When Williams's abstractions are applied to the particularities of masculine representation in *Times Like These*, their concordance becomes immediately helpful in considering the novel through a gender-specific eye. Three mine managers, Sir Hugh Thomas, Henshaw and Webber, emerge as textual critiques of a patriarchal 'dominance' which defines masculinity through the construction of hierarchy and the performance of power. The miners and Denis Shelton, a more sympathetic pit boss, incarnate 'residual' forms of masculinity which 'are significant both in themselves and what they reveal in the characteristics of the "dominant"'. The gender-defining practices of the miners, who significantly are never represented working underground as colliers, are frequently positioned within a residual continuum of collaborative, homosocial pastoral. Denis Shelton, employed as a mining agent,[12] but the second son of a Berkshire landed family, who himself inherits the family estate at the end of the novel, is located within the tradition of eighteenth-century genteel patriarchy and 'politeness'.[13] Notably, the 'residual' masculinities of Shelton and Jenkinstown men are associated with cultural traditions extending beyond the sphere of heavy industry, Shelton by birth, the others by their collectivist pastoral activities, and they complement each other in their contrasts to the dominant, grasping hegemony. The figure of the ambitious businessman, Broddam, who merits at most a passing reference in the small field of comment extant on the novel, becomes, within this frame, an essential component of the text's gendered architecture. Not only does he operate outside the sphere of heavy industry, thereby adding further breadth to the novel's framework, but as an 'emergent' masculinity, he attempts to negotiate the challenges of evolutionary self-formation inherent in a class-based society. Through Broddam the novel illustrates how emergent identity is 'never only a matter of immediate practice (although it is also that); indeed, it depends crucially on finding new forms or adaptations of forms'.[14] Broddam's 'immediate practice' is modulated through his careful study and imitation of Denis Shelton as an example of the 'gentleman'.

Published in 1936, a decade after the strike that impelled its creation, *Times Like These* is at once embedded in the historical process of material production and a personal commentary on it. Pierre Macherey writes that novels are 'influenced by the formal function of the writer and by the problems of his individual existence'.[15] The interfusion of the 'formal function' and the 'individual instance' in Macherey's comment offers an approach to *Times Like These* where an expected emotional cohesion and ideological consistency in the writer are not the principal sources of its value. A gender-specific reading appreciates the formal breadth of its masculine representation and the 'problems' animating the writer's 'individual existence', his own 'emergent' identity – from miner's son to university lecturer – as someone himself negotiating two culturally different worlds. It places the novel not only in its historical context but examines the competing energies in the narrative's own construction of history. In other words, the gendered and social tensions present within *Times Like These* are activated by and reflect the very tensions that bring it into being.[16] As Macherey reminds us, 'a book never arrives unaccompanied',[17] and in Gwyn Jones's case it appears likely that 'the individual instance' – his recollections of the 1926 strike – helped determine the 'formal function' of the construction of the mine managers in the novel.

Times Like These critiques the discourses and ideologies of dominant industrial masculinity through gender-specific representation of three members of pit management: Sir Hugh Thomas, the pit owner and chairman of directors; Henshaw, the Cwm colliery manager; and Webber, the under-manager who later replaces Henshaw. Having little time for the values associated with Denis Shelton's gentlemanly 'politeness', they share patriarchal assumptions of the interconnectedness of power, decisiveness, agency and masculine identity. All three embody textual expressions of industrial hegemony for whom the exercise of systemic, uncompromising control within the coalfield is integral to their perceptions of self. David L. Collinson and Jeff Hearn write of such figures:

> attempts to establish a stable and well-defined sense of masculine identity frequently involve defining oneself and one's masculine/hierarchical difference, status and power through the subjective process of *identifying* with some men [...] while simultaneously *differentiating* themselves from others.[18] (original italics)

None of these three characters is ever seen in the company of a woman, unlike Denis Shelton. And none is situated in a context outside his public role. Presented as Sir Hugh's creatures, Henshaw and Webber identify with and disseminate his patriarchal conceptions of power and pragmatism. To begin with, they exhibit common signifiers. Arguing with Shelton over the crisis in the pits, Henshaw complains, 'Where are the markets? Two years ago we could send seventy-nine millions abroad, this year we'll be lucky to touch fifty.' Webber concurs: 'There must be some way out if we only had the wit to see it' (p. 74–5). Both regard the problem as purely economic; neither questions it as a destabilising, systemic feature inherent in a market-led ideology. Later, the text is careful to identify points of gendered departure in each one. In doing so, it carefully constructs a broadly framed critique of the behavioural norms functioning in a model of monolithic industrial patriarchy which both controls and empowers them. None of them is a complicated character creation, but together they constitute a damning indictment of contemporary industrial practice.

Thoroughly interpellating both Henshaw and Webber into such a system of gender identity, the novel demonstrates how they enact its divisive contradictions. Differentiating themselves from the miners, who, Henshaw tells Shelton, are 'too pig-headed' (p. 76) to understand basic economics, they paradoxically include them in a common cause: 'We've all got to make sacrifices' (p. 75). Needless to say, the common cause is an appeal to an abstraction of nationhood capable of rhetorical manipulation. Without such sacrifices, Webber informs Shelton, 'the country'll lose' (p. 75), the 'country' at once incorporating the miners and their families in its predicament, as it simultaneously excludes them as the enemy within. Henshaw and Webber's appeal to nationhood features as a strategic rhetorical figure employed by agents of the state in later anglophone Valleys' novels. The proto-fascistic sentiments of the police inspector Ernest Evans in *Strike for a Kingdom* (p. 129), for instance, and Adam Smith-Tudor's poisonous fustian in *Until Our Blood is Dry* (p. 96) are later fictional developments of the same power-driven thread, where sacrifice is expected of those with least to give for the benefit of those with most to lose.

When Shelton tells Henshaw that 'some things are more important than figures', Henshaw's mantra that 'You can't get away from figures' (p. 74), is at once a declaration of his own self-proclaiming, no-nonsense pragmatism and a textual pointer of his reduction to mere functionality in a system where 'a man is not seen as a human being [...] but as a unit in the cost of production regulated to maintain profit margins'.[19] The text leaves overt criticism of Henshaw unmarked, exposing his limiting conceptual framework through his own discourse. Having him parade his unflinching resolve and implicitly contrasting it with what he regards as Shelton's milquetoast 'politeness', the novel exposes how he is unable to distinguish between steadfastness and inflexibility, or to recognise any difference between large-scale warfare and an industrial dispute: 'It's like the last war – it wouldn't matter a rap to me personally if fifty Archdukes were shot in different parts of Europe – I shouldn't care much even if they were English – but once I joined up, I went flat out to smash Jerry' (p. 75). So much, then, for his belief in national unity. As the product of a patriarchal model where violence sanctioned by war elides effortlessly into his discourse regarding industrial relations, Henshaw predicates his masculinity on his unwavering intransigency without ever questioning the ethical or proportional principles underlying his pride in his own agency. In Henshaw's construction, *Times Like These* is less concerned with his own reductivism than with its implied consequences on the lives of those he manages.

Although Webber shares a repertoire of gender signifiers with Henshaw, the novel is careful to avoid replication by constructing him as a deviant psychology given licence by the diktat of a patriarchal hierarchy. As David Leverenz comments, 'any intensified ideology of manhood is a compensatory response to fears of humiliation',[20] and Webber illustrates the corrosive effects of such anxiety. His masculinity, like the more fully developed Elliott Bowles's in Roger Granelli's *Dark Edge* (1997), is predicated on the pathological interfusion of power and a form of sado-masochism. Brutal in his dealings with the striking miners, he uses humiliation as a dramatic assertion of his own hegemony:

> A ridiculous regulation of the dole authorities was that every collier had to go to the pit once a week and have a stamp on his card to the effect that he was genuinely seeking work and that there was no work for him [...] Webber's conduct was more than usually obnoxious on these occasions. Instead of making arrangements to give the men a speedy dismissal, he kept them loitering near the office, sometimes for an hour on end, without shelter and bitterly conscious that he was treating them so deliberately. (p. 246)

Sir Hugh identifies in Webber 'a strong man, with none of Shelton's sentimentality and irresolution' (p. 287). Whereas Henshaw prides himself on what he regards as his rationality, Webber's identity is enacted through a perverse display of power, and the masochistic pleasure he takes in 'the knowledge that the men hated him' (p. 287). However, the novel's declaration that 'Mastery was a sensation to him rather than a privilege' (p. 287) acknowledges an intellect not in control of itself, and capable of buttressing its own fear of humiliation only through the calculated humiliation of others. Sir Hugh Thomas's refusal to distinguish Webber's strength from his sociopathology is only one example of the newly made knight's convenient moral elisions.

In the figure of Sir Hugh Thomas, the mine owner, *Times Like These* conflates two opposing perceptions of hegemonic patriarchal practice that dominated the Victorian period and whose residual influence lingered into the twentieth century. They are Spencerian social Darwinism,[21] and the constitutive elements of the patriarchal 'man of character' (as opposed to the Georgian 'man of sentiment' presented through Shelton). Stefan Collini sees the 'man of character' as embodying 'self-restraint, perseverance, strenuous effort, courage in the face of adversity', all of which have an 'intimate dependence on the prior notion of duty'.[22] In Sir Hugh these ideal qualities emerge as competing strands to expose his hypocrisy through a power system enabling greed to be redefined as moral obligation. Whereas for Henshaw, industrial relations exist in the same sphere as war, in Sir Hugh they are the residue of nineteenth-century social Darwinism, one thread of which was the justification of a laissez-faire capitalism where the powerful dominate the weak as part of a natural and therefore amoral process. In the lexicon of Sir Hugh's predatory masculinity, 'it is necessary to smash the trade unions, and absolutely pulverise the miners' (p. 112) because it is 'jungle law, pure and simple' (p. 114). Within moments, however, the text shows how he cloaks his Spencerian 'survival of the fittest' amorality in the casuistry of a taxing ethical responsibility. While his fundamental social Darwinism necessarily regards moral principle as non-existent, his self-positioning requires that he adopt the pose of a patriarchal 'man of character' burdened by the demands of duty. Safely engirdled in his self-righteousness, he finds no difficulty in reformulating the base metal of his greed into the golden piety of unblemished moral responsibility and collective patriarchal patriotism, as one of 'those of us who feel we have a duty to the nation rather than to one class of it' (p. 112). When the pits return to work after the strike and profits rise under the brutally repressive regime of Webber, 'Sir Hugh, a religious man, thanked gracious heaven that the Cwm was thus becoming a model pit' (p. 287). In the figure of Sir Hugh Thomas, *Times Like These* critiques not only a rapaciously greedy individual. Its target is the facility with which a dominant patriarchal culture manipulates a political theory of nature as an amoral phenomenon into the service of a divinely approved order. Without textually marking the difference between the two characters, *Times Like These* further positions Sir Hugh Thomas's expedient hypocrisy against Oliver Biesty's probity. When Oliver, a striking miner, reminds his wife of his belief in a fundamental moral obligation that 'We been sent to do our duty, Polly' (p. 196), he puts principle above self-interest, for which he is eventually sacked by Webber. [23] For Sir Hugh, duty and greed conveniently align, and allow him, in Shelton's mind, to 'live like a prince twelve miles from the nearest colliery' (p.187), careless of the conditions in which his miners work, while piously thanking heaven that he has done his duty.

Writing of how 'power operates in and through discourse', Judith Butler asks rhetorically: 'Is there a community and history of such speakers not magically invoked at the moment in which the utterance is spoken?'[24] In speaking for himself Sir Hugh Thomas speaks for both Henshaw and Webber, and for others who appear later in Valleys' novels like *Dark Edge* (1997) and *Until Our Blood is Dry* (2014). In such a hierarchical system of industrial organisation, Sir Hugh Thomas incarnates the oppressive signifiers of the patriarchal alpha male. Henshaw and Webber dutifully follow him, both of them appropriating and further circulating their master's aggressive discourse. The novel's forensic presentation of these three representatives of patriarchal masculinity identifies what Berthold Schoene-Harwood calls a 'kind of masculinity [that] endlessly produces and consumes "others" against which its superiority is defined'.[25] In the starkness of their representation, the novel provides a searing critique of the deformative rituals, both discursive and performative, of power-driven masculinity. In the pastoral activities of the miners and Denis Shelton's 'Georgian' sensibility, the novel constructs 'residual' masculinities diametrically opposed to this reductive paradigm.

The importance of green spaces in Valleys' fiction is evident throughout the twentieth century. Writing of English fiction in the 1930s in particular, Chris Hopkins devotes a chapter to Welsh pastoral in which he remarks: 'Welsh texts of the time themselves often use a pastoral model for their narrative of the Welsh experience of industrialisation'. This is true, of course, but Hopkins continues: 'Thus, novels such as Lewis Jones's *Cwmardy* (1937) and Richard Llewellyn's *How Green Was My Valley* (1939) both refer to the agricultural life which is replaced by South Wales industrialism.'[26] Strangely, Hopkins makes no mention of *Times Like These*, which predates both novels, and in which pastoral is not only present but functions as a crucial semiosis, a strategy through which one discourse of masculinity is framed as a juxtapositional critique of another. Pastoral is an ideal mode for examining assumptions and conventions representing a continuum of practices defining somatic masculinity for, as Andrew V. Ettin reminds us, 'Pastoral society is predominantly male.'[27] The novel's explicit references to pastoral figures and activities are used to establish a clear fissure between opposing definitions of masculinity, where 'an ability to be unconsciously creative and festive' functions as a direct indictment of a de-humanising, reductive patriarchy exhibited in industrial practice.[28] But pastoral in *Times Like These* is not only a vehicle celebrating a somatic, collaborative masculinity different from that of figures like Hugh Thomas. It also constructs performative spaces in which recurring patterns of male behaviour may be practised 'so as to insist upon the importance of pattern and repetition in the order of things'.[29]

One of the notable features of *Times Like These* is the way gender differences are mapped onto such pastoral spaces. Pastoral tropes in the novel serve not only to distinguish two types of masculinity – demonstrated through the restoratively pastoral and the reductively industrial – but to identify one of the defining elements of masculinity itself, where, as Michael Kimmel states, 'Masculinity is a *homosocial* enactment'[30] (original italics). In *Times Like These*, pastoral and its associated activities are inseparable from homosociality. They involve physical activity and manual dexterity and, in contrast to their industrial counterparts, are innocent, cordial and mutually supportive. The novel is strewn with examples: the several occasions when men and boys are at the swimming holes; men engaged in felling a large tree (pp. 44–51); strike meetings where 'The men sat around three sides of a natural amphitheatre' (p. 94); striking miners relaxing on the Common (pp. 186–90). If men and women are present together – at the Whit Monday festivities and the rugby match, for instance – there is gendered collaboration. Significantly, in these contexts, patriarchy is devoid of inter-gender tensions of the kind that recur as central features of later novels like *Strike for a Kingdom*, *Dark Edge* and *Until Our Blood is Dry*. But pastoral is not sentimentalised in *Times Like These*. In his monograph on the pastoral, Peter V. Marinelli comments that pastoral innocence and human experience exist in a perpetual and unresolved dynamic: 'Like pastoral itself [...], the myth of the golden age arises when gold has only too clearly been discovered',[31] the gold in this novel's case being the rich seams of anthracite and bituminous coal that ran beneath the surface of the south Wales Valleys.[32] The harmony between nature and the human presence offers an implicit contrast with the ugly village, built without regard for its inhabitants, 'just where the prevailing south-west wind would carry [the Cwm colliery shafts'] smoke towards the village' (p. 33). And one of the most distinctive features of the presentation of pastoral in *Times Like These* is what Hopkins calls, 'a continuing organic community (if not one which is unchallengeably so) displayed in these gatherings'.[33]

The socially collaborative form of pastoral in *Times Like These* serves as a reminder that 'Rulership and even leadership are generally inimical to pastoralism',[34] and the novel's emphasis on masculinity performed through decorum, concord and restraint consistently distinguishes its harmonious pastoral modality from the combative patriarchy it creates in Sir Hugh Thomas, and the deviant hegemony of Webber. Pastoral simplicity intersects with Christian celebration after the Whit Monday procession, for example, when 'the shepherds reached for their crooks and sought their wandering flocks' (p. 65). As the day wears on, 'an innocent intoxication fermented in the veins of the adolescents' (p. 65), but not even 'the gloomiest elder frowned on so carefree a relation of the sexes' (p. 65). The Whit Monday festival is only one set piece of pastoral affirmation, however. There is in the novel a carefully designed, consistently articulated representation of masculinities engaged in a variety of pastoral activities emphasising androcentric cordiality, communal activity and gender confirmation. The novel's use of such a thematic manoeuvre has been the subject of critical disapproval. James

A. Davies finds the articulation of pastoral episodes in *Times Like These* particularly unfortunate in its reference to a river lido known locally as the Horse Washings. The text reads: 'To this new Horse Washings, as to Arden, many young men did flock every day, and fleet the time carelessly, as they did in the golden world' (p. 205). In Davies's view, the close textual association of the Horse Washings and Arden, and a later reference to the Arcadian freedoms permitted by the strike come 'close to the mock heroic, the dangerously satirical'.[35] Stephen Knight concurs on the uncertain effect created throughout the novel 'when the narrator uses classical imagery to describe the humble pleasures of the industrial environment'.[36] Neither commentator remarks how the pastoral mode is a recurring and always valorised element of the novel's architecture. This extends from the obviousness of a character called Theocritus Jones to the convocation of relaxing miners on the Common, the pastoral festivities on Whit Monday, the felling of Theocritus' tree by Oliver Biesty and others, and the association of the mischievous Ben Fisher with a faun, a male figure from Greek mythology associated, like Ben, with roguish high spirits.

Davies and Knight imply through their comments that pastoral in *Times Like These* is a discrete mode of representation overlaid onto material that is topographically and discursively inappropriate. But any seeming dissonance between subject and mode is purely connotative and culturally constructed, a view of pastoral as representing idealised 'enamell'd Fields' inflected through the English poetic tradition.[37] Terry Gifford rightly identifies 'retreat and return' as a central dynamic of pastoral,[38] but while in early modern and later English pastoral they are the constituents of an imaginative, aesthetic engagement with a literary artefact, a pleasing fabrication for the reader, in *Times Like These* they constitute a dynamic interfusion more central to the realities of the characters represented. As the text pointedly remarks, in the reality of home to which the young swimmers return after their retreat to the pleasures of the lido, there is 'no actual evidence of starvation, but that such a lack should need substantiation was significant' (p. 205). Written for an educated elite, and appropriated and colonised by early modern English poetry, literary pastoral itself is littered with the relocation of classical pastoral into an idealised English context: John Milton could situate Corydon, Thyrsis, Comus and others in an English landscape.[39] Andrew Marvell advises little T. C. not to upset Flora in an English garden.[40] And two centuries later, in 1865, Matthew Arnold could describe how he and Arthur Clough, roaming the Oxfordshire fields in the guise of Corydon and Thyrsis,

> With the country-folk acquaintance made
> By barn in threshing-time, by new-built rick.
> Here, too, our shepherd-pipes we first assay'd.[41]

Nothing so fancifully self-indulgent as Arnold's pastoral inhabits *Times Like These*. The metrics of the river lido where the miners swim are scrupulously mapped: 'thirty yards long by twelve to fifteen yards wide with a maximum depth of five and a half feet' (pp. 204–5). And although the water runs clear when the strike has reduced its pollution, 'many of the hollows were known to contain tar' (p. 204). As Terry Gifford comments, 'Pastoral authors are inescapably of their own culture and its preoccupations',[42] and *Times Like These*, unconstrained by the formal idealising of English pastoral poetry, makes use of pastoral's residual values of retreat and return to shape a distinctive Welsh form, grounding its masculinities in a realistic topography. Marinelli states that 'perfect felicity is never the subject of pastoral when it is truly serious, and complacency is not the feeling from which it arises'.[43] Indeed, rather than construct an idealised, escapist version, as Matthew Arnold does, the novel offers a gendered, Welsh, working-class inscription of an enduring pastoral myth, and the swimming hole episodes link the youth of Jenkinstown, beset by economic and political variables beyond their control, with the respite from care which pastoral has offered humanity through the ages. Myth here informs the 'real' present, for the text identifies through its lyrical prose, 'an overriding trajectory of nature as fecund, generative and transformative',[44] captured by 'the soft swirling of bodies in the water, the soft pad of feet on turf, the crumble of brown soil, sappy chew of grass, the fly and leaf stippling the smooth river pools' (p. 205).

Celebration of the male body is evident in the first lido episode (pp. 33–5), which is represented as an observed celebration of physical expression. The bodies of the young swimmers are naturalised – they are 'naked', 'glittering' and 'silver' – as they emerge from the coal-blackened water, 'everyone there knew everyone else' (p. 34), and there is 'bawling and screaming of greeting' (p. 34) when others join. Anthony Easthope remarks of male banter that it 'works as a way of affirming the bond of love between men while appearing to deny it',[45] and this is evident in the way unspecified speakers display a strong sense of male fellowship: 'That's our 'Arry, on the grey 'orse! Go and put u shirt on u little rascal' (p. 34). When the young 'bloods' arrive at the Horse Washings and strip off to swim, their 'vitality [is] kindled anew, Antaeus-like, at the touch of their bare feet on the grass by the river [and they] lark, horseplay, and dive like lunatics' (p. 35).[46] The novel identifies three significant details here: their enjoyment is expressed through uninhibited physical ebullience; the recuperating effect of direct tactile contact with the grass; and the use of a classical figure, Antaeus, to position this recuperation within an unbroken, if challenged, continuum of human experience. That this reference is no mere attempt at what James A. Davies calls 'juxtapositional dignity' is evident from the way the episode closes.[47] With a winning display of respect on the arrival of their elders at the pond, 'All the youngsters then left the pool, and sat bare or shirted, watching their particular heroes as their strongly-muscled bodies rolled under the coaly web and sweat spray' (p. 35). Until the last two phrases the description could be of a pastoral landscape by John Constable. In its blend of riotous fun and instinctive decorum it represents, through the creation of a Welsh pastoral, a vision of Welsh masculinity rescued, if only temporarily, from the physically destructive demands of capitalised labour. That these fine specimens of young manhood have no option but to swim in coal-polluted water, the text suggests, is an indictment of an industry, not a mockery of them. And as for Antaeus, surely the power of myth lies in its capacity to encapsulate and encode an experience of being human, whether young miner or young English aristocrat. In this final scene, male bodies are the objects of an approving multiple gaze where the implied reader is invited into sympathetic collusion with the scene: the reader's gaze is generated through the narrative voice's gaze which creates the image of the boys gazing on the bodies of their heroes while themselves being presented as 'bare or shirted' (p. 35).

In the third swimming episode (p. 209), a reference to a classical figure is once again employed, this time to celebrate an identity created through the male physique in a natural setting, rather than an underground miner's stall, when Ben Fisher emerges naked from the water to confront a clothed Snooker Kelch in a quarrel over a girl. As in the earlier episode, the male body is subjected to close and approving observation. The qualitative difference between Ben and Snooker as men is represented solely through their contrasting physical appearance: 'Snooker rusty in brown, Ben glitteringly naked' (p. 209), the luminous masculinity of the one at variance with the dourness of the other. Definition of Ben's masculinity is provided through further physical representation: 'His wicked, handsome face, strong white shoulders, and the curling black hair that covered his legs, thighs and lower belly, and thence ran in a thin tetter up the middle of his chest gave him an oddly faun-like appearance' (p. 209). Ben's upper body conforms to desirable masculine signifiers, but his physique is removed from the merely contingent and placed within a wider historical and cultural perspective. As a young man, Ben is constructed as confident, buoyant and winningly roguish, whose association with a faun positions him in a pastoral continuum of mischievous subjectivity. In the swimming hole episodes, *Times Like These* celebrates through its pastoral inflection the boisterous socialising of young men, but emphasises, through direct textual representation the good humour and natural decorum of the occasions, and by making simple use of a few classical analogies positions such activities as abiding presences within a cultural and historical continuity detached from and inimical to the precepts of a demanding political and economic stratification.

But the enticing prospect of indolence is also one of the staples of the pastoral mode and is given an important and distinctive inflection in *Times Like These*. Patrick Cullen reminds us that Arcadian pastoral 'takes as its ideal the *pastor felix* and the soft life of *otium*: correspondingly, it locates its characters in a landscape of varying degrees of idealisation [...] but at the same time vulnerable and precarious'.[48] *Times Like These* subverts the notion both of the *pastor felix* – Sir Hugh Thomas is no kindly shepherd – and the topographical idealisation of Arcadian pastoral is impossible: the fair country has already been raped. However, the text valorises 'the soft life of *otium*' in a green space, which offers an alternative to a striving hegemonic identity embodied in Sir Hugh, while acknowledging its ephemeral nature within the prevailing socio-economic model. The fact that the miners' leisure is enforced by the strike, and that they scarcely exist in a golden age functions textually as a critique of an economic regime which de-humanises them, and as testament to their capacity for delight in communal leisure and a rebuke to the philosophy that work is the sole source of meaning and purpose in life. The opening pages of chapter XIV, for example, juxtapose two representations of masculine definition to make its point. The first is presented through the eyes of Sir Hugh, the male as dominant self-achiever, coercive and decisive: 'We've got to show the miners where they stand' (p. 187). This modulates almost immediately to a second scene, on the Common where the miners, by a semantic twist, are not 'standing' for anything, but instead are lying down and at ease; males as uncompetitive and gregarious, distracted by their conversation from 'the great roll of tree-pocked fields sprawling below them, the thousand greens that blocked the eyes in each direction' (p. 189).

In this invitingly pastoral context, narrow patriarchal prescriptions are suspended, and any marital friction is absent. The family men, 'with their wives' connivance and discreet encouragement took young children [to the Common] over the week-ends and later throughout the school holidays' (p. 187). Once on the Common, they would 'find a pleasant spot under a tree and stretch themselves, interminably yarning the same old stories' (p. 87). The picture is remarkably similar to John Milton's tale-telling shepherds relaxing in hawthorn glades, although Milton's is a literary trope in which Corydon and Thyrsis themselves are likely to pop up at any moment, whereas *Times Like These* offers pastoral embedded in a material reality. A sense of rapport runs through the entire passage. While spaces still define gender – the women are at home, the men at large – there is a mutually understood benefit to both; fathers engage with their children and mothers have some small respite from care. On the Common, 'the kiddies of the different households, banded together, played without undue noise at the safe little brooks that ran along most of the hollows' (p. 187). Dog walkers 'ramble along in leisurely fashion' (p.188), before gathering to 'discuss the points of dogs' (p. 188). Even their dogs appear to join them in a 'harmony of spirit' (p. 188). Whereas in *Cwmardy*, strikes are rendered through representations of male confrontation, agency and violence, in villages here, during the 1926 strike, the focus is on a quite different portrayal of masculinity in a verdant setting.

However, as Theocritus' *Idylls* illustrate, manual work is not absent in the pastoral world.[49] In *Times Like These*, the tree-felling in chapter III, overseen by the appropriately named Theocritus Jones, employs elements of pastoralism to offer a residual alternative to the capitalist ethic and its impact on male identity formed through work. In an *al fresco* space, distinctive features of male bonding are evident. These include masculine self-definition through physical strength; manual dexterity; collaborative effort; problem-solving; and intergenerational banter. Although it is only Luke Biesty who is asked to help fell the tree, it presents a problem which interests and leads to the eventual participation of Luke, Luke's grandfather Evan Thomas, Oliver Biesty, Charlie and Ike Jones, Ben Fisher and Spot Oakman. Key signifiers emerge of cooperative masculinity manifested within the context of the unified group. Together, they illustrate how pastoral foregrounds recurring cultural patterns of mutuality in male behaviour and the consequent securing of identity, and by implied contrast the distorting effect on the self of industrial practice posited on competition and power. Each of those present has his own opinion of the best way to complete the task, and their hard-won experience as sensible working men is evident in their all having come to the same conclusion independently. One of the recurring features of the novel, evident also in the swimming hole episodes, is the deference shown by males to their elders (Oliver's daughter, the ambitious Mary, being a significant, gendered, exception). Ike is anxious to get started, but 'Out of deference to Oliver's seniority' (p. 46) he seeks his opinion first. Deference to Oliver springs from an instinctive decorum here; it is demanded by a patriarchal industrialist like Sir Hugh Thomas. As Judith Butler observes of a speech act such as Ike's: 'It not simply that [it] takes place within a practice, but that the act itself is a ritualised practice.'[50]

Whereas boisterous homosociality defines the lido episodes, here the emphasis is on identity revealed through a residual form of non-mechanised male strength and physical dexterity. The educated Theocritus Jones, spectator not participant (rather like the educated Gwyn Jones himself?), is rather less of a man – 'an ineffectual help' (p. 47) – than the others, and a bystander when the tree is eventually pulled down. The text makes an unmarked connection regarding somatic masculinity here between the cerebral Theocritus and the upper middle-class Shelton, neither of whom is engaged in physical work. Both identify imaginatively with an unambiguous embodiment of physical self, Shelton with the powerful rugby player, Skuse, and Theocritus with the manually dextrous Oliver. At the rugby international, Shelton subjects 'the rolling of muscles through [Skuse's] torso' (p. 119) to his admiring gaze and for a moment, 'Skuse was Shelton' (p. 119), and, watching Oliver as he 'chopped so beautifully', Theocritus 'felt like crying out' (p. 48).[51] Manual work in such a context becomes a creative expression of self and acquires an aesthetic dimension. When Theocritus picks up 'a spotless chip and rubbed it between his fingers', he seeks a fleeting identification with Oliver himself and a tactile communion with a fragment of uncontaminated nature (p. 48).

When Ben Fisher and Spot Oakman appear and help fell the tree, the novel illustrates how homosocial banter acts as 'an example of masculine style'.[52] On this occasion it features as a carnivalised intergenerational ritual allowing young men to mock the status of their elders within mutually understood and accepted boundaries. It is another example of how decorum governs the novel's representation of pastoral masculinities. Within a male group of differing ages but shared values, Ben's irrepressible self-confidence is liberated so that prevailing norms of decorum may be waived. His breezy comment to Theocritus, his former teacher, 'Time you were back in school, ain't it? I reckon I'll have to send Inspector Breeze to whip u in' (p. 49) is modulated by the respectful way he addresses the schoolmaster as 'Mr Jones' both before making the remark and again a moment later. When he eventually departs, leaving 'these here others to clear up the light stuff' (p. 50), it is significant that he does so 'lost amidst the trees' (p. 50) and singing. Both details locate his masculinity within a tradition of implied classical pastoral: fauns were woodland spirits, and Ben's similarity to these mischievous beings, as noted above, is textually acknowledged later (p. 209) – and, like the exuberant young man that Ben is, any number of pastoral figures sing in Theocritus' *Idylls*.[53]

The entire occasion is marked by a free giving of time, a demonstration of skill and an exhibition of working-class male homosocialising. Oliver's reluctance to leave the job half-done – 'We can't leave him like this, though' – is interrupted by an approving textual judgement, 'The idea of an untidy job was hateful to Oliver.' Only then is he allowed to complete his comment: 'He wants a bit of trimming, naturally' (p. 50). The contrast here with the novel's opening sentence illustrates how deeply the practices of mechanised labour permeate *Times Like These*. Work in this pastoral context finishes when the job is completed to the participants' satisfaction. At the start of the novel, the miners' night shift finishes promptly when the 5.30 a.m. hooter blows. As Marx states of this kind of constraining framework, work becomes 'not the satisfaction of a need, but only a *means* of satisfying other needs'[54] (original italics). When thanked by Theocritus, Oliver's simple reply carries the weight of a cultural *modus vivendi*: 'Not at all. A fellow don't mind helping' (p. 51).

Times Like These takes key elements of classical and neoclassical pastoral and relocates them within a specifically, and seemingly unlikely, Welsh industrial context. The presence of these liberating 'residual' features, 'effectively formed in the past, but [...] still active in the cultural process' offers an implicit contrast to the materialistic and humanly reductive demands of capitalised labour.[55] It is through this prism that the narrative deepens its critique of reductionism where money is given precedence over human fellowship, where a Sir Hugh can advise a Shelton to cheer for Ben Fisher at a rugby international, 'and then go back to the Cwm like a sensible fellow and see if you can knock sixpence off [his] wages' (p. 115). It is an ethic where 'a sensible fellow' lives at odds with himself. The text's respect for generosity of spirit and honest dealing embodied in the residual values of men like Oliver is evident, too, in its depiction of the socially superior Shelton, who finds Sir Hugh's advice 'simple brigandage' (p. 115).

The son of a landed English family, Denis Shelton not only embodies a link with enduring pastoral values in the novel but is, unusually for Welsh mining fiction, 'a sympathetic figure from the manager class'.[56] The source of this sympathy, Stephen Knight suggests, is Shelton's respect for the miners and his dislike of their treatment by Sir Hugh Thomas. But if this were all, there would be no need for Shelton to be a scion of a landed English family. Within the gendered landscape of the novel, however, it is essential that he is. As with the miners of Jenkinstown, he embodies a textually inscribed residue of 'certain experiences, meanings and values which cannot be expressed or substantially verified in terms of the dominant culture'.[57] In Shelton's case it is the weight of a residual tradition of pre-industrial genteel patriarchy which, like pastoral, is inimical to the values of laissez-faire industrial capitalism of the sort advocated by Henshaw and embodied in Sir Hugh Thomas.

If Gwyn Jones draws on the rich repository of classical and later pastoral embodied in the striking miners to shape his critique of the patriarchal power systems of the mine bosses, he expands his criticism by drawing the figure of Denis Shelton from a different though equally suggestive cultural archive. 'One can see in the decision of some writers to focus on non-Welsh subjects', writes Katie Gramich, 'an inspiration deriving from an academic or scholarly interest (such as Professor Gwyn Jones's interest in English Augustanism)', and it is that interest that determines Shelton's nationality, inscribes his values and shapes his form of masculinity.[58] Indeed, Jones's scholarly interest in English Augustanism predates his rise to a university chair. In 1935, a year before the publication of *Times Like These*, he had published *Richard Savage*, a fictional biography of the real-life eighteenth-century poet, philanderer and claimant to noble descent, in which Alexander Pope appears as a character, and another poet, James Thomson, is called as a defence witness at Savage's trial for murder in 1727, at which he was found guilty, but eventually pardoned. Helen Yallop states: 'The hegemonic form of masculinity extant in this period [was that of] the "polite gentleman"',[59] and Shelton's identity, manoeuvred into an industrial context, is based on the modes, manners and values of such a figure, and is thoroughly at odds with Savage's. It is, therefore, no coincidence that both Oliver Biesty (p. 273) and Sir Hugh Thomas (p. 274) recognise Shelton as a 'gentleman', but with widely differing appreciations of the term's semantics.

During the inter-war years, perhaps as a release from the mechanised slaughter of World War I, and as a diversion from the rise of Nazi Germany in the 1930s, there was a cultural affection, a nostalgia even, for what Michael Bunce calls 'pre-industrialised ways of living [...] a world in which social relations were defined by a benign rural class system'.[60] Bunce refers to the 'proliferation of books, articles and radio programmes on English country life and heritage',[61] in which 'National character [...] became associated with ancient rural virtue'.[62] Shelton's construction certainly reflects aspects of a cultural inter-war *zeitgeist* noted by Bunce, but, as a close examination of *Times Like These* reveals, he is no incarnation of a nebulous, romanticised history. He is, in fact, a modernised representation of a non-idealised Augustan 'gentleman' a 'man of sentiment', of refined sensibility and moral consciousness. As Stefan Collini reminds us, 'sentiment as a derogatory term is a nineteenth-century usage – the eighteenth century had known a more favourable sense – and manliness expressed a deep, possibly in some cases a revealingly pathological, aversion to this trait.'[63] In Collini's distinction between the 'Georgian' sentiment of Shelton and the 'Victorian' manliness of Sir Hugh Thomas lies the fulcrum on which their figures are positioned. *Times Like These* is, of course, set in a post-Victorian period, but residual 'Victorian values' of self-improvement through competitive endeavour permeated British consciousness until well into the twentieth century, and were the declared political credo of at least one post-war prime minister.[64] These cultural and historical differences are the *données* from which their textual significance emerges. For instance, Sir Hugh Thomas exhibits the masculine characteristic of stern, pragmatic self-control when he declares he will cheer any collier of his who scores a try in the rugby international the next day, but asserts that 'when he walks off the field, he walks out of my heart' (p. 115). Shelton, by contrast, exhibits his 'sentimentality' when, at the same match, he 'hoped Brimble [his chauffeur] was already in, for they would be closing the gates soon' (p. 117). Out of sight is not out of mind for Shelton. The incidents, seemingly tangential to the mainstream events of the novel, are significant because they encapsulate two radically opposed practices of masculine definition. As John Brewer says, the qualities of Georgian sentiment and politeness were not regarded as connoting a vapid lack of masculinity. Rather, they were among the markers that 'saw human affections [feelings] rather than reason or judgement as the basis of moral life'.[65] As a representative of a later age, Sir Hugh Thomas regards Shelton's 'sentimentality and irresolution' (p. 287) as markers of a feminised disposition.

One of the principal components of Georgian politeness was agreeable conversation, ideally in surroundings that were, as John Brewer notes, 'unquestionably convivial'.[66] *Times Like These* is assiduous in distinguishing Shelton's discourse from that of his more aggressive colleagues. Sir Hugh's language is characterised by its abrasive pontificating energy. And so when he proclaims to Shelton that violence lies at the heart of industrial relations because violence is 'human nature, and you can't change that' (p. 114), he naturalises brutality as the defining male signifier, unaware of the irony that he is speaking to someone whose very identity flatly contradicts him. Shelton's discourse is 'residually' more accommodating, as an exchange with the socially ambitious Broddam illustrates. Emerging from a trying meeting in Cardiff, he bumps into Broddam and asks on impulse:

> 'Have a drink?'
> 'Yes, I will. I've got time.'
> 'Thing I never do actually – drink in the daytime.'
> 'No more do I,' said Broddam, laughing.
> 'Is that really so?'
> 'Yes.' They both laughed. 'Let's make it tea or coffee, shall we?'
> 'Every time.'
> They had tea at the Kardomah, rather below Shelton's usual style. 'Decent little place', he commented. 'Nice brown sugar for coffee, eh?' (p. 139)

The contrast with Sir Hugh's forthright dominance is immediately evident. A mutually satisfying agreement is reached to avoid alcohol and, significantly, to visit the Kardomah, a coffee house (coffee houses in the eighteenth century were regarded as 'a permeable public institution where familiars and strangers could make polite conversation').[67] The arrangement is negotiated through collaboration, compliance, self-confession and humour, so that neither participant loses manly face, while Shelton's compliment on the choice of café reveals his sense of decorum, combining honest restraint with nicely judged praise.

Shelton's relaxing with Broddam in what for him is a *déclassé* space, where he enjoys himself enough to order a second cup of coffee, is only one example of the text's practice of distinguishing him from his colleagues, whose power-driven masculinities are defined solely through their hierarchical professional performativity.[68] Once again, the difference extends beyond the novel's validation of Shelton as an individual to his larger representative status. The post-Romantic/modern axis saw, Collini notes:

> a significant shift away from eighteenth-century ideas of the moral and cultural primacy of leisure. For the Georgian gentleman, and thus for all those who aspired to that status, the most prized human qualities could only be developed in the enjoyment of 'society' in the older meaning of the term.[69]

One of Shelton's defining characteristics in the novel is that although he is present at meetings with Sir Hugh, Henshaw and Webber, and discusses his work with his wife, he is seldom depicted as being at work in a day-to-day sense before the strike. He is, however, present in more relaxed environments, most often at home with his wife Louise, but also at the theatre, at the rugby match, where he likes 'the feel of a gathering crowd' (p. 117), and, as above, in a café with Broddam, a figure connected with commerce rather than heavy industry. And driving past groups of striking miners on the main street of Jenkinstown, he 'would have enjoyed being able to mix among them for a while to hear their views' (p. 165). A 'sociable man' in the Augustan sense of the term,[70] he is at once far removed from the miners of the south Wales Valleys, and yet discursively aligned with them in seeing engagement with others extending beyond the confining practice of hegemonic industrial enterprise. Two differing examples illustrate how juxtaposition in the novel is used to make the point. The first concerns the unlikely pairing of Shelton and the young miner Snooker Kelch in one significant and illuminating respect. The latter half of chapter XV is devoted to the bare-fist fight between Snooker and Ben Fisher over a girl.[71] They are equally matched, but it is Snooker who mistakenly believes he has won, that Ben is 'out on his feet!' His response is brief though telling: 'If Ben's out, I 'ont hit the poor bucker' (p. 215). Early in the following chapter, Shelton expresses his disapproval of the brutal treatment miners can expect when the strike fails: 'It goes against the grain to hit a man when he's down, Louise, and that's what we are going to do' (p. 218). When he presses Sir Hugh to show magnanimity, he is rebuffed: 'It's the word fools use for weakness' (p. 225). Juxtaposing the two responses to a defeated opponent, the text connects two male figures, separated by class demotic and material privilege, but united in a residual code of decent behaviour that has no place in the world of an industrial patriarch like Sir Hugh Thomas, where you 'look out for yourself [...] and let the other fellow go hang' (p. 138).

Equally unlikely unifying correspondences between Shelton and the impoverished, unemployed miner Luke Biesty further act as a binding agent in the novel, constructing masculinities separated by class, but diverging from male-empowered industrial patriarchy. The intimacy with which Shelton relates to his wife Louise is of a piece with his 'sentimentality': 'His vanity was satisfied by his wife's perfection' (p. 239), while she believes 'He was a husband in a million' (p. 89). The text's discursive ennobling of Luke's devotion to his wife Olive is equally effusive: 'Knights less tongue-tied have dedicated themselves to service without reward, but few more sincerely than he' (p. 141). Shelton's 'sentimental' devotion to Louise and Luke's knight-like wish to serve Olive contrast with the attitude of the 'new-made knight' (p. 274) Sir Hugh Thomas, for whom the notion of service without reward is sheer folly. As Ben Knights suggests of potent masculinity, 'Intimacy is so threatening to the jealously bounded identity that the only way of coping with it is to retain intellectual and emotional distance even when physical intimacy is taking place.'[72] But in Shelton and Luke, *Times Like These* remarkably constructs two figures whose wives are not adjuncts to their lives, but inhere with them to form a shared identity. Once more, juxtaposed passages are used to identify thematic contrasts and correspondences. With Shelton and Luke, they fuse both the emotional similarities and material differences between the two figures. After a visit to the theatre in Cardiff with his wife and daughter, where they had 'extremely good seats' (p. 239), Shelton retires 'to Louise's room very happy', the text implying that physical intimacy will follow (p. 240). Immediately after this passage, and set on the same evening, the novel focuses on Luke and Olive, who walk home from the cinema 'their eightpence spent'. Lying in bed, 'they experienced a complete tenderness and joy in each other' as they bond through small talk and expressive affection (p. 240).

Positioned to represent male values located within a modernised concept of the eighteenth-century gentleman where 'politeness embodied an idea of what the true gentleman [...] should be',[73] Shelton incarnates a trenchant criticism of divisive patriarchal capitalism.

Given to a belief in 'fair play, consideration, magnanimity', which Sir Hugh dismisses as 'irritating catch-words' (p. 275), he fails to demonstrate through aggressive performance the signifiers of a satisfactory competitive masculinity. 'Conciliatory in spirit' (p. 74), Shelton understands that he is a man out of his place and his time, that he 'wasn't the man for a job like this' (p. 89), and knows that his fellow managers regard him with contempt. As such, he is manoeuvred by the events of the narrative into an ideological impasse where the coordinates of his private selfhood come into conflict with the expectations of his public role. It is an impasse which confronts the figures of Len Roberts in *Cwmardy*, D. J. Williams in *Strike for a Kingdom* and Edwin Bowles in *Dark Edge*, whose masculinities it defines. Whereas they strive to negotiate their own resolutions with varying degrees of success, *Times Like These* solves the problem for Shelton. In a piece of textual sleight-of-hand, Jim, Shelton's elder brother and owner of the estate, becomes Louise Shelton's 'god out of the machine' (p. 274). In a device Raymond Williams calls 'the inheritance plot',[74] Jim's timely death, notably in Georgian Bath, enables her to escape from the valley she detests and allows Shelton 'to take over a fair-sized estate, on which they could live almost as well without salary as with salary at the Gate House. Besides, it was the sort of place they could always let' (p. 274). The significance of the device extends beyond a simple, Victorian manipulation of events to achieve satisfactory closure, however, for it reconnects Shelton with a space in which the 'residual' values of pre-industrial patriarchy will conflate in him to become 'dominant' values. Although Shelton's form of genteel masculinity functions in diametric opposition to that of Sir Hugh and his lackeys, it also has a significant effect in offering a desirable model to the businessman Broddam, who is ambitious to become a dominant figure in his chosen career. His seemingly tangential presence in the text is crucial in reading the novel as one concerned with the dynamics of social process, and illustrates how Williams's 'dominant', 'residual' and 'emergent' energies conflate and are manipulated in creating new identities.

Broddam's presence in *Times Like These* has been noted by several commentators on the novel, but his function has never been inspected in any detail. The closest enquiry into his presence comes from James A. Davies who, though not uncritical of the novel elsewhere, regards Broddam as an important figure because his presentation (along with

Shelton's) as 'a self-made businessman' places *Times Like These* as 'one of the few Welsh industrial novels to move beyond a relentless concern with working-class life'.[75] Elsewhere, Broddam has merited a passing judgement by Stephen Knight who sees him as 'an upwards-mobile bus owner',[76] while for Tony Brown he is a 'successful businessman'.[77] But Broddam's presence, instead of being extrinsic to the primary 'industrial' concerns of the novel, is crucial to its formal patterning of masculinities, and to reading it as study of how the dynamics of social formation and individual identity interact. Whereas the striking miners, Denis Shelton and even the three hegemonic bosses are located within recognisable paradigms of cultural and historical practice and identity, this is not the case with Broddam, who embodies what Raymond Williams calls 'the complications of improvement'.[78] A dedicated self-improver inhabiting the more fluidly defined world of business and commerce, he is a study in the opportunities and dangers present in the creation of an emergent self. In Broddam, *Times Like These* articulates a version of the predicament of the ambitious Welshman, a deracinated, culturally hybridised, anglicised figure, confident and successful in his business identity, but cautious and alert in his informal relations as he works to negotiate his way into a higher social class.

Broddam's business career reads like the trouble-free *cursus honorum* of the successful self-made entrepreneur. The son of a Chepstow plumber, he has progressed from starting a small bus company in Jenkinstown and working as a driver himself, alongside 'mechanics and men with bits of dribbled candle in their baskets' (p. 124), to controlling the Gridd County Services from Newport. By the end of the narrative, he will have moved to London to a senior managerial post in the London Pan-Centric Transport Board. As Shelton says admiringly of him, 'He must be a born businessman, the way he's got on' (p. 111). Yet the novel's disparaging reference to his fellow 'mechanics and men' hints that Broddam's ambition to rise in business is accompanied by, and arguably indivisible from, his determination to rise in the class hierarchy.

As an ambitious figure, Broddam's cultural significance resonates beyond his relatively few appearances in the text. In this he is like his secretary, the equally ambitious Mary Biesty. But whereas the novel consigns her, as a woman, to recognisably subordinated clerical roles in a world in which power structures are devised and populated by men, the methodology of Broddam's construction differs from that of any other character in the novel. The constituents of his occluded, liminal self are offered in the text largely by veiled indirection. A seemingly innocuous detail of his birth county as Monmouthshire (as with Gwyn Jones himself), a county neither entirely Welsh nor English at the time, hints at a figure who himself occupies an undefined, hybridised space. A brief exchange with his secretary, Mary, when he asks her if she would consider working in London, resonates with subtextual pointers regarding the problematics of self-improvement. Her excitement at the prospect does not surprise him but his brisk lexis is at once formal and, to a reader at least, designed as much to impress as to inform:

> 'There are your people, of course', he warned, with the wisdom of his early days. 'How would you feel about it, Miss Biesty?'
> 'If I can have the job, I'll go, Mr Broddam!'
> 'Your people?' (p. 220)[79]

His use of the high-status term 'people'[80] insinuates into the text his ambition to climb the class ladder by appropriating the sociolect of the 'polite' class, a point discussed more fully in later paragraphs. Removal from his family and his background, the novel tantalisingly implies, was not friction-free and he has not forgotten its psychic abrasion as his warning to Mary indicates. But while the novel shares the insight with the reader, Broddam is unable to position his warning to her on a more personal level. In one respect, his formal restraint is at one with the times and reflects their business relationship, but here and elsewhere in the novel his discourse hints at a fear of exposure springing from his insecure identity.

In his project of self-creation, Broddam finds it essential to seek a model that both satisfies his career advancement and complements his social ambitions.[81] He clearly rejects the coarse-grained industrial power model of a Sir Hugh Thomas, for while that might promote his ambition to succeed, it would come at the cost of the identity he wishes to create. Instead, he adopts and adapts as his model the traditional figure of the 'gentleman', expressed through speech and manners, as a means of anchoring a 'consistent "mode of being" [that] relates future to past'.[82] Not his own past, of course, but the past as defined by the notion of the 'gentleman' and embodied in the figure of Denis Shelton. Tellingly for an 'emergent' figure such as he, the novel's implication is that he achieves only the quiet desperation of inauthenticity. His acquaintance with the Sheltons is crucial in his strategy of self-formation. In his upward trajectory he realises that his biggest challenge lies in achieving acceptance into a higher social echelon, getting to know 'the sort of people who knew the sort of people he had little expectation of knowing' (p. 124). To someone assured of her social position like the astute and snobbish Louise Shelton his ambitions are immediately clear: 'he was a man who, as he rose from one grade of society to another, always had his eyes upon the one above, observing and learning' (p. 116). For him, the acquaintance with the Sheltons, especially Denis Shelton, who belong to a 'superior social layer' (p. 124), is an invaluable resource for what Anthony Giddens calls 'the appropriation of mediated information'.[83] The Sheltons offer not only the alluring prospect of entrée into a more sophisticated social layer, but crucially the opportunity to observe and strive to acquire the modes, manners and speech congruent with 'polite' behaviour. But in the brief space it accords Broddam, *Times Like These* pushes much farther in its representation of social process, for it embeds in him the dangers to the self in the conflict between authenticity and self-formation in a class-based, patriarchally structured society. To make its point, the novel once more harks back to historical precedent to demonstrate the risk involved. Shelton's form of masculinity easily combines characteristics of Georgian 'politeness' and 'sentiment', the one a performative display of the civilised self, the other 'a feeling whose value did not depend upon its being observed by others'. But for Broddam, always aware that as he observes so he is being observed, his 'politeness' is a form of public behaviour 'intended to impress others rather than spontaneously generated',[84] a 'performative display of the civilised self', rather than the easy expression of a genuine feeling.

Fifty years after *Times Like These* was published, John Mortimer's *Paradise Postponed* (1985) similarly exposed how deeply embedded was the continuing 'soft power' of class gradation through sociolect and manner in the figure of the working-class arriviste Leslie Titmuss, as he contends with the snobberies of young Conservatives.[85] Broddam's trajectory is radically different from the acquisitive Titmuss, who, depicted as lacking any moral compass, becomes a successful property developer in London and a minister in a Thatcher government. Broddam is far less repellent, and his friends the Sheltons are more sympathetic, but the comparison with Titmuss is instructive because both he and Titmuss are in the precarious business of self-transformation. For Titmuss, like Broddam, a career arc of his kind is inseparable from the acquisition of socially validated linguistic signifiers, but his clumsy use of high-status discourse, like 'awfully' as in 'awfully nice to meet you', 'a frightfully jolly party' and 'a fellow' rather than a man or person, 'people' rather than 'family' are greeted with snobbish mockery.[86] Broddam is more fortunate in his companions, although recognising and striking the appropriate tone in conversation are still for him something of a challenge. In a conversation he has with the Sheltons regarding rugby (p. 116), for example, he remarks that he once 'played a bit in Jenkinstown'. Shelton is impressed by his modesty and replies conversationally, 'They've got a good side now, Broddam.' The tone of Broddam's initial response, 'That may be why,' is promisingly concise, light-hearted and appropriately self-deprecating. No more need be said, but his difficulty arises when he attempts self-justification: 'They picked me because they had no one better. I was too slow for the game, I'm afraid – the sort of player who remembers after the match what wonderful things he could have done had he only thought of it at the time'. (p. 116). In attempting to be amusingly dismissive of his ability, he becomes unsure of his tone and clumsily verbose, mired in a network of ponderous sub clauses.

Although *Times Like These* unfailingly supports Broddam's ambitions through the interventions of the narrative voice and finds his general attitude 'a sensible and admirable one' (p. 124), it reveals, too, that throughout he is enacting a performance rather than expressing a 'feeling'. Anthony Giddens notes that in the 'reflexive project of the self, the narrative of self-identity is inherently fragile',[87] and one of Broddam's recurring fears is of making 'himself look ridiculous' (p. 124). However, the novel conveys his fear of exposure most notably not through his acquaintance with the Sheltons, though that fear is never far away, nor with Mary Biesty when she worked for him as his secretary and where their respective roles were clearly defined, but with Mary Biesty when they meet socially and by chance at Newport station, he catching a train to London for Christmas, she returning home from her new job there (pp. 254–6). Aside from brief, suggestive incursions by the narrative voice, the passage is rendered in direct speech, so that the almost programmatic strands of Broddam's strictly performative masculinity are both implied through discursive indirection and developed incrementally.

Mary is hardly a stranger to him, and their association with each other, the novel teasingly hints throughout, is not without a suppressed mutual attraction, thwarted by her gendered hesitation in making the first move, and his existential fear of exposure through commitment. He quickly judges with approval that since her move to London her accent has 'improved' and 'her clothes were more stylish and yet in good taste' (p. 255). Where she is concerned, he is a man who notices such things. But bereft of a suitable medium of informal discourse for such an occasion, which a Shelton would manage more assuredly, his only resource is staid formality as a means of defence. His stilted lexis has all the decorous signifiers appropriated later by a Leslie Titmuss. He exclaims 'Good heavens' on seeing her; he thinks it is 'Splendid!' that she likes it in London. He is impressively modest and appropriately concerned when she thanks him for his help getting her the job there: 'It was very little to do, really. You are quite settled now, of course.' As it is Christmas, he has noticed that 'There are fearful crowds about'. His employment of stylised discourse with high-status connotations is complemented by his over-punctilious manner, with the overall effect that the novel manages to imply both a wish to maintain a formal distance and a pleasure he experiences in her company. As the novel has made clear elsewhere, Mary Biesty is a strong-minded young woman, yet Broddam treats her like the archetype of vulnerable maidenhood, taking protective control of the direction of the meeting. Because of the crowds, he will 'see that you get a seat all right' on the bus home. When he asks if she is being met, he immediately corrects himself for such presumption with, 'Or am I being very rude to ask?' Assured that neither is the case, he politely insists that '[you] must let me get you a cup of coffee'. And afterwards, although Mary has been capable of boarding a train from London to Newport and dealing with 'fearful crowds' herself, 'He took her the short distance to the bus station' to get the bus to Jenkinstown. Once there, he performs for her the role of dominant male and assures her that 'You'll get home quite safely now', although she has expressed no anxiety about the matter.

    Norman Fairclough observes that 'having access to prestigious sorts of discourse and powerful subject positions enhances publicly acknowledged status and authority'.[88] However, through Broddam's stilted sociolect, so different from the ease of Shelton's expression, the text constructs him as a form of de-centred masculinity aping a style that he feels confirms his status in a class-conscious society. However, as Raymond Williams observes of performative modes, 'What they exclude may often be seen as the personal or the private.'[89] Even within the more regulated, male-determined social decorums of the 1920s, Broddam's excessive formality indicates his need to control the interpersonal register of the meeting. But in keeping with its strategy throughout his construction, the novel also offers veiled suggestions of the tensions between his protective wall of formality and the tug of his desire for greater intimacy. (The speed with which Mary counters his question whether she is being 'met' suggests that the desire is reciprocated.) Her presence pleases him, but in inviting her for coffee, 'The idea occurred to him that, all things considered, he was not acting wisely; but he dismissed it' (p. 255). When Mary comments, 'I do hope you enjoy yourself' in London (p. 255), this piece of phatic communion 'rather pleased him', and the texture of his language softens: 'It's very nice of you to say that, Miss Biesty. I hope I do – and you, too. How are your father and mother these days?' In an earlier exchange, we recall, they were 'Your people' (p. 220). Through such nuances the text hints at a level of feeling in Broddam that he represses for fear of displaying it. The competing elements of his character are once again hinted at in his farewell to her: 'It's been very, very nice to meet you once more' (p. 256) suggests the pleasure he finds in her company, while his qualifying 'once more' prompts doubts about the wisdom of meeting her again. Having seen her onto the bus, his self-control dominates, the brief encounter is over and 'she saw him turn at once towards the station', out of her sight and out of the novel. As it does elsewhere, the novel resorts to juxtaposition to make its gendered point. In the paragraph immediately following their farewells, Mary comes under the less complicated male gaze of the bus conductor: 'Smart piece, he thought appreciatively', to which a confirming narrative voice adds, 'Undoubtedly, too, he was right' (p. 256). The switch defines three forms of masculinity in which the forthright response of a minor, unnamed character, together with the *ex cathedra* judgement of an equally impressed narrative voice, functions as a choric commentary on how Broddam's role play requires a caution that comes at the cost of spontaneous expression.

Broddam adds a significant dimension both to the forms of masculinity represented in *Times Like These* and to the novel as a study in the historical and cultural precariousness of emergent identity in south Wales. Acutely aware of the dangers involved in self-formation, he is a figure existing within an insecure negotiation of self, at once confident that 'before long he would be among the topmost branches' (p. 124), yet ineradicably fearful of making himself look ridiculous in the process. Erich Fromm writes of the individual who 'adopts the kind of personality offered to him by cultural patterns',[90] and the pattern Broddam adopts is that of the English gentleman as represented in the text by the 'Georgian' behaviour of Denis Shelton. But adoption is not the equivalent of assimilation. In Broddam, *Times Like These* unsentimentally constructs a version of the ambitious Anglo-Welshman, an emergent masculinity, seemingly confident in some contexts but lacking a stabilised emotional identity and a convincing repertoire of performative signifiers. He remains incomplete, a simulacrum rather than a successful hybrid. It is a challenge Edwin Bowles will face in *Dark Edge* written sixty years later. As for Broddam, a Judith Butler comment positions a figure like him as a 'shadow' masculinity in which 'Practices of parody can serve to reengage and reconsolidate the very distinction between a privileged and naturalised gender configuration, and one that appears as derived, phantasmic and mimetic – a failed copy'.[91] This may appear hard on Broddam, but it is he, we remember, who regards Denis Shelton as 'the real thing' (pp. 123–4).

The qualified critical praise accorded *Times Like These* has resulted largely from reading the novel as a fragmented industrial narrative lacking political passion and ideological consistency. James A. Davies acknowledges that while it has some fine episodes, it suffers from a 'lack of vision'.[92] A gender-specific approach, however, shifts the focus from the visionary to the representational, from the coherently ideological to the pragmatically observed. Within this context, analysis of Sir Hugh Thomas, Henshaw and Webber addresses the novel's trenchant criticism of a form of patriarchal masculinity as reductive, hypocritical and even pathologically disturbed. But a gender-specific study also reveals a wider, historicised examination of Valleys' masculinities during a decade characterised by paradoxes and contradictions, aspiration both individual and communal, and instability both private and public. The competing elements of the novel's discourse inscribe and reflect the differentiated masculine formations of the age in which it is set, but it locates them in a historical perspective that both shapes and reflects the culture it presents. Pierre Macherey's view of the genesis of a novel, that 'it is a figure against a background of other formations, depending on them rather than contrasting with them', is instructive in reading *Times Like These*.[93] Its masculinities are formed not only within the particular circumstances of their own time, but embody modifications, adaptations and attempted assimilations of patterns of male identities, whether consciously selected or not, reaching from the past to inform the present.

Published in London first in 1936 and reissued in 1979, *Times Like These* has not been published in Wales at the time of writing this book, and it exists within a liminal space occupied more centrally by ideologically energetic or socially rumbustious 1930s narratives. The contributor to *The Oxford Companion to the Literature of Wales*, for instance, searching for a way to conclude the entry on a novel that 'describes the humdrum life of Jenkinstown', writes that it 'remains notable chiefly for its understatement and its vivid evocation of the commonplace'.[94] By this measure, a touch of Jack Jones-type ebullience appears to be a desired ingredient of a Valleys' novel. This chapter has moved away from a reading of *Times Like These* premised on the expectation of a novel depicting masculinity through patterns of industrial conflict. Instead, it has positioned the novel's diverging masculine discourses within a larger social frame of what Raymond Williams has called 'the complexity of a culture', where recognition of 'the internal dynamic relations of any actual process' is essential to its understanding.[95] Williams's terms for this process, the 'dominant', 'residual' and 'emergent', opened a pathway into analysing how *Times Like These* exposes profound differences in masculine construction, but also reveals, within the dynamic of history, how elements of the residual are incorporated into dominant and emergent masculinities, and how the residual in one context becomes the dominant or the emergent in an ongoing process of historical movement. And so the 'residual' values of the past not only shape the aspirations of the 'emergent' businessman Broddam, but also of the 'dominant' patriarch Sir Hugh Thomas, the 'new-made knight' (p. 274) who despite his contempt for Denis Shelton's 'residual' values, nonetheless manages to accommodate a 'residual' title.

Because Shelton's presence in the novel has attracted little critical attention, the significance of his residually 'Georgian' function has passed largely unnoticed, but it may be read as an essential element in the novel's gender representation and its narrative design, as does the use of the pastoral mode. Taken together, Denis Shelton's neo-Georgian benevolent patriarchy and the miners' pastoral collectivism extend their textual function beyond a specific critique of industrial exploitation by representing them as forms of extant masculinity lodged within lengthy historical traditions. In doing so, *Times Like These* adopts a doubly retrospective viewpoint. Written in the decade after the events it describes, it reaches farther into the past for its animating ideas of two differing though not oppositional forms of masculinity, the Georgian and the pastoral. Tempered by their historic positioning, they exhibit a stability of identity under constant challenge from the institutional patriarchal hegemonies of Hugh Thomas, Henshaw and Webber, but are of inestimable value in themselves. Shelton's disappearance from the novel does not inscribe the end of the values he embodies. His 'residual' qualities in industrial Jenkinstown become 'dominant' values as he moves back to Berkshire, and as such expose the 'dominant' values of industrial patriarchs like Sir Hugh as social constructs rather than immutable principles.

The wide representation of masculinities, inflected through the breadth of its non-industrial perspective, distinguishes *Times Like These* from Lewis Jones's more socially narrow *Cwmardy*, published a year later. *Cwmardy* employs a different methodology in constructing its masculinities. *Times Like These* celebrates the physical masculinity of its pit workers through a pastoral continuum of collaborative endeavour. *Cwmardy*, by contrast, exposes through the macho Big Jim Roberts and his physically feeble son Len how a form of competitive masculinity endemic in patriarchal capitalism requires a conformity of physical practice that leaves little room for individual difference. It is arguable that the juxtaposition of the two novels' publications – 1936 and 1937 – has privileged the immediate drama of one over the 'more distanced' voice of the other,[96] rather than celebrating the diversity of Valleys' narratives, and the masculinities they construct.

2
Genre and the Tribulations of Masculinity in Lewis Jones's Cwmardy (1937)[1]

Cwmardy's panoramic opening paragraphs present a motionless lone male resembling a 'Wild West desperado', whose eyes 'roam over the splendour of the mountain landscape', as 'a soft breeze' plays on his manly chest. Introduced by his colloquial alias Big Jim, he is immediately positioned outside the conformities of 'civil servants and army authorities'. A slight change of perspective discovers a small boy standing nearby, gazing at him. This *tableau vivant* of two figures fixed in a landscape then gives way to cinematic action as the man turns, and spits 'a large mass of tobacco-stained saliva'. What does this uncouth spitting signify? In which unidentified landscape is this scene taking place? Who is Big Jim? The novel reveals him to be a Welsh miner. When his eyes roam the expanse of the mountain, they seek reconnection with his distant past, 'the days long ago, when I did used to walk the fields of the North before I came down here to work in the pits' (p. 1). Meanwhile, the boy, his young son named Len, strains his eyes towards a distant seascape, and 'wondered what the ships it held looked like, and vainly tried to magnify the black dots that dotted the ribbony gleam' of the waters (p. 2).

For a novel which, according to Carole Snee, privileges 'the shared experience of the collective life',[2] *Cwmardy*'s impressive opening focuses instead on the consciousness of two distinctive individuals. With enviable economy, the novel directs the reader to their inner selves, to their shared sense of yearning. Despite his renegade appearance, the 'pensively motionless' (p. 1) Big Jim reflects wistfully on the freedom of a past recollected but irrecoverable, while Len hungers for wider prospects, both visual and imagined, expressed through his rapt fascination with an alluring distant horizon. Both figures are physically where they are, and imaginatively are somewhere else. 'The desire to change places', writes Jane Tompkins, 'also signals a powerful need for self-transformation',[3] a need thwarted in Big Jim and his son by the coercive power of industrial capitalism – its economic exploitation and mechanisation of the human presence. When the novel returns the figures from the mountain to their village, the perspective narrows from horizons both glimpsed and remembered as their bodies become irradiated by the 'palpitating throb of the pit engines' (p. 4). Like R. S. Thomas's Cynddylan on his tractor, they then become 'part of the machine',[4] as *Cwmardy* shifts its focus from the introspective, individual human to the corporately structured functionary. By doing so, the narrative prepares itself to present male characters who are commodified and rendered emotionally intransitive by an industrial capitalism whose 'purpose', as Steve Bodington suggests, 'is not a human purpose'.[5]

Published in the same year as *Cwmardy*, George Orwell's essay 'Down the Mine' famously distinguishes coal mining from other work as 'an almost superhuman job by the standard of an ordinary person', and miners themselves as characterised by 'their most noble bodies; wide shoulders, tapering to slender supple waists, and small pronounced buttocks and sinewy thighs'.[6] In lauding miners' exceptionalism, Orwell collectivises them into an iconic homogeneity centred on their bodies. For Raymond Williams, such generalising has an obverse face, where collectivised identity accommodates a 'political formula by means of which it seems possible to convert the majority of one's fellow human beings into masses'.[7] *Cwmardy* challenges this humanly degrading 'political formula' by emphasising how the individual predicament of the working-class male is a subject worthy of intense fictional examination.[8] Because *Cwmardy* is generally read, when it is read at all, as a doctrinal text, the literary merit required to effect this examination is largely marginalised.[9] David Bell, for instance, regards it as his critical duty 'to explicate the doctrinal message of the novel'.[10] This chapter begins from the premise that *Cwmardy* is the product of a novelist engaging through his own complex, fissured self with an economic enterprise requiring humanly reductive, individually corrosive and morally pernicious masculine conformity. It is a novel, as Aidan Byrne says, 'of loss and alienation rather than of transformation and settlement'.[11] The estrangement examined in this chapter is not only the alienation of the worker from his work, but the male individual estranged from himself when confronted by the limiting paradigms of coercive gender definition required by patriarchal capitalism.

This chapter proposes that, when read as a creative novel, the power of *Cwmardy* lies less in its doctrinaire conformity than in its humanistic critique of the challenges patriarchal capitalism imposes on individual self-integration. In this reading, Big Jim Roberts becomes miner as victim, not miner as hero. *Cwmardy*, I argue, examines how his fragile sense of superior 'otherness', nurtured by his experience as a soldier of Empire, requires the repression of his empathetic self so that he may continually demonstrate his difference from/superiority to other men, either with his shovel at work or his fists in the pub. This narrow definition governs his identity. His son Len sits at the opposite end of the masculine spectrum from his father. Physically frail, traumatised when young by the death of a sister for whom he felt a confused, transgressive love, he finds a public identity as a miners' representative that is incompatible with the novel's insistence on his passivity and 'temperamental unsociability' (p. 232). Experiencing alienation from what he sees as the powerful forms of masculinity around him, beset by what *Cwmardy* tantalisingly describes as a never satisfied 'vague emotional hunger' (p. 2), and a prey to his vivid imagination, he self-deludingly believes he has fashioned himself into a stabilised class activist by the close of the novel. In Gramscian terms, both characters strive for a 'modifying [of] their own habits, their own will, their own convictions' in order to conform to the physically demanding coordinates of an industrial masculinity.[12] In this reductive context, neither character is offered the opportunity for creative self-development, but only a reiterative enactment of self-limiting, pre-determined roles. By distinguishing the two individuals so clearly, *Cwmardy* transcribes a gender arc exhibiting how thoroughly the precepts defining working-class masculinity are propagated, nurtured and percolated through a dominant patriarchal culture to the economic and organisational benefit of those who disseminate them and the individual detriment of those required to enact them.

Thematic and structural unity are often seen as markers of classic English fiction. Carole Snee, for instance, takes the view that the novel as a genre has 'to create an internal "real" world of the text, which has its own coherence and "explanations"'. For Snee, *Cwmardy* fails to achieve this totalising coherence and, as a consequence, its individual successes 'never become part of a unified whole'.[13] This is certainly one way of looking at it. But *Cwmardy* is a novel articulating a Welsh, not an English, experience, and more particularly a Valleys' experience. Pierre Macherey offers another approach to reading a novel like *Cwmardy*, in which 'coherence' is not the source of its value. Macherey argues that a literary work is 'never entirely premeditated; or rather it is, but at several levels at once, without deriving monolithically from a unique and simple conception'.[14] Indeed, when *Cwmardy* is read as a novel from a gender-specific viewpoint rather than as a political manifesto, it becomes apparent that various forms of fragmentation generate its power as a novel, define its architectural shape and become one of its key motifs. As a motif, it defines the novel's critique of industrial capitalism where fragmentation of the self within self takes different forms in Jim and Len Roberts, and neither can unify nor progress under the prevalent economic model. All Jim and Len are left with in their behavioural rhythms is 'the flat repetition of existing patterns'.[15]

Cwmardy is a novel in which, at the level of individual identity, there is not, and cannot be, the expectation of coherence within self, whatever dubious coherence may exist within the ideology of industrial capitalism itself. When approached this way, *Cwmardy* offers a frame for a gender-specific reading beyond the 'unique and simple conception' of the text's declared aim: 'to "novelise" [...] a phase of working-class history'.[16] Implicit both in its construction and its representation of fragmented masculine identity, *Cwmardy* exposes what Macherey describes as 'the fallacy of the rules [and] the fallacy of harmony'.[17] Instead, *Cwmardy* creates a hybrid form in which the generics of *Bildungsroman*, veiled autobiography, socio-political history, and family saga are manipulated and contribute in a dynamic, if fragmented, form, allowing for a representation of fragmented masculinities.

In the formal hybridising of *Cwmardy*, writes Rolf Meyn, 'proletarian fictional autobiography and proletarian *Bildungsroman* overlap'.[18] There is doubtless a confluence of these two generic streams in *Cwmardy*, though the autobiographical current may be read in a different way from Meyn, who places his emphasis on 'the close resemblance' of Lewis Jones to Len in their career trajectories where, somewhat fortuitously it would appear, Len's eventual death in Spain (in *We Live*) is 'almost prophetic' of Jones's own early death. Furthermore, Meyn continues, there is also 'some psychological connection between Jones's illegitimacy and the familial structures in the novel'.[19] Stephen Knight brings a different approach to *Cwmardy* as veiled autobiography. He detects features of the *roman à clef*, where 'the title *Cwmardy* has a general, even allegorical effect, referring to the mining town of Maerdy', and the characters are as symbolic as the title where 'Len has the role of Lewis Jones', and Ezra Jones, the miners' union leader, seems 'to combine aspects of Mabon with Noah Rees'.[20]

47

Of more relevance to this chapter than identifying specific autobiographical patterns within the novel's carpet is Lewis Jones's interest in Len's complex, insecure masculinity. R. W. Connell's observation that the 'sense of the fragility of adult masculinity [is] founded on the tragic encounter between desire and culture' proves instructive here.[21] Len's tragic encounter with the 'desire' generated by his hypersensitive unsociability and the performative impositions placed on him by his 'culture' are imaginatively generated elaborations and explorations of the same tensions between 'desire and culture', the inner and outer self, that exist in Lewis Jones himself. It is in this arena that the depiction of Len as a form of autobiographical exposition becomes most fruitful, for it replaces the autobiographical novel as a series of detectable and determinate correspondences with autobiography as contributing to a creatively expansive, fictional exploration of cultural coercion generated and validated by personal experience. In the words of John Pikoulis, *Cwmardy* becomes 'a more complicated work than the reference to "novelising" life in Jones's preface might imply',[22] for as much as it is a novel of political commitment, it becomes also an inquiry, through the characterisation of Len, into an extreme form of liminal, conflicted masculinity unusual, if not unique, in anglophone Welsh industrial fiction.

But readings privileging either *Cwmardy*'s ideological or autobiographical axis undervalue its literary merit. Len is no fictional *doppelgänger* of Jones, who was more gregarious than Len, and displayed an uncontroversial male ability to dominate public space.[23] Unlike Len, he was something of 'a man's chap',[24] assiduously cultivating a bravura image of the rakishly engaging male.[25] However, his masculine performativity coexisted with an expressive emotionalism of which unrestrained adult tears, similar to Len's, were a visual and recurring feature. The most striking aspect of Lewis Jones's character, according to his friend Billy Griffiths, was not his carefully cultivated jauntiness, nor a conventionally masculine rationality expressed through abstract political dogma,[26] nor a dashing iconoclasm, but an acute sensibility. In an interview with Hywel Francis, Griffiths stated that Lewis Jones's principal quality was 'love of people and compassion. I have seen Lewis […] sitting down listening to two old people telling him about their troubles and tears running down his cheek.'[27]

It is from the tensions peculiar to Lewis Jones's own masculinity, between *eros* and *agape*, communist theory and humanist practice, passionate oratory and lachrymose sensibility, 'man's chap' and creative novelist that the fissured character of Len Roberts springs, and it is these tensions which constitute the novel's most intriguing autobiographical focus. To extend what Pikoulis states,[28] valuing *Cwmardy* as a historical document misplaces its achievement in creating such hypersensitive masculinity in Len Roberts in an arena where mental and physical resilience and display were the expected and revered norms. Such a focused, intense representation required a reformulation of the *Bildungsroman* which drives Len's narrative. The traditional *Bildungsroman* articulates the bourgeois conception of the autonomous figure, the 'emergent self', who progresses towards full self realisation through an exercise of the will. In *Cwmardy*, the overarching power of capitalism reduces, even obliterates, individual autonomy, so that individual uniqueness becomes irrelevant to the industrial process, and progressive integration of self with self becomes virtually impossible. As the political theorist Steve Bodington states, 'Human individuality is "noise" disrupting the harmony of capital as organiser.'[29] In order to reinstate the tragedy of the unique individual amid such 'noise', *Cwmardy* utilises the *Bildungsroman*'s consoling assumption of individual progression towards fullness of self to expose it as a myth.

Susan Rubin Suleiman points out 'that we may define a story of apprenticeship (of *Bildung*) as two parallel transformations undergone by the protagonist: first, a transformation from *ignorance* (of self) to *knowledge* (of self); second, a transformation from *passivity* to *activity*' (original italics). Furthermore, 'the story of the apprenticeship ends on the threshold of a new life for the hero – which explains why in the traditional *Bildungsroman*, the hero is always a young man, often an adolescent.'[30] Rolf Meyn adds to this definition that in a proletarian *Bildungsroman* the protagonist's self-knowledge is 'never an end in itself, but part of a "totalising" truth in the form of political values'.[31] The transformations of Émile Zola's Étienne Lantier fit the paradigms that Suleiman and Meyn construct. Towards the close of *Germinal*, Étienne has acquired the self-knowledge, purposefulness and all the achieved unity of the 'totalised' male:

> He thought about himself, and knew that he was now strong, matured by his hard experience down the pit. His apprenticeship was over and he was going forth fully armed as a fighting missionary of the revolution, having declared war on society, for he had seen it and condemned it.[32]

Len regards himself at the close of *Cwmardy* in much the same univocal way as Zola presents Étienne. Having just displayed his proficiency in class-warrior-speak on the mountain where his narrative began, he squeezes the arm of Mary Jones, his lover and political comrade, 'with a warm confidence' (p. 310) and appears armed for the future struggle. But Étienne and Len inhabit different forms of *Bildungsroman*. The form Len inhabits addresses Bakhtin's 'problems of freedom and necessity',[33] problems which in Len's case expose unresolved tensions between passivity and action, public duty and private withdrawal, subjective absence and objective presence, self-knowledge and self-ignorance that, unlike Étienne, he is unable to resolve. Central to these tensions is Len's perception of himself as a man.

Readings of Len Roberts frequently privilege the politically public over the sensitively personal. David Bell, for example, concedes of *Cwmardy* that 'Len's development as an individual in physical and emotional terms is also present but subordinate to the prime objective of the acquisition of the doctrine'.[34] Central to this 'prime objective', Bell explains, is the novel's need 'to constrain interpretation to a desired outcome',[35] the 'desired outcome' being Len's totalised progression towards political activism. Unlike Bell, Emma Smith focuses on Len as a problematised individual, but like him regards Len's progression to full political consciousness as a teleological inevitability. For Smith, *Cwmardy* 'destabilises hegemonic forms of masculinity only to then reassert them', and requires Len to 'negotiate his way through a series of situations and relationships designed to threaten not only his productive activity as a political subject, but also his "masculinity"', before he develops into 'an ideal "masculine" autonomous political subject'.[36] Len's 'journey' in this reading follows the direction of the traditional *Bildung* figure where he successfully nullifies his emotional turbulence to stand at the close of the novel as the emergent representative of a new dawn. Each of these critical positions privileges a predetermined reading of the novel where the formal conventions of the text are as tightly regulated as the revolutionary ideology they espouse.

But Len's form of masculinity runs counter to the notion of steady, if necessarily vexing personal development, of obstacles confronted and successfully overcome, that is the paradigm of the *Bildungsroman*. Rather, he is created from what Susan Suleiman describes as 'the coexistence of "several discourses" in a single (inter)textual space'. Recognising that such discourses can be conflictual, Suleiman explains that they 'confront each other without cancelling each other out and without being integrated into a single unified discourse'.[37] The confrontation in *Cwmardy* exists in its presentation of a Len Roberts who apparently progresses towards political maturity and a Len Roberts who is a study in continuing psychic impairment. Read this way, the latter is not a distraction from the former as Bell argues,[38] but a means of examining the repressive effect of a dominant industrial ideology on a complex individual driven by confused and inarticulate longing. Ambivalence is inscribed into Len's characterisation. *Cwmardy*, therefore, has two stories to tell of Len, two competing modal registers, and it is essential to the text's success that they have no means of integrating. John Pikoulis is one of the few critics to argue the case for the divided Len, one of whom is the 'golden-tongued' political subject, the other a disturbed, fragmented figure – sexually insecure, hypersensitive, and passive – 'who, if Jones were really writing a political novel, would be quite superfluous'.[39] Len's anguished attempts to cross from the margin of his passive self to the centre of the public stage and 'become a man' are persistently undermined by his inability to engage with – let alone accommodate – his debilitating sensibility. In dramatising so powerfully his sense of personal failure and his incapacity for self-reflection, *Cwmardy* critiques the capitalist commodification of the self into a unit of production through its universalised conception of manhood.

Regarding male subjectivity, Peter Middleton observes: 'With its emphasis on the male as active agent, norms of masculine identity have not developed a comprehensive discourse for self-interrogation. And reflection.'[40] And so, for all Len's 'natural tendency to introspection' (p. 14), he is never represented as able to question adequately the particular nature of his own emotional and psychic complexity.[41] He is angered and puzzled by Evan the Overman's son's refusal to marry Jane, his pregnant sister, and he 'pondered the problem of Jane' (p. 52); but he lacks the vocabulary to address his own incipiently transgressive feelings for her. Instead of internalising 'the problem', or even recognising a potential rival in his affection for her and the complications that presents, he externalises it, so that 'The hatred he felt for Evan the Overman's son slowly diffused itself into a hatred of all those classed as officials' (p. 53). The irony in his construction, therefore, is that while he is depicted as introverted, prevailing norms of masculinity provide no means for critical introspection of his own emotional sensitivity. The novel finally grants him a limited realisation that 'he was more of a nervous being than a consistently thinking individual' (p. 293), but this is very much a partial *anagnorisis*, arising from Ezra's comment, 'You see things as you desire them to be at the moment instead of as they actually are' (p. 293). Thought and feeling occupy different realms of individual consciousness in Len, but the novel's point here is that he is able to affirm the insight only by standing outside himself, through what Peter Middleton describes as 'the alienated form of [oneself] as the object of someone else's judgement'.[42]

In order to perform satisfactorily to the requirements of industrial capitalism Len Roberts needs to demonstrate certain signifiers of normative masculinity. As Andrew Tolson noted in an early venture into masculine studies, 'the qualities needed by the successful worker are closely related to those of the successful man.' Among these qualities 'physical strength or mechanical expertise [and] ambition and competitiveness' are among the most notable.[43] Of these, strength and expertise are evident in somatic performance, whereas ambition and competitiveness require inner mental determination in the undeviating progression towards a fixed purpose. Len Roberts displays none of these attributes. He is even, as Pikoulis notes, a 'reluctant politician, one who would much rather consult his own interests'.[44] Yet immersion into the coded fellowship of unified 'manhood' is the prize for which he is represented as striving throughout the novel, unable to question, despite his undoubted intelligence, the reasons for his demonstrable inability to be admitted to it, or noticing the cruel irony that by striving to conform to the prevailing model he sustains the very capitalism he opposes.

Cwmardy states categorically that with Jane's death came 'the end of his boyhood' (p. 67), but in which sense remains obscure, for Len remains persistently vexed by the adult world. The bipolarities of his individuality – political commitment and temperamental introversion – remain intransitive, the one progressive, the other static, so that his commitment to an emancipatory politics is not accompanied by a release from his enfeebling sensitivity. Having introduced the particular constituents of his young masculinity at the outset of the narrative, *Cwmardy* produces a series of structural continuities which position his reflexive sensibility against his progressive rationality from the point when he leaves school to work in the pit. Concentrating primarily on the representation of the 'private', troubled Len, the Len who subverts the *Bildungsroman* with its progression to maturity, the following paragraphs examine the manner in which *Cwmardy* probes Len's masculinity to reveal how its defining characteristics remain constant and irreconcilable from boyhood through to adulthood.[45]

At the funeral of the miners killed in the explosion (chapter VI), the young Len is depicted as understandably, but exceptionally, emotional and confused. As his 'brain twirled in a vortex' (p. 104), he animates the pit into an ogre with an insatiable appetite for miners' bodies, and as so often when emotionally overcome, he is shown closing his eyes to abstract himself from a reality he cannot confront. Despite this traumatic experience, so alluring are the prevailing norms of masculine identity that he completely underestimates the lasting horror of the funeral, and the consequences of his flight from school to the harsher regime of work underground, a site for him of incontestable masculinity. This cultural naturalising of oppressive gender norms is evident as he publicises his intention of leaving school for the pit, and delights in becoming 'a hero' (p. 106), the man-to-be, to his schoolmates. Judith Butler observes that 'Universalist claims are based on a common or shared epistemological standpoint',[46] and, for Len, integration into a communal identity is represented as a desirable alternative to the depersonalisation and alienation he had experienced at school. But *Cwmardy* illustrates how remote such an 'epistemological standpoint' is for Len. To achieve recognition and integration, he 'conjured up for [his schoolmates] a romantic vista of what work meant' (p. 106). Monochrome reality, as so often with Len, conflicts with his own preference for the colour of romance, for abstraction from the material world into an idealised, imagined landscape.

Cwmardy destroys such romantic vistas for him when he begins work. In a lengthy narrative exposition, it clinically exposes the brutally de-humanising nature of the labour required, and Len's own extreme physical and temperamental aversion to it. In an example of his recurring naivety, the narrative has him believe that the simple act of turning up for work will instigate an immediate 'instantiation of masculinity',[47] a status mysteriously conferred rather than performatively achieved. His receipt of his miner's lamp is, he believes, a ritualised moment of transfiguration. Convinced that he is progressing from innocence to experience, from junior to senior status, he '*at once* felt himself a man' (p. 107, my italics). *Cwmardy* employs two strategies to disabuse him: his involuntary 'terror-stricken, hysterical' weeping when he discovers the harsh reality of mining, which brings a sharp reprimand from his father (p. 116); and the introduction of an enlarged referent of stabilised youthful masculinity in Will Evans. Will's narrative function is to serve as a composite assemblage of youthful phallic signifiers, all of which Len lacks. He functions as an exaggerated exemplar of the practice in which 'working-class masculinity becomes a kind of "performance"' where, as he grows up, a boy 'develops a repertoire of stories, jokes and routines'.[48] Six months into his role, Will Evans has already become a confident, strenuously self-promoting practitioner. Thoroughly credulous, Len stares 'with admiration' (p. 117) as Will parades his repertoire by blaspheming, spitting, demonstrating his familiarity with workplace jargon, and boasting of his prowess with pit ponies. And Len responds 'amazedly' (p. 117), as he often does, when Will informs him that he intends buying his own horse. Len's self-positioning as the uncritical, imperceptive acolyte connotes his own lack of performative confidence. Whereas Will publicly mimics the adult masculinity he admires and will later himself represent, the novel, in a deft touch, has Len, solitary once more among a crowd of miners as he returns home from his shift, glance surreptitiously into 'every window' (p. 120), anxious to catch a glimpse of his coal-blackened self. His repeated need to confirm his desired identity is a telling moment of Lacanian apperception. But like a mirror, the windows simply reflect a surface that is momentarily reassuring for him but as insubstantial as the masculinity he craves, despite the coal dust on his face.

Len's unwanted difference from his male peers and from the masculinity they embody features in two further examples occurring later in the text and illustrates the continuity of his conflicted representation. In the first example, the narrative once again uses Will Evans as the norm against whom he is inspected when, as a young adult, he meets Will and three others on the mountain. Aidan Byrne makes the point that 'Jones's mountains remain oppressively masculine',[49] and for Will and his companions they are a site of determinate masculine action, for on this occasion they are hunters, intent on luring a sheep to a cave and killing it for food. However, for Len, the mountain is associated with passive withdrawal and confused memories of his sister Jane. As a correlative of his inner lack of direction, the text notes that, unlike the purposeful Will, Len is 'wandering aimlessly' (p. 208) on the mountain, a recurring trope with him, after a disagreement with Ezra Jones, the union leader. The novel here starkly juxtaposes Will's progression from early mimic to authentic embodiment of physical masculinity alongside Len's arrested emotional development and continuing distracted unworldliness.

Despite the several visual clues of their intent before him, Len remains as naive as always: he 'had not the faintest idea' (p. 209) of what is going to happen until he sees the figure of the sheep. When Will rugby tackles it and cuts its throat, he demonstrates the power and self-control concomitant with normative masculinity when under the gaze of others. Len's reaction is predictably unique among those present, though reminiscent of his earlier 'sick giddiness' at work (p. 114).[50] Close to vomiting, he feels 'faint, and sharp dazzles twirled before his eyes' (p. 210). The episode closes with an unembellished diegetic comment, rich in suggestive insinuation regarding Len's place in the male community. On their way down the mountain, 'they met other groups of men laden as they were' (p. 210). Will's group is therefore only one of several engaged in sheep rustling, leaving unstated but implied the conclusion that Len was not invited to join any of them.

Len's precarious selfhood, labile susceptibility to persuasion, his sexual prudery and withdrawal from reality are all given prominence in a second example later still in the novel when, persuaded against his better judgement by Ezra and his daughter Mary, to whom Len is attracted, he decides to enlist for military service in 1914 (pp. 262–3). Textual implication and direct statement combine to expose what Berthold Schoene-Harwood describes as 'a societal frame of *Bildung* under whose systemic pressure individuals aspire to become the men and women they ought to be'.[51] Animating the entire episode is the repressive, naturalised agenda which demands conformity to 'the configurative standards of a societally acceptable masculinity'.[52] It is an example, rarely commented on, of *Cwmardy*'s individually humanistic focus, and reveals clearly how the novel continues to deny Len the progression of the traditional *Bildung* figure to maturation. His humiliation when Mary declares, 'I wish I were a man and able to go [to war]' (p. 257) acknowledges epistemological gender binaries, but equally importantly accepts that masculinity is recognised and validated by a limited range of characteristics, central to which is participation in violence.[53] How limited these characteristics are and how inapplicable they are to Len become evident when he himself attempts to enlist. Just as he was impressed as a boy by young Will Evans's boastful performativity in the pit, so he 'marvelled at [the] breezy nonchalance' (p. 262) of the young men queueing with him for a medical examination, unable to recognise in their careless repartee a homosocial displacement strategy for nervousness. He knows practically all of those present, but the novel focuses instead on his detachment and embarrassment when he is asked to strip for his medical. Kevin Devaney observes that coal face workers not only faced constant physical danger but also high temperatures in deep mines, and so 'Nakedness is accepted by miners', but for Len it is an obstacle to be overcome.[54] Revolted by the nakedness of the other volunteers, and discomforted by their sexually suggestive banter, he hopes for some privacy before undressing. In another of its seemingly innocuous but highly significant encodings, *Cwmardy* constructs a passage where Len's fear of physical exposure competes with his fear of ridicule if he seeks privacy. On an occasion where male agency is required, Len vacillates, is rendered acquiescent and, unable to act, mutely accedes to stripping himself in public (p. 263).

Failure confers an identity on him which he is unable either to rationalise or oppose when he learns he has failed his medical examination and is rejected for service. As happens elsewhere, his setback modulates into trauma and trauma modulates into retreat. Overwhelmed by 'a strong feeling of inferiority' (p. 263), he retires to bed, weeps, as he did on his first day at work, but finds consolation by removing himself from the agonising moment and constructing an alternative, romantic narrative as he did much earlier in his life. In doing so, he demonstrates what Peter Middleton calls a Lacanian 'neediness of desire',[55] the need to desire the desire of the other, the 'other' being the more militant Mary. Seduced by the male 'glamour of war', he 'imagined himself performing valiant deeds that won Mary's approbation and the applause of all the people' (p. 263). Through these powerfully articulated episodes, *Cwmardy* demonstrates how coercive is the dominant model of gender identification, and how antithetical to Len Roberts's particular hypersensitivity.

Graham Dawson notes that 'Imagined entities are shot through with wish-fulfilling fantasies',[56] and in its acute analysis of Len's divided self *Cwmardy* represents how he remains a 'queer lad for his age' (p. 14), whatever his age. In his schizoid representation, he is both a serious political activist – a 'pretty big figure in the strike' (p. 273) to a police inspector – and an immature adult, 'just a boy groping for something you are not even yet aware of' (p. 234) to the perceptive Mary. Immobilised psychologically when under pressure, craving self-justification through 'the applause of all the people', yet morose and solitary, unable to control either his imagination or his emotions, offended by displays of robust homosociality, he continually exhibits his distance from the kind of male identity Ben Knights describes as 'naturally characterised by strong boundaries'.[57] For him, failure to comply with the dominant discourses of masculinity is to fail the test of manhood, to make him feel 'an outcast' (p. 263). One of *Cwmardy*'s notable achievements is its refusal to offer the reassurance of progression. Through his desire to enter the gravitational pull of an industrial form of normative masculinity, and the torment he experiences in his recurring failure to do so, the narrative dispenses with the *Bildungsroman* as a Meynian 'totalising' development towards self-realisation. Instead, it manipulates a bourgeois form to expose 'the autonomy of the individual self in the presentation of character'[58] as a reassuring fiction, and Len Roberts stands as an acutely observed, individualised victim of a repressive socio-economic model.

In a moment of textual brilliance, *Cwmardy* provides a final reminder of how partial Len's progression from Suleiman's paradigm of '*ignorance* (of self) to *knowledge* (of self)' has been, how remote he is from a *Bildungsroman* hero in the Étienne Lantier mould of 'strong boundaries'. Near the end of the narrative, *Cwmardy* returns to a landscape with figures, this time with three figures – Len, Mary and Ezra – gazing down at the blighted valley. Suddenly, 'A hooter from below sent its wailing note up the mountain. Len *started, as if the sound were strange to him*' (p. 308, my italics). For all his grasp of the doctrinal rhetoric he mouths moments later, the outside world, the world of daily struggle continues to be an abrupt intrusion from which he remains temperamentally estranged. There is no need for textual interjection to explain where he was in his abstracted landscape when he starts at the familiar sound of the hooter. It is enough that its 'wailing note' brings no such psycho-physical shocked response from the more focused Mary or Ezra. In a wonderfully circular movement, the incident reminds the reader of the lingering 'vague emotional hunger that made him sad' (p. 2) in his childhood. The novel closes in an upbeat manner, but in a final modifying touch we note that although he 'squeezed Mary's arm with warm confidence' he and she have to negotiate a 'rocky path that led back to Cwmardy' (p. 310). Len's path through *Cwmardy* has been persistently rocky, a recurring pattern of intentions and expectations frustrated when confronting grim realities. When a young boy, he believed that receipt of a miner's lamp would magically confer masculinity on him; when rejected by the army he sought refuge in romantic dreams of derring-do. Lewis Jones closes *Cwmardy* on Len's intentions and expectations. But we are left wondering where he will be in his imaginative hinterland when the next hooter sounds.

If the architectural framework of *Cwmardy* subverts the progression to selfhood of the Étienne Lantier *Bildung* figure, the novel also moves in a different direction in the attention it accords Len's individual subjectivity. Because critical attention has focused largely on *Cwmardy* as political doctrine, little attention has been given to the care with which it constructs the determining features of Len's damaged psyche.[59] By consigning Len to 'representative status',[60] such readings marginalise the contribution *Cwmardy* makes in depicting the tormented subjectivity of a working-class male in a culture where gender conformity is the unstated expectation. Through Len, *Cwmardy* implicitly challenges the assumption that psychological depth and emotional sensitivity are characteristics of bourgeois refinement only.[61] The culturally generated assumptions of miners as Orwellian supermen is one formulaic construction that compels a Len to live with demons he cannot contain or express. Readings of *Cwmardy* that marginalise this more problematic aspect of Len's representation minimise the novel's power as both a social critique and as a work of imaginative fiction, fiction without the accompanying half-explanatory, half-apologetic descriptors of 'proletarian' or 'working-class'.

Cwmardy is usually positioned unproblematically within the realist novel form, a form that Carole Snee suggests is 'the most readily available mode of expression for writers not schooled within a literary tradition'.[62] But in constructing Len's individual masculinity *Cwmardy* often veers away from determinate realism towards experimental symbolic signification revealing a literary imagination seeking freedom to explore a highly distinctive consciousness – and subconsciousness – rather than remain within the more straitened form of the *roman à thèse*.[63] Len's displaced connection with empirical reality through his use of imaginative figuration is one method the novel uses, but so is an imbricated network of tropes with gender connotations with which he becomes progressively associated, and through which his variance from normative masculinity is defined. The following paragraphs examine these two methodologies to suggest that while Lewis Jones may not have been 'schooled within a literary tradition', in constructing Len Roberts's masculinity he was no unsophisticated novice either.

Throughout *Cwmardy*, Len responds to the external world through the prism of figurative association. Although the text offers several examples of his vivid imagination, there has been little critical inspection of the influence this has on the construction of his character in general, or the nature of his masculinity in particular. Yet it is a recurring feature of his cognitive functioning, and it signals his need for a retreat from a drab, oppressive reality and a re-engagement with it in a redefined, more sensuously imaginative formulation. The novel establishes this characteristic at the outset, and at this early stage of Len's development it identifies a mind creating a reality through free association. Returning from a mountain walk with his father, he comments that the swirling smoke eddies from the pit 'brought to his mind thoughts of the broth he had often seen his mother make' (p. 4). The simple analogy 'tickled Big Jim' (p. 4). In rapid succession, the mountain track leading to the pit becomes 'ashamed of its eventual destination' (p. 4); 'to his imaginative eyes' the rail tracks from the pithead resemble 'veins of quickly coursing blood' (p. 5); the whirlpools in the river 'do look like it is quarrelling with itself' (p. 6); and 'twinkling lights from the windows looked like far-away stars' (p. 9). School 'had become a monster that was going to rob him of his mountain rambles' (p. 25). These images have a more than ornamental function in Len's construction, for figurative language, as Suresh Srivastva and Frank J. Barrett, inform us, 'can communicate an emotional reality that lies just beyond our conscious awareness'.[64]

As he grows older, Len's sense stimuli become attuned to a more intense reality that connects him graphically with the brutal reality of his existence, so that 'the resonance of possible associations and connotations [construct] a new contextual meaning'.[65] The pit becomes an 'inhuman monster' (p. 104); underground roadways are imagined as the pit's 'knotted arteries', with men reduced to functionaries 'circulating in these like blood' (p. 219). And when the hooter sounds at the end of the novel, startling him back into the present, it is to figuration that he immediately falls to shape his reality: 'Hear the whip crack? I wonder if all those who respond to its lash tonight will come back up in the morning' (p. 309). Srivastva and Barrett contend that metaphorical associations 'are clues to the underlying paradigm of a given social system'.[66] Len's figurative responses to sense stimuli articulate a masculinity deviating from denotative masculine rationalism, but they offer him an alternative means of engaging with 'the underlying paradigm of a given social system'. As these examples illustrate, Len's connotative imagination is the filter through which he interprets the material world. But as Peter Middleton notes, 'Masculinity has a vested interest in blocking unheroic, masculine self-analysis.'[67] Within its compositional framework *Cwmardy* constructs in Len a figure whose industrialised culture, predicated on gender asymmetry, denies him the means to question the constituents of his own masculinity. And so instead the novel associates Len with a series of locations and experiences carrying a complex meshing of connotatively gendered significations. From the outset the narrative acknowledges Len's heterosexuality, while associating him with emotive and psychic configurations traditionally coded as feminine.[68] These configurations are articulated metonymically through the suggestive associations of his bed, the mountain, water and various other forms of deliquescence. Individually, each of these has its own culturally generated dimensions, but they combine discursively to acquire accumulated resonance as the narrative unfolds. Their recursion adds a level of suggestive significance which the text never formally acknowledges, but which contributes to Len's representation as a divided, complex subject. Each of the three tropes is associated with a network of culturally feminised principles that connect to Len, and each is associated with his relationship with his sister Jane, and with Mary Jones.

The bed which Len and Jane share as brother and sister becomes in *Cwmardy* a site of multiple associations for Len, embracing passivity, security, incipient sexual desire, womblike regression, and repressed gender anxieties. Jane is five years older than Len – the text is imprecise about their actual ages, although she is sixteen or seventeen when she dies in childbirth. The novel focalises through Len what happens in the bed and lends itself to a Freudian reading of Oedipal desire transferred from Len's mother, Siân, to his sister.[69] As Len lies passively watching Jane undress, she becomes for him an elemental concretisation of two key female principles: fecund young womanhood and maternal affection. He is fascinated by her maturing body, especially, and significantly, the growth of her breasts, which he enjoys fondling. Following Freud, Ben Knights comments:

> The state of being male – so far from being self-contained and sure of itself – is actually a state of longing, for transformative contact with an object that would enhance and irradiate your being, assuaging all that sense of loneliness and lostness.[70]

For Len, Jane is at once an object and a subject: a sexualised object of his masculine gaze and a subject of his own gender completion. When he 'pressed the hot wick of the candle into the oily grease' (p. 40), and a weeping Jane 'drew his wavy head to her bosom, which he clasped with a loving tenderness' and she takes care not to remove his hand, the text constructs a complex matrix of Freudian implications, conflating 'dormant mother-love' (p. 40), gender interdependence, innocent babes in the wood, and sexualised gratification.

From the outset, Jane is associated in Len's mind with the mountain, which is itself invested with gender significance. As he watches her undressing, his 'mind again traversed the mountains' (p. 15), where he is able to wander liberated from the gender prescriptions prevailing in the valley below. Providing an alternative but equally viable interpretation of gendering through landscape, Katie Gramich writes that, in Welsh fiction 'the hills are feminised, breast-like protuberances, giving succour to sensitive males wounded by the brutal masculinity of their culture'.[71] In *Cwmardy*, the mountain itself has several symbolic functions and in this particular context it becomes a 'vast bed which nestled [young lovers'] bodies to its breast' (p. 170). It is no accident, then, that when Len mourns Jane's death in childbirth he wanders aimlessly on the mountain, on which he lies and cries. Given the associations between Jane's breasts, Len's desire for tactile contact with them, and the mountain as both a mothering breast and a bed, he lies on the mountain so that bodily connection with it becomes, at a deep level of psychic need, a communion with Jane herself. It is a site where he becomes both masculinised and feminised, desiring her, but also weeping and 'pierced' (p. 67) by the coldness of dusk.

The connection between their shared bed and the mountain continues even after Jane's death as the means of exploring Len's gender definition. Daydreams and 'absences' function as indices of his need either to remove himself from the material world or to reformulate it, but it is through his anxious nightmares that the novel scrutinises most vividly the repressed complexity of his gendering. Fretful after a conversation with Ezra Jones, for example, he seeks the consoling comfort of his bed, where thoughts of Mary, Ezra's daughter, run through his mind 'like a burning thread' (p.224). The connection between Jane and Mary through a particular anatomical feature becomes apparent as he dreams that he and Mary were walking over the mountain hand in hand:

> He saw Jane waving to them, beckoning them on. They started to run, but Mary stumbled and fell. Stopping to pick her up, he saw her clasped in the arms of Evan the Overman's son, one breast hanging loose and flaccid through her blouse. Len moaned and tossed in his sleep as the dream gripped him. (p. 224)

But in the phantasmagoria of the dream, latent connections powerfully evoke suppressed aspects of Len's subjectivity which his conscious mind is unable to articulate. The dream is at once wish-fulfilment – he and Mary are walking hand in hand – and horror story located on the mountain, a space connected in his mind more with Jane than with Mary. In the unanchored state of the oneiric, subliminal associations reveal the deeply troubled state of Len's subjectivity. Jane's sudden appearance on the mountain coded as feminine indicates that the dream is about love, desire, rivalry and loss, the mountain representing Jane's body that Len desired and felt completion alongside. The sudden appearance of Evan the Overman's son, the father of Jane's dead child, with Mary 'clasped' in his arms, and the sight of Mary's breast conflate the iconography of Jane's seduction by Evan with anxieties about Mary, and fuse old, unresolved anxieties and hostilities with current insecurities. The verb 'clasped', both here and earlier when it was Len who 'clasped [Jane's bosom] with a loving tenderness' (p. 40) in bed after her seduction by Evan, connotes the conflict and fear in Len's mind that Mary will be lost to him just as Jane was. There is nothing neutral about the site where this dream occurs. In appearing on the mountain, Evan invades a dream-space associated in Len's mind with what Jane represents for him, and in that space robs him of another woman. Just as Len's bed offers no assurance of escape from an intrusive world so, on the dream-mountain with its multiple signifiers, Len is confronted with a ghastly past replicated in the possibility of an empty future.

The detailed probing of Len's anxiety dreams reverberates with gendered significance. 'A familiar theme in patriarchal ideology', as R. W. Connell writes, 'is that men are rational while women are emotional.'[72] The novel has already challenged this convenient patriarchal binary in a gender reversal where Len is 'more emotional than Mary [...] less inclined to critical analysis' (p. 224). His dream of Jane, Mary and their respective breasts (p. 224–5) offers powerful confirmation of his inability to control, through reason, the boundaries of his own subjectivity or to submit himself to critical analysis. He awakens the next morning 'feeling heavy and lethargic, while his head throbbed painfully' (p. 225), but as the product of a masculine culture he is unable consciously to turn his gaze inward and reflect upon his inner self. Instead, the text has him suppress his demons in the collective activities of the public space of work, where 'the main topic in the pits was the "federashon", as the men called it' (p. 225).

The complex associations of Len's bed and the mountains require contextualisation in the novel in order to evoke their particular symbolic function, for there is nothing culturally determinate in either beds or mountains to associate them exclusively with features traditionally regarded as feminine. The text's employment of liquid as a suggestive motif is different, and *Cwmardy* repeatedly constructs Len's permeable self through associative images of deliquescence. Marianne DeKoven argues that in patriarchal iconography water is 'the feminine element par excellence [...] It is incapable of form but is the necessary medium upon which form imprints itself.'[73] On more than a dozen occasions Len either weeps or is close to tears when emotion overwhelms him. Located in a liminal space when he daydreams, his mind 'floats' (pp. 15, 115). He timidly kisses Mary with 'all his body melting into the caress' (p. 250). After a disagreement with her regarding the justification for war, he finds himself 'floating in a mental whirlpool' (p. 286). From the outset, the sea has a particular fascination for him. On a visit to the seaside, he experiences 'an aching urge to ride its crests and hollows' (p. 34), the embedded sexuality of the representation allusively suggesting the complexities in his gender definition. Just as earlier, he 'loved to impress his "photo"' on the impermanent snow by lying 'prostrate' on it (p. 18), so his wish 'to ride' the waves is at once positionally masculine relative to a female element. Yet immersion in the waves simultaneously offers a dissolving of gender boundaries, a complex pyscho-physical state where traditional distinctions are at once recognised and negated.

In her essay on *Cwmardy*, Emma Davies sees Len as representing 'the evolution of masculinity at the beginning of the twentieth century'.[74] But it can be argued that *Cwmardy*'s considerable achievement lies elsewhere. It takes an imaginative novelist, employing 'experimental fictional interventions',[75] such as those discussed above, rather than a political polemicist to reveal that there is no evolution in Len's capacity to engage with his emotional self. Rather, *Cwmardy* explores through Len how, within a patriarchal model, 'masculinity represents an imperative ideal of systemic perfection that obstructs rather than facilitates the liberation of the self'.[76] What has changed over time is not so much an evolution of what men are essentially like, but what they are allowed to be within the norms of a particular culture. It is society's willingness to begin dismantling gender imperatives that 'facilitates the liberation of the self', but any possibility of its happening – as begins to happen with Iwan Jones in *Until Our Blood is Dry* (2014) – comes too late for Len and, as the following paragraphs suggest, much too late for Big Jim.

Writing of a period of English literary history more than three centuries earlier than the version of Welsh mining history presented in *Cwmardy*, and within an entirely different social milieu, Stephen Greenblatt notes:

Whenever I focused sharply upon a moment of apparently autonomous self-fashioning, I found not an epiphany of identity freely chosen, but a cultural artifact. If there remained traces of free choice, the choice was among possibilities whose range was strictly delineated by the social and ideological system in force.[77]

Greenblatt's comments apply as much to the construction of the fictional miner Big Jim Roberts as to Edmund Spenser or Thomas Wyatt, for *Cwmardy* defines Jim Roberts through the two working-class social systems available to him, soldiering and mining. *Cwmardy* employs both of these fields to illustrate how his masculinity is shaped and approved by expansionist and capitalist ideologies above and beyond him – by the army in the service of Empire, and by the pits in the service of capital. Jim's constant references to his service in the Boer War – the first appears as early as page 6 – have attracted little critical attention, but they contribute significantly to the matrix of interweaving and often contradictory masculine practices through which he denies the 'pensively motionless' (p. 1), reflective self, introduced at the start of the novel and indicated in glimpses elsewhere.

Jim's function in *Cwmardy* has seen him framed either as a simple contrast to the febrile Len or, as an uncomplicated stereotype within a doctrinal text. For Carole Snee, he and Siân represent 'all the finest attributes of the working class'.[78] Stephen Knight, in an illuminating discussion, sees him as a Rhondda version of 'The Big Hewer', a folk-hero like the Canadian logger Paul Bunyan or the Australian drover, 'The Man from Snowy River'.[79] For David Smith, he is 'an entirely representative type' who is often 'insensitive to the needs and frailties of his immediate family'.[80] He may also share the same heroic space as Big Bad John, the miner from the 1961 song.[81] All of them embody physical strength, courage and manual dexterity. All of them are cultural artefacts and all of them live in a vividly represented man's world. Jim Roberts's representation is easily mocked, too. Writing of 1930s proletarian fiction, Valentine Cunningham observes: 'Nowhere does the Bigness cult run bigger than among these fictions. The Big Worker – almost the same Big Worker – pops up everywhere. It's true that not quite *all* the big proletarians are actually called Jim.'[82] Surely, the amused tone conveys fundamental misrepresentations. In areas of heavy industry, it is hardly surprising that a respect for 'Bigness', for the fineness of a strong, big male body should be evident. Furthermore, the Big Jim figure was a popular folk hero for the working classes in Britain, America and Australia. And as for his name, the character construct James Roberts in *Cwmardy* simply carries the two most popular boy's names in the decade the novel was written. Big Jim may be a representative working-class he-man; James Roberts, however, is representative of something less easily dismissed.

A gender-specific reading of his construction reveals how the novel deconstructs this most seemingly iconic representation of unified working-class masculinity through a series of humanising contradictions to reveal the coercive imperatives of industrial capitalism laid on the individual. A better example of a masculinity performing to a regulated script in *Cwmardy* would be the miner Bill Bristol. Thoroughly interpellated into a system of industrial production, his *modus vivendi* is entirely straightforward: 'Without masters us cawn't have pits, without pits us cawn't have wages, and without wages us cawn't have beer and baccy and grub' (p. 14). In the company of men, as he is here, he defines himself purely through items of male activity and consumption; his young wife, who will later mourn his death underground, is not mentioned, nor is his child.

Like Bill Bristol, James Roberts is also a deracinated figure. His nostalgic memories of his homeland in north Wales are one of the first things the text tells us about him. Unlike Bill Bristol, he is divided within himself, a textual embodiment of antagonistic influences through whom, as Pierre Macherey states, 'conflict is not resolved or absorbed but simply *displayed*' (original italics).[83] In *Cwmardy* his gendered predicament is presented through two fields of exposition: his home, where he is the titular head of a house to which he is both intimately connected yet liminally positioned; and his relationship with fellow miners in public spaces where his prickly pride and massive body tolerate no insults. The 'Wild West desperado' of the novel's opening paragraph is in fact a figure whose strenuous masculine practice is less a demonstration of his stable hegemonic self than a perpetual appeal for attention and gender validation.

As with Len, the intransitive elements of his identity are revealed side by side without much in the way of direct narrative comment; they are simply displayed as the inevitable consequences of a required cultural conformity. Yet the frequency with which this happens suggests that it is part of a narrative manoeuvre whose effect reveals fissures in Jim as a subject. He has been regarded as a simple, unified construction whose textual function is ideologically driven, and who provides through his functional simplicity a few smiles along the way. There are several episodes in *Cwmardy* for instance, where the Jim-at-home figure provides what in one context may be read as a little light relief as he is reduced to adolescent impotence by Siân. When he thinks she has discovered a small cache of money he has hidden for himself (which she has), for example, he gives her 'a scared look', and 'he submitted meekly' (p. 31) when she forgives him by maternally straightening his tie. In a later episode, she scorns him for bringing home 'boy's money', so that he 'began to wheedle' in a form of adolescent pleading: 'Come, nghyariad i [*sic*], give me my pocket-money' (p. 69). But the reversal of roles in such incidents carries a far deeper and more serious intent than simple droll diversion. They expose the theoretical precepts of patriarchy to be pragmatically untenable and relationally problematic. The male-at-work figure, subordinated within a larger hierarchical patriarchy, does not become, by a seamless congruence, the settled patriarch at home. Through Jim Roberts's ambiguous position at home in Sunny Bank, *Cwmardy* critiques a model of social construction that inhibits the male cultivation of a full adult sensibility and denies women a role outside the home.

In one of its most remarkable passages, *Cwmardy* reveals how the precepts of patriarchal masculinity thwart the fullness of male self actualisation when Jane, the daughter Jim adores, gives birth to a stillborn child and dies herself. The bedroom where this occurs becomes an exclusion zone for him, a female enclosure occupied by Siân and her neighbour Mrs Thomas, who, as older women, have been initiated into the mysteries of childbirth. The Siân/Jane connection, which has already suggested a matrilineal domestic succession, is strongly evoked here as Jim is relegated to the kitchen, where his desperation and isolation are fuelled by an ignorance he cannot satisfy and find frustrated expression in pointless agitated movement. In a series of tautly written physical actions, *Cwmardy* strips Jim of his carefully cultivated masculine presence and reduces him to helpless impotence. There is 'no intimacy in most male friendships and none of what intimacy offers: solace and support,'[84] writes Michael E. McGill, and Jim's solitary predicament is given graphic illustration, where upstairs in Sunny Bank Mrs Thomas offers Siân support and, later, solace when Jane dies. In the feminine space of the kitchen, Jim has no company except his bewildered son. In a powerful, multilayered image, the novel notes how he 'began a soft, regular swaying as though trying to soothe a child cradled in his arms' (p. 54). Craving the comfort of physical embrace himself, yet wishing also to offer it to his daughter, his body pathetically attempts to provide it for itself. But cradling an imaginary child is a poor substitute for cradling Jane as she screams in pain in the bedroom above. Valentine Cunningham regards the episode as one instance among several in *Cwmardy* of Lewis Jones's love of 'Deaths sudden, deaths gruesome'. But his judgement that '*Cwmardy* has Jim's young daughter dying most spectacularly' surely sensationalises the scene,[85] for the novel's perspective distances what is happening upstairs. Not only is a helpless, lonely Jim separated from the drama, but so is the implied male reader who becomes necessarily implicated in Jim's inarticulate agonies. What we are invited to witness instead are the damaging consequences to the male when the systemic conditioning required to function as a patriarch conflicts with an overwhelming desire to express himself as a nurturing parent. He becomes a 'hermetic being, closed up in himself',[86] excluded from the drama happening upstairs. In his own home. Ensnared in an epistemological void of gender definition, Jim is unable to connect to himself, lacks the means to reach out to others and loses all the masculine agency through which he defines himself. With Jane close to death, when Siân instructs him to get ready for work she tacitly confirms his supernumerary status, and he complies 'without a word' (p. 55). As he leaves the house,

> His eyes were blind to the black bordered streaks that ran across the sky at the bottom of the valley [...] His ears were deaf to the loudly shrieking pit hooters that raped the early morning air with violent echoes. He paid no attention to their frenzied demand that he hurry to the pit. Imperceptibly his body melted into the silent, shadowy line of men that wound its way up the hill to the colliery. (p. 56)

Unable to express his own grief, it is the narrative voice that powerfully communicates it for him, through images that reduce him psychologically to insentience and physically to insubstantiality.

Using a few deftly chosen comments on Jim's behaviour after Jane's death, *Cwmardy* illuminates the coercive influence of hegemonic masculinity on a sensibility that requires, as Peter Middleton states, the display of 'strength and invulnerability' and the 'suppression of feeling'.[87] Jim soon enacts 'the usual routines of his life' (p. 68) – drinking in the Boar's Head and fighting – in order to buttress his macho image. It is left once more to the narrative voice to articulate for him, in a telling litotes, a response he cannot acknowledge to himself or to others: 'the death of his daughter had shaken Big Jim' (p. 68). By quickly reverting to his macho role in the public space of the Boar's Head, he demonstrates his apparent imperviousness to pain, whether from loss of a daughter or from blows in a fight. The novel's taut representation of his earlier agonies, however, inscribes a different narrative and a different Jim. That different Jim, James Roberts, an emotionally illiterate but instinctively sensitive individual, emerges several times in the novel. In an echo of the scene above, but occurring in a different space and in different circumstances, it is Jim who puts his arms 'gently beneath the poor mangled body' (p. 139) of Bill Bristol, fatally injured underground, and lays him down with the tenderness of a breast-feeding mother for her child. The ironic contrast with his separation from his dying daughter is powerful, but even here in his masculine world his tenderness must be internalised and redirected through the objectifying distance of banter: 'you will soon be all over the old' ooman as strong as ever' (p. 139). Whether at home or at work, Jim's circumstances deny him the full expression of a more complex self, and by situating him frequently in public spaces, *Cwmardy* exposes the sustained pressure he feels to confirm the public image he has constructed as the iconic, stable hegemonic male.

Interestingly, Jim's notions of what constitute masculinity were formed, approved and settled outside the context of the mining Valleys. It is his service as a soldier of Empire that has shaped his dominant, boastful, emotionally repressed self. His recurring references to his experiences in the Boer War, and the many 'finger soiled' copies (p. 11) of *The History of the Boer War* that lie in conspicuous presence on a kitchen shelf, attest to its lingering influence on his self-perception. [88] As John Tosh explains, it was the imperial call to arms that 'beckoned young men in reaction against domesticity'[89] and its feminised associations. Having joined the militia, 'just prior to Jane's birth', Jim volunteered for active service 'immediately the Boer War was declared' (p. 11). In doing so, he not only reacted against domesticity; he paradoxically fled from it into an enterprise whose controlling ideologies of power and presence remain constitutive elements in his public identity throughout the novel.

Perhaps foremost of these imperial influences was 'enabling the imagining of English-British adventurers as triumphant heroes in relation to various colonised "others", [and] the real possibility of living out those imaginings in everyday experience'.[90] The masculine 'imaginings' given to the 'English-British' coloniser is one on which Jim builds his precarious identity. He explains to Len, for instance, that it is only black miners who work in deep mines in South Africa, because 'us white men be the bosses' (p. 6). The absence of narrative direction makes Jim's imperception all the more telling, but by 'othering' black miners as inferior, Jim, who himself is little more than a lowly wage-slave of capital, self-deludingly incorporates himself into the imperial myth of white supremacy. *Cwmardy* here offers a powerful link between the alterity intrinsic to imperialism and Jim's construction of his hegemonic self by his constant 'othering' of whoever is available. As John Tosh notes, hegemonic codes of manhood serve 'to strengthen the power and security of the governing class' but they apply 'not only to elites, but to subordinated classes' who seek power within those groups.[91] And so, in Jim's view, the local 'natives' like Dai Cannon, Bill Bristol, and the innumerable unnamed men with whom he fights and argues, are always restless, always embodying a challenge to him. In true imperial fashion, Jim's public image of himself is never subject to renegotiation, as he can never allow himself to be bettered. Even Bill Bristol's half-mocking remark underground that an official's lame excuse is 'like the battles Big Jim used to fight in the Boer War, always finishing miles further back than where they started' (p. 135) is met with the threat of immediate retaliation – 'Jim started to his feet at this insult' (p.135) – and is stopped only by the intervention of another workman. The insecure self-promoter can tolerate no ragging.

But Jim also seeks to dominate the public space through his own self-mythologising – he frequently refers to himself as Big Jim: 'Have anybody ever seen Big Jim losing?' (p. 39) – and through distinctive visual display. A body, as Judith Butler reminds us, is 'a signifying practice within a cultural field of gender hierarchy and compulsory heterosexuality',[92] and Jim's stiffened, bristling moustache, so different from Dai Cannon's 'drooping' specimen (p. 7), not only blazons his sexual potency, but is a visual reminder of his military service. Between the 1860s and 1916, Queen's Regulations required soldiers to grow moustaches that were 'clipped and trimmed until they curved like sabres and bristled like bayonets' in order to enhance their warlike appearance.[93] In retaining his moustache, Jim's formative military service is never far from his mind, nor intended to be far from the minds of others. He regards his military service as a 'source of masculine authority and a privileged arena of male activity',[94] which justifies his exclusionary masculine practice. And so, when he leads miners into a conflict with officials it is in the guise of the imperial warrior: 'Good Old Africa [...] the man who can fight Boers can fight blacklegs any day' (p. 166), and not surprisingly, when praised for his martial spirit, the novel notes that 'he solemnly twirled the ends of his long moustache' (p. 167).

By giving pre-eminence to Jim's craving for attention, *Cwmardy* constructs him as a figure inherently self-contradictory, the antithesis of the stabilised male. Unprepared to concede dominion at any time to his fellow workers, contemptuous of 'bosses' (p. 165) and assertive of his own individuality, he nonetheless parades himself as a respectful product of military discipline, 'batman to an officer' (p. 11), ironically, a servant of a servant of Empire. The public masculinity he constructs is therefore context-dependent, determined by the opportunities offering greatest self-exhibition. His defiant posture is represented at the outset of the novel when, in transnational mode, he constructs himself as an approximation of the *hombre* figure of the American western. Anti-authority and undomesticated, the *hombre* was a renegade, 'a rough fellow, a tough',[95] for whom, as Jane Tompkins observes, the open space of the American west 'seems to offer escape from the conditions of life in modern industrial society',[96] as the mountain does for Jim. In a few brisk sentences, *Cwmardy* contextualises him within this cultural domain. Implicitly hostile to convention, he lets his coat hang 'uncouthly' from his arm, and although he is 'known to civil servants and army authorities as James Roberts', he cultivates a less institutionalised identity through his alias, 'Big Jim' (p. 1). His bristling moustache gives him a 'fierce, reckless appearance' and he resembles 'a Wild-West desperado with the red silk scarf dangling loosely from his neck' (p. 1).[97]

Yet, later in the novel, the different context of an industrial dispute constructs a different, though equally grandiloquent, Jim when he volunteers to carry a note of truce to the police chief after a *mêlée*. Introducing himself proudly as an 'Old soldier. Served through the Boer War with the old 41st and proud of it' (p. 186), he acknowledges military hierarchy, stands to attention, addresses the uniformed policeman as 'sir' and salutes him twice. Savouring the distinction from his fellows conferred on him by this display, the irony evades him that he is saluting an agent of the state apparatus responsible for his economic exploitation. What matters more is the revival of 'His old war days' and his pleasure when 'the strikers made a clear path for him' (p. 186).

Jim as anti-authority *hombre*, and Jim as ex-imperial soldier proudly saluting a senior figure immediately exposes a rift in his own masculine definition between defiance of socially established norms and compliance with military regulation. To cite Greenblatt once more, the choices available for self-definition are 'strictly delineated by the social and ideological system in force',[98] and whichever masculinity Jim chooses, anti-authority figure or uncritical son of Empire, to reject one culturally determined form is simply to accept another, even when they conflict. Commodification of the self, the novel implies, is intrinsic to the ideological forces that govern him. *Cwmardy* powerfully articulates this phenomenon when Jim arrives home from war service in 1918. After visiting the Boar's Head, he returns, drunk and boastful, to Sunny Bank and declares 'it's good to be home, mun', while 'his eyes roamed longingly over Siân's body' (p. 300). Having satisfied one need through drink, Jim commodifies Siân as there to provide a different form of satisfaction. However, in a graphic irony Jim is about to be further commodified himself. Mining has become mechanised since he left for the war. From being the 'best skilled man in the pit' (p. 13), Jim becomes subservient to the rhythms of the mechanised conveyor. He discovers that 'however much coal they put in, the conveyor was always empty when they turned to it again', and 'conversation became impossible in the tumult' (p. 305). Jim had been excited by the prospect of returning to work because that 'do make me feel as if I now be home real, mun' (p. 304). Instead, he discovers only the further alienation of a worker who 'at work [...] feels homeless'.[99] As a skilled miner, Jim faces not only obsolescence in a new regime but, as the mechanised servant of a machine, the erosion of his status also. At least in the army he was a servant to a man.

In Jim Roberts, *Cwmardy* constructs an industrialised male alienated, whether at home, at leisure or at work. Subordinated at work, emotionally repressed at home, aggressive/defensive of his status at leisure, he exists in a state of perpetual non-realisation of self. The novel provides glimpses of his capacity for emotional empathy – tears fill his eyes, for example, when a young man loses his arm underground (p. 308) – but the military discipline inculcated by the Empire and the 'superman' culture of the miner— prohibit such public displays. In Jim Roberts, *Cwmardy* inscribes a masculinity at once iconic and individual, always poised between a constant craving for self-affirmation through action and a constant threat of self-implosion through defeat. Perhaps Jim's only salvation is that *Cwmardy* denies him clear-sighted awareness of it.

In focusing on two such differing forms of masculinity as Jim and Len Roberts, *Cwmardy* illustrates how male identity, whether somatically powerful or psychically complex, is fractured under socio-economic patriarchal paradigms which promote monolithic gender inscription.

The confidence Len displays at the end of the novel conceals his temperamental inability to deal with the brutality of his working life. He acquires political *nous* as the narrative develops, but remains a divided subject to the end. Jim Roberts, rather than being the uncomplicated 'Big Hewer' of his usual representation, is a subject displaced from his home in north Wales, whose need to display his dominant masculinity has been influenced by imperial ideologies of supremacy and utilised by a capitalist economy until his magnificent body is 'thin, bent and slow' (p. 309). To privilege doctrinal readings of *Cwmardy* is to make rigid what is a more pliant, subtle text. Despite the disclaimers in its Foreword, it is the work of an impressive imagination, as much as an acute demonstration of political theory. Artistically, it is energised by its probing imagination, its humanism, its subversion of the *Bildungsroman* precept of the autonomous male, and its construction of Len's masculinity through allusively suggestive symbolic association. David Smith notes that in June 1933 Lewis Jones published 'The Pit Cage',[100] a dramatic short story of a pit cage crashing two thousand feet to pit bottom, and he points out how Jones 'moves inside emotions to probe imaginatively rather than simply vent his savage indignation'.[101] Written by a man for whom what 'was more important than the politics […] was the humanism and compassion',[102] *Cwmardy* continues this imaginative probing.

3

Investigating Genre and Gender in Menna Gallie's Strike for a Kingdom *(1959)*[1]

Set in the western coalfield pit village of Cilhendre during the 1926 strike, Menna Gallie's whodunnit *Strike for a Kingdom* (1959) centres ostensibly on a humorously incompetent police investigation into the death of an authoritarian colliery manager. Its blend of intrigue, wit and lively characterisation was rewarded by its place as joint runner-up for the later-renamed Crime Writers' Gold Dagger Award. However, as with much popular generic fiction, after the spotlight moved elsewhere it retired into the backstage shadows. It required a combination of factors – the emergence of genre and gender as subjects of serious literary inquiry, and the desire to revive and assess the work of Welsh writers in English – to lead later to re-evaluations of Gallie's *oeuvre*. Yet while scholars like Angela V. John, Jane Aaron, Katie Gramich and Stephen Knight have brought Gallie's work to greater notice, in Wales at least, much of this critical discussion takes the form of introductions to republications of her novels, general essays on her work,[2] and brief overviews in surveys of Welsh fiction. As Gill Plain notes in another context, 'All of these approaches are necessary; the problem is not their existence, but rather the absence of substantial text-based analyses that would supplement their debates.'[3] Attempting such an investigation of *Strike for a Kingdom*, this chapter reads the novel as more than an ephemeral whodunnit. It proposes that its value lies not only in its 'rich [...] comic rhetoric',[4] but in its coded representation of how colonising anglocentric power systems displayed through structural patriarchy, class hierarchy and accompanying rigid gender differentiation, were appropriated but ran contrary to less combative, indigenous forms of masculinity in the western mining Valleys. The novel announces the particular nature of its gendered framework from the outset. Whereas *Times Like These* opens with the march of miners' boots in the early dawn as the men return home from the night shift, and *Cwmardy* locates two male figures alone on a mountain, *Strike for a Kingdom* begins with a group of young children – all girls – playing a skipping game in a Cilhendre street. A troubled neighbour emerges from his house to request 'in a funny choking voice' if they would play somewhere else because they were 'making a bit too much noise for Gwen' (p. 3). His supplication is successful, and from this point on, *Strike for a Kingdom* articulates a radical reconfiguring of Valleys' culture in which the power structures that validate hegemonic masculine behaviour, embodied principally in a self-important police inspector, are juxtaposed and critiqued alongside textually endorsed 'feminised' and 'juvenalised' forms of masculinity in the striking miners. However, Menna Gallie's remarkable achievement in her regendering of the 'heroic' miner cannot be fully appreciated without first considering how indelibly linked it is to the subversion of the generic form, the whodunnit, through which its narrative is channelled.

Clue-puzzle whodunnits were a feature of genre fiction in the inter-war years and, as *Strike for a Kingdom* illustrates, they continued to enjoy popularity beyond that period. While not forming a homogeneous group, they employed what Stephen Knight describes as 'a coherent set of practices which were shared [...] by most of the writers then at work',[5] and anticipated by readers who bought into the format. In such novels, readers were usually invited to collaborate, even compete, with the investigators in solving the mystery without having their social assumptions fundamentally challenged.[6] In writing *Strike for a Kingdom*, then, Gallie entered a field of literary endeavour in which the components of the generic form she chose were not neutrally transparent and conveniently dissoluble; they were ideologically laden and culturally conformist. Julian Symons notes, for example, that throughout the interwar years much crime fiction presented a world in which 'the General Strike of 1926 never took place, trade unions did not exist, and when sympathy was expressed for the poor it was not for the unemployed but for those struggling along on a fixed inherited income'.[7] Modifications to the genre, such as a greater engagement with social process, occurred during the 1950s, and were not entirely absent even earlier, but the prevailing cultural ethos of both genre and implied reader remained bourgeois. The challenge Menna Gallie faced in constructing *Strike for a Kingdom* was to manoeuvre a working-class, politically left-wing narrative into the infrastructure of a socially conservative generic form. In other words, how the novel was to be read, and by whom, became central to its success.

In the *Pleasure of the Text*, Roland Barthes outlines two different forms of textual reading. the *lisible* – one that 'goes straight to the articulations of the anecdote' and reads with the narrative in order to reach closure – and the *scriptible*, an 'applied' form of reading that reads into the narrative and attempts to respond to its 'layering of significance'.[8] Gill Plain observes that while genre narrative is generally associated with the first form of reading, when crime fiction is given an 'applied' focus, 'then both the text and its pleasures are rendered profoundly different'.[9] Gallie herself hinted that *Strike for a Kingdom* was amenable to such bifocal readings when, pointing to substantive differences in purpose and method between a novel and a whodunnit, she claimed that *Strike for a Kingdom* was 'a novel which disguised itself as a thriller'.[10] Gallie, then, manipulated the form of the clue-puzzle whodunnit so that *Strike for a Kingdom* becomes a sustained alibi, a declaration of generic innocence in a powerfully subversive novel.

Gallie's choice of the whodunnit form was purely pragmatic. It was a genre in which writers like Agatha Christie, Margery Allingham and Ngaio Marsh had already established a strong female presence, and as an unknown female writer herself Menna Gallie considered it the best route for her 'to get my toe in the door, to get myself a publisher'.[11] But it was a genre that presented Gallie with the immediate challenge of locating an ideologically charged novel in a genre that is expected to 'prioritise [readers'] pleasure and entertainment'.[12] As Gill Plain observes,

> the political efficacy of crime fiction re-stages the conflict between form and content, asking whether radical characterisation and plot construction will inevitably be undermined by the constraints of generic form: namely, closure, resolution, and restoration of order.[13]

In a novel like *Strike for a Kingdom*, set even in the distant 1926 strike, any 'closure, resolution and restoration of order' were likely to be circumscribed. Careful negotiation and a cautious narrative voice were required by Gallie to situate a discourse that challenged the apparent ideological neutrality of such patriarchal norms as gender differentiation and traditional marriage. For, as John Scaggs remarks of whodunnit readers, 'it is the home-owning bourgeois reading public whose interest it is to see the dominant social order of which they are a part maintained, and their stake in it protected.'[14] Acknowledging such constraints, *Strike for a Kingdom* constructs a sphere of activity where recognisable features of the whodunnit format reassuringly appear for its readers. Cilhendre, a cocooned mining community, replaces the country house favoured by many crime novels, and maps instead a physical landscape viewed through the comforting lens of romantic fiction:

> Cilhendre was a little huddle of pigeon-coloured houses following the curves of the River Tawe, which plaited its way among them, with the road and railway for company. The sun polished the walls of the houses. They were built of river stones, lavender grey, cloud grey, sea grey, pink and purple. One side of the valley faced the sun and was golden and pink in the warmth. The hills on the other side were in deep shadow, deeply blue. (p. 5)

Unlike the pit villages of much Welsh fiction, beset by social upheaval, coal dust and polluted rivers, in Cilhendre's harmonised topography nature and industry, river, road and rail keep each other company in good fellowship, and its tonal palette functions as a metonym for its radical reconstruction of Welsh miners' masculinity.[15] Vastly different in status from the country house as a locale, Cilhendre nonetheless offers a locus of closely interconnected characters in a relatively confined area, from among whom the culprit is to be unmasked. And while its working-class residents are positioned centrally in the narrative rather than cast as peripheral functionaries, as usual in whodunnits of the period, they offer no apparent political threat to Scaggs's 'home-owning bourgeois reading public'. Indeed, Gallie makes this point early in the novel with the reassurance that Cilhendre miners 'were not Marxists out to destroy Capitalism'. They are instead juvenalised as powerless 'Oliver Twists and the Owners had much in common with the Beadle' (p. 13). Presented in such a manner, the novel appears, in Barthes's terms, to promise a straightforward *lisible* narrative with a suitably reassuring finale.

The novel's strategy to present, if not harmonise, its competing elements was to leaven seriousness with parodic humour, to construct harmless miners who offer no potent threat to the socio-political status quo: to present a comically self-opinionated policeman and then allow the strike to recede progressively into the textual undergrowth as the narrative progresses. By foregrounding the police investigation over the politics of the strike in the second half of the novel, the narrative offers the prospect of expected cathartic closure when the crime is solved. And this is what apparently occurs. The compliant people of

Cilhendre return to their daily routines having 'accepted all that had happened' (p. 156). At the funeral of Gwen Evans, in a reassuring image of Wales as a socially conservative, easily comprehended land of song, the (predominantly male) mourners are depicted as being collectively vitalised by hymn singing. Later, at home, the poet/miner D. J. Williams feels a poem 'bubbling within' (p. 160). Undemanding in their needs and comforted by choral singing and poetry, Cilhendre miners appear to conform to a convenient stereotype where they are restored to normality through a therapeutic and cathartic release commensurate with what Dennis Porter calls the whodunnit's 'defence of the established societal order'.[16]

Yet the hybrid nature of the narrative resists such an easy, univocal resolution. It appears to confirm the simplistic picture of the Welsh as devoted to bouts of hymn singing and given to poetical impracticality only to undermine it. Within this whodunnit, closure can only be provisionally satisfying, for the larger social transgression, the strike, lurks unresolved and unresolvable within the frame of the narrative. And as the novel progresses towards decoding the clue-puzzle, echoes of disruption are manoeuvred into the text to give a modernist sense of incompleteness, rather than what Plain describes as a generically expected 'mode of textuality designed to comfort and reassure'.[17] Through a 'layering of significance' in three sequential episodes the text fails to offer unambiguously satisfying closure. Returning from Gwen Evans's funeral, the uplifted mourners feel that an 'inner need was satisfied', and the community has been reintegrated, but the narrative voice functions as both recorder of the event, and sceptical commentator upon it to observe that 'the opium of the poor was a powerful drug, and they left the chapel refreshed and belonging and reassured for the time' (p. 157). The indirect reference to Marx and the inference that their contentment is a temporary drug-induced detachment from a deprived social reality, experienced only 'for the time', insinuates not closure, but continuation of communal and individual rupture into a temporal space reaching beyond 'the time', and therefore beyond the text. This episode is followed immediately by a form of curtain-lecture confrontation between the indolent Jack Look-Out and his wife, in which she complains of his thoughtlessness, scolds him publicly and beats him over his head with her broom before retiring to the female space of the kitchen. He, having accused her of infidelity by having a 'fancy tart' (p. 158), retires to the male haven of the pub. The comic trope of the browbeaten husband and the unfaithful wife has a lineage going back to Chaucer and earlier, and can be read here as little more than an amusingly stereotypical reversal of traditional gender power in an amusingly written whodunnit. Read more deeply into the semiotics of the text, however, the episode illustrates once again its encoding of critique through humour. The restoration of a pre-crime status quo, a generic expectation of the whodunnit, is referenced here not through the prospect of harmonious reconciliation, but through a cameo of continuing marital friction. As later discussion shows, in a text which throughout presents patriarchally defined marriage as an incarceration of hapless men and women, humour does not deflect and diminish the presentation of marriage as mutual torment, but rather magnifies it and reflects it back. The scene acts as the novel's final, rebarbative judgement on a social arrangement where a marriage, a fundamental principle of structural patriarchy and domestic order, is exposed, like the strike, as a source of continuing, unresolved attrition.

From domestic fissure, the text then moves finally to the contemplative haven of D. J. Williams's kitchen. As he is the novel's study of the reflective Welsh bachelor, the poet/miner Williams is accorded uncritical approval throughout. Furthermore, he is instrumental in solving the crime, and so it is here, if anywhere, that a sense of textual completion might be expected. Yet, through him the novel's conclusion becomes ambiguous. Feeling 'released and relaxed' (p. 159), and poised at the moment of poetic creation, Williams reaches for his pen and paper, confident that the 'poem was coming' (p. 160). But the one line he inscribes, and on which the novel ends, 'Earthbound and slothful, barely venturing forth ...', constructs only images of hesitancy, torpor and confinement. And the ellipsis concluding the novel is semiotically paradoxical. While it hints at the promise of continuance, it also suggests a stasis, an endpoint without a future, as though he has, quite literally, come to a full stop. Like the figures on Keats's urn, he appears trapped in an uncompleted moment, incapable of progression or resolution. Taken together, these three sequential though tonally differing episodes inscribe an alternative closure. They map a bleak prospect for Cilhendre, where there is no promise of a brighter future, poetry offers only a qualified catharsis, and marital conflict is a micro-version of a patriarchal power system signified by continuing industrial strife.

One of the substantive achievements of *Strike for a Kingdom*, then, is to manipulate form, tone and language to conscript a popular bourgeois genre into representing a de-politicised Welsh mining masculinity, rendering it sympathetic and harmless. It uses such devices to embed within the narrative a powerful gender-specific critique of externally generated male power structures operating within a Valleys' context and the effect on miners who suffer under such a power system. Having devised a means of manipulating the novel's form, Gallie goes further in radically regendering how mining masculinity is presented, so that gender binaries are dissolved, or perhaps were never developed in Cilhendre in the form that they were in the colonising culture of England. Indistinguishable from both women and children, Cilhendre men therefore remain untouched by the patriarchal 'rite of passage' into instrumental 'adult' manhood.

Gallie's route to challenging prevailing gender and political orthodoxies which found coded expression in *Strike for a Kingdom* may be traced through three interconnecting, deeply personal threads: her childhood memories of the 1926 strike 'seared' her into adulthood;[18] her growing dislike of a certain type of strident masculinity; and a growing interest in what she preferred to call 'women's lib' rather than feminism. For Gallie the distinction between the two terms was important and enabled her to construct male characters without what she regarded as the more fundamentalist approach of ideological feminism. In an undated address, Gallie explained that writing *Strike for a Kingdom* was an attempt to expiate the guilt she felt for her experience as a child in the 1926 strike. Her father was not a mineworker at the time, and so she did not share in the privations and humiliations of being a hungry schoolchild fed from a communal soup kitchen. 'When I wrote [*Strike for a Kingdom*]', she recalled in a powerful moment many years later, 'I was trying to take part in that strike, that fight; here was my belated shot at solidarity; here was my contribution that, to my shame, I felt my father had never made; here was I at last taking soup with the other children.'[19]

It was living in England between 1950 and 1954, where her husband was Professor of Philosophy at what is now Keele University, that Gallie 'lifted Wales off my shoulders',[20] and where her hostility to a dominant form of masculinity began to crystallise. She records, 'It needed England to indicate to me the boredom, the irritation, the need to smack down the rugger type. Their inherent fascism hadn't actually struck me then.'[21] The metonymic 'rugger type' here signifies a form of boisterous masculinity posited on demonstrative heterosexuality, and the assertion of self through 'othering'. In *Strike for a Kingdom* it is represented by the anglicised Inspector Ernest Evans – who 'spoke Welsh but preferred not to let it be known that he suffered from this disability' (p. 85) – and through him carries the novel's embedded critique of a masculinity shaped by English-British imperial exceptionalism, committed to the domestic subordination of women and the public exhibition of power. If Menna Gallie's residence in England began to clarify her attitude to a dominant anglicised Welsh stereotype, it was in Northern Ireland that she began to inspect critically her own status as a Welsh woman. In 1954, she moved to Belfast, where her husband had become a professor at Queen's University, and it was during this period that several currents in her life converged to propel her towards writing. She records that, living as she did outside Belfast, her nearest neighbour, Viscountess Bangor, 'took us up'.[22] Gallie's pointed understatement that 'the gentry are not ideal informal friends',[23] suggests that the relationship of patronage was not congenial to her. Initially lonely and socially isolated, she records that her hours of solitude led her to writing *Strike for a Kingdom*. Positioned thus in a subaltern role as the wife of an academic, she writes that 'it was then that the full force of women's lib struck me'.[24] The draft title of *Strike for a Kingdom,* 'Say the Pink Bells'*,* taken from Poem XV of Idris Davies's *Gwalia Deserta,*[25] indicates how Gallie employed the colour connotations of pink and 'pinko' to endow her narrative with both a self-consciously gendered and a left-wing political awareness.[26] Its use of 'pink', a colour coded as feminine, also hints at a more allusive approach to 'women's lib' than the emerging ideologies of second-wave feminism were to construct. But if Gallie was critical of aspects of the feminist movement, it was not through gender timidity, but because she felt that it was ideologically hidebound.

In a talk given in the early 1970s, Gallie revealed her coolness towards, and her willingness to challenge, what she regarded as the more insistent aspects of second-wave feminism, especially what she considered its sometimes too fervid attacks on men: 'I'm not much of a one for the stridency of women's lib', she stated, and added provocatively, 'Indeed, I find my bra the most comforting of my garments.'[27] Her refusal to align herself with a more ideological form of feminism (a refusal that also enabled her to write so sympathetically of male characters in *Strike for a Kingdom*) remained evident when she reviewed Germaine Greer's *The Female Eunuch* (1970) while her husband was a professor at Peterhouse, Cambridge. She did so in a manner designed to offend the sensibilities of the conservatively male cohort of the Senior

Common Room with her declaration that 'this book contains a lot of cock, in both senses'; and angered more ideological feminist readers when she took uncompromising issue with Greer for what she felt was her Manichaean premise, 'Man is the enemy; so is the family and so is marriage.'[28] Yet if neither man as a genus nor the family was the enemy for Gallie, as *Strike for a Kingdom* consistently illustrates, she was herself no uncritical advocate of the regulatory conventions of marriage, as she forcefully states in the same review:

> I'd like to suggest that what is wrong with marriage – as we know it – is the word adultery and the insistence on monogamy. We have a duty not to leave the feminist revolt to Miss Greer's chums with cliteromania, but to try and get a general acceptance of the fact, which even British Law has sanctioned, that adultery is not the end of marriage, for either sex. We must come to terms honestly with sexual pleasure, within marriage or outside it, for sex is one of our few physical joys.[29]

Written into the narrative discourse of *Strike for a Kingdom* years before this review is the potential barrenness of conventional marriage that incorporates men like Jack Look-Out, as well as women, into its victimhood. Jess Jeffries' adultery, for instance, is treated sympathetically in the text. She sleeps with the colliery manager not only because 'The money was lovely for the children', but because, rather like Polly Garter, she is generous-hearted, and 'it was a pity for the poor man and she liked to do a favour when she could' (pp. 11–12). Monogamy suppresses her sexuality. Notwithstanding her motives, the novel shows how the repressive formalities of social convention generate her 'greatest terror' (p. 102), that the chapel deacons, those male custodians and enforcers of female respectability, will 'bring her case before the members and have her publicly cut out of the chapel' (p. 102). And it is this form of institutionalised, demonstrative masculinity that Gallie criticises throughout the novel.

Even when adultery does not feature in the novel, the textual import is that the regulatory conventions of marriage that serve a patriarchal power system position women into living with men they either despise, like Mrs Nixon, the widow of the dead colliery manager, or by whom they are cowed, like the police inspector's wife. In a telling moment, when she is appropriately positioned in the feminised space of her 'milk-and-water kitchen', Mrs Evans 'grew smaller, out of sight' (p. 127) as her normatively angry husband 'shouted for his breakfast, kicked his wife's dog, cursed his porridge and said the tea was cold'

(p. 127). It is notable that both Mrs Nixon and Mrs Evans are married to prototypically dominant, domineering men, incarnations of patriarchal empowerment who incur textual disapproval. By contrast, the text's two loving inter-gender relationships diverge significantly from these fractious patriarchal models: D. J. Williams's with his mother, Ann, is framed within a loving mother/son perspective. And although the novel never confirms that the consanguineous love of Gerwin Evans for his sister Gwen is physically incestuous, it leaves little doubt that it is so.[30]

Angela V. John, in her introduction to *Strike for a Kingdom*, observes, 'Men and women in Cilhendre appear to inhabit separate worlds'.[31] This is true, for physical spaces have gendered associations, as Jack Look-Out and his wife's quarrel has already indicated. However, his haven of the pub and her return to her house also serve as correlatives in the novel of a much larger cultural assumption, as the Inspector illustrates in his behaviour to his wife, that men and women also require different physical spaces because subjectively they belong to 'separate worlds', determined and normalised by their different genders. But this patriarchal model of gender asymmetry as part of a natural order of being is contested throughout the novel. Its discursive space repeatedly merges native Cilhendre miners with women and children into a triad that shares common structures of feeling and shared behavioural patterns at odds with, but overlaid by, dominating cultural assumptions about what constitutes performative masculinity.[32] The only living male character who assumes a normatively instrumental male role in the novel is Inspector Evans, though the murdered manager was another. Elsewhere, it is the differences between Cilhendre men and the repressive scripts of an alien normative masculinity that operate. David Glover and Cora Kaplan, for instance, identify characteristics ranging from 'supposed excesses of feeling to passivity to a degree of nurturance' as being generally regarded as 'inappropriate to Anglo-Saxon masculinity',[33] inappropriate because they smack of the 'feminine'. In *Strike for a Kingdom*, however, the three examples of feminised behaviour Glover and Kaplan identify – emotionalism, passivity and nurturance – are precisely those qualities that are textually valorised and embodied in D. J. Williams and Gerwin Evans, both Welsh members of that incontrovertible 'masculine' occupation, coal mining.[34]

D. J. Williams's relationship with the emotionally distressed Gerwin Evans, the very loving brother of a very loving sister, is nurturing throughout the novel. Anxious to console Gerwin, who fears for his sister's health, Williams displays just such expressive qualities when 'he put his scarred hand on [Gerwin's] arm to strengthen him, *to be with him*, [and says], "Come into the house to talk a bit, Gerwin"' (p. 24, my italics). The implication here is that while such modalities deviate from Anglo-Saxon inscriptions of what constitutes normative male behaviour, in Cilhendre it is those inscriptions that are alien and abnormal. In D. J. Williams, Gerwin has a friend with whom he shares his intimate concerns. We remember that the tormented ultra-male Big Jim Roberts in *Cwmardy*, shaped by and restricted by the masculine ideologies of Empire and anglo-capitalism, had no one 'to be with him' when his young daughter Jane died in childbirth.

This feature of a reformulated, expressive masculinity extends throughout the novel. The 'supposed female virtues of sympathy and nurturance' that Glover and Kaplan note as inappropriate elements in Anglo-Saxon definitions of masculinity are evident in Cilhendre policemen, too.[35] After a confrontation between police and striking miners, when they are freed from their Inspector's pathological love of violence, the police 'organised cups of tea for the men, *sorry* for the bruises and *feeling responsible*' (p. 64, my italics). The sergeant takes the bewildered Glanddylan Price 'on one side and *begged* him not to worry' (p. 64, my italics). A statement resonating with significance in this gendered context notes that away from the Inspector, 'the policemen won back their manhood and their humanity' (p. 64). Contrary to the hegemonic anglocentric model that Glover and Kaplan identify, manhood here is signified by tolerance, compassion and sympathy. The text's premise that the police recover not only their broader humanity but their very manhood implies that demonstrations of macho violence are a perversion of their own indigenous culture, thrust on them by a repressively dominant model – embodied in the Inspector – which serves the functioning of an industrial, patriarchal system of power.

Patriarchy, as Susan Rowland notes, valorises agency and heroism in men,[36] but in Cilhendre it is passivity and pusillanimity that govern most male structures of feeling both individually and *en masse*. D. J. Williams, himself an uneasy hybrid of striking miner and establishment JP, is never far from experiencing fear of authority. Despite the front he puts on, 'inside [he] was afraid of the bobbies' (p. 18) and the centrally conferred power they embody. The protest march itself is constructed as an act of quiet despair, and confronted by the local police on the common the miners are afraid of them (p. 58). The police, as a corpus, reciprocate, being 'themselves as frightened as women', and 'all of them [were] terrified of the Inspector' (p. 58). When they are ordered by their militaristic Inspector to charge the miners, the nurturing instincts of the female narrative voice are revealed: 'they, poor frightened things, did as they were told' (p. 58). In the novel's extensive use of male fear of exposure, fear of violence and fear of authority as discursive tropes through which miners' and police behaviour is represented, the novel mobilises a powerful critique of the social construction that promotes and activates fear, and the gender model that nominates 'excesses of feeling' as 'unmanly'.[37]

Even when not focused on emotional similarities between the male and the female, the narrative contextualises male behaviour within a proximate female discourse. The minor figure PC Wilkins, for example, 'picked his way like a girl in high heels up to the door of the cottage' of the Town Cryer (p. 73), and PC Thomas draws comfort from buttoning up his uniform 'as a woman does from her corset' (p. 127). For a brief moment, even the police Inspector, loaded with flowers by an extra-generous villager, looked 'like a May Queen' (p. 96). For the most part, these figures are unproblematic rhetorical analogies which contribute progressively to diluting normative, accepted gender boundaries. However, there is a marked occasion when the narrative proposes a more semiotically layered representation of gender fluidity. At the Cilhendre carnival parodic cross-dressing critiques gender dualism by hybridising the two traditionally differentiated genders in a comic visual format. Carnival cross-dressing fashions a liberating opportunity to perform an alternative gendered identity, one where, as G. G. Bolich observes, ludic transgression may pass unquestioned:

> Cross-dressing as *social* play – consequences shared with others – offers an important safety-valve opening by Carnival to relieve cultural pressure. But it may do more. Such play, by showing the fluidity and artificiality of things like gender role expectations, may make them easier to endure on re-entering the mundane world.[38]

Bolich acknowledges that gendered performance is artificial and implies in his closing sentence that binary definitions of gender are unnatural and repressive. However, whereas he sees carnival cross-dressing as a temporary Bakhtinian release from mundane gender formation, for Judith Butler physical semiotics inscribe a more abiding problematic. She closes an essay on gender construction with the comment that if gender is mistaken for a 'natural or linguistic given', the cultural field will be expanded bodily 'through subversive performances of various kinds'.[39] Positioned within a community where patriarchally mandated gender difference formally applies, cross-dressing at the Cilhendre carnival functions as a semiotically disruptive performance. It is a distilled subversive example of which the entire narrative is a carnivalesque inscription, modulated by prevailing temporal and cultural influences but resulting in a significant gender hybridising. In such a community, both Moc and the footballers take pains to confirm their male credentials within a traditionally gendered schema, Moc as a tribal African who chases children with his wooden spear, and the footballers 'dressed like young ladies' (p. 15) who behave like roaring boys. Yet their appearance, albeit comically exaggerated, inevitably constructs an ironic perspective on the gender purity of their actions.

The frequency with which these features appear in *Strike for a Kingdom* suggests that, as the cultural anthropologist Gayle Rubin has stated, 'The idea that men and women are more different from each other than they are from anything else must come from somewhere other than nature.'[40] The 'somewhere other than nature' from where gender polarities are constructed in *Strike for a Kingdom* is a form of patriarchal capitalism, implicitly anglocentric, through which differences between men and women are naturalised as the *sine qua non* of social hierarchies and gender identity. Running counter to such culturally contrived differentiation, the novel inductively represents the natural similarities existing between Cilhendre men and women, and men and children, thereby implicitly challenging the boundaries, both gendered and generational, that an anglicised model of industrial patriarchy establishes and regulates. Within this ethnographic context, the fictional representation of Valleys' masculinities is radically reformulated by being feminised. What emerges from the text's feminising discourse is not only a rewriting of mining masculinity in the Welsh novel, but a narrative in which gender commonalities are suppressed by a dominant model of hierarchical masculinity requiring the 'othering' of women. The economic and cultural power of such a practice interpellates the Cilhendre miners into the subject status appropriate to its ideology, but as the feminised narrative voice implicitly insists, this is an alien model. As if to emphasise the extent to which Cilhendre masculinity deviates from a normative anglicised stereotype, where progression into work is heralded as a rite of passage from boyhood to manhood, as the young Len Roberts in *Cwmardy* believes it is, the text aligns male behaviour not only with women but with boys to draw them into a conspectus of unified gender alignment. The tone through which the narrative voice articulates this viewpoint is neither satirical nor sardonic, as it is with the police inspector. Instead, it is bifocal in the way it both penetrates and embraces.

Stephen Knight remarks that many Welsh male writers in English deal 'with a boy'. He attributes this gendered feature principally to 'the isolation and powerlessness the authors feel', leading them to 'find an objective correlative in a character subject to forces beyond personal control'.[41] Among the 'forces beyond personal control' is the sense of cultural and gender inferiority, of being assigned a subaltern status in a hierarchical structure of gender and colonial definition. *Strike for a Kingdom* also includes a boy, John Nixon, whose gendered function in the novel is discussed later, but as a Welsh female writer working in English, Menna Gallie appears more interested in the multivalent significations of the terms 'boy' and 'boys' in defining Cilhendre masculinity than in finding a correlative for her own social displacement. David S. Gutterman addressed the semantics of the term 'boy' when he wrote:

> it is useful to conceive words like *boy* not as nouns but rather as adjectives, that describe a subject. By doing so one can more easily and deeply appreciate the contingency of the meanings attached to the word *boy*. Being a boy is different in cultures/families/contexts and will mean different things to individuals as they grow older.[42]

Some forty years before Gutterman's article, *Strike for a Kingdom* had already extended the word's cultural possibilities in a peculiarly Welsh context to show how the term can 'mean different things to individuals as they grow older'.

Within the demotic of the south Wales coalfield, 'boys' is not exclusively an age-specific term; rather, it is a figure of egalitarian familiarity commonly used by men of other men. However, its function in *Strike for a Kingdom* is more context-dependent, where it is appropriated by the narrative voice in three different ways: as a literal nominator – the young John Nixon is 'a good, superior boy' (p. 122); as a colloquial nominator – the police sergeant who organises cups of tea for the miners is 'a good boy' (p. 64); and as a descriptor to signify the man-as-child – Elwyn Jeffries's legs hang 'like a boy's' over his bed (p. 60). These different significations are then conflated with the text's frequent mimetic use of the term: D. J. Williams, for example, gently reprimands two plotting miners to 'Stop it now, boys' and 'Don't indeed, boys' (p. 131), where the word signifies communality and a shared system of values. Given that the novel was published in London for distribution to a largely anglophone readership, the term's semantics differ on how the word is read. On one level, it presents the striking miners as lacking the autonomy and agency of 'adult' masculinity, and thereby functions textually to reassure a socially conservative crime novel readership. On another level, it encodes a masculinity where to refer to fellow men as boys is not to insult them, but to liberate an age-related term and incorporate it into a signifier of age-unrelated sodality. The effect is not only to construct a divergent form of Valleys' masculinity from the competitive, hierarchical paradigm, but to subvert the fundamental structural principle of the *Bildungsroman* that 'men' are different from 'boys'.

Dispensing with male-generated notions of rites of passage, a feature that Jonathan Rutherford calls 'a cultural pathology',[43] the text elaborates a continuity between boyhood and adulthood by easing the miners' signifying positions along an unbroken temporal continuum from babyhood to boyhood, from infant dependency to schoolboy performativity, and thence to adulthood. Early in the narrative, two male characters, Moc Cow-and-Gate and Gerwin Evans, are discursively infantilised. Both are like babies: Moc resembles the Royal Baby used in a Cow-and-Gate promotion as 'the food for royal babies' (p. 15),[44] and Gerwin Evans acts like one (p. 27). Later, a troubled D. J. Williams is like a 'child feeling sick on the little horses in the fair' (p. 57). At work in the police station, PC Thomas 'copied out in Best Writing a list of names' (p. 71) of striking miners. An anxious mine official is reassured by a colleague that the hot-tempered dead colliery Manager can't eat him (p. 127), as though he is an ogre from a fairy tale. The imaginative landscape of two mischievous miners is defined by 'the *Wizard*' (p. 131), a comic for boys. And later still, a group of officials searching for dynamite stolen from the colliery are like Boy Scouts who 'set off in couples to play detective' (p. 143). The effect of such a strategy is dramatic if understated. Adult masculinity in Cilhendre becomes part of an organic progression where the child, if not father to the man, may be seen in the man.

Whereas feminised tropes in *Strike for a Kingdom* are articulated through diegesis, offering an omniscient corrective to a hegemonic model, juvenile tropes are more deeply integrated into the textual fabric, so that the female narrative voice appears merely to reflect the normalised discursive practices of the miners themselves. Pierre Macherey remarks that a novel 'cannot say everything at once; its scattered discourse is its only means of uniting and gathering what it has to say'.[45] Distributed throughout *Strike for a Kingdom*, such scattered discourse unites in a consistent vision of gender and developmental fluidity oppressed by an alien model of structural masculinity. However, the novel goes further in anatomising the consequences of such a restrictive model through two seemingly different characters, D. J. Williams and the dead manager's son, John Nixon.

The gender theorist Todd W. Reeser suggests that central to the continuance of gender binaries promoted by patriarchal masculinity is the coming-of-age ritual, where a boy becomes a man as he passes through various symbolic and non-symbolic processes.[46] As we have seen, through references scattered throughout the novel, the 'natural' evolutionary development from boyhood to manhood implicit in this model, where a differentiated form of completed, potent being emerges as though from a quiescent chrysalis, is treated as a myth in *Strike for a Kingdom*. More specifically, through its construction of D. J. Williams and John Nixon, its rejection of a coming-of-age paradigm is generic as well as gendered. Generically, the crime novel's limited time frame, where detection rather than the *Bildungsroman*'s evolution of the protagonist into manhood motivates and accelerates the plot, allows *Strike for a Kingdom* to inspect, within a tightly regulated temporal schema, two male figures of differing ages who share common structures of feeling. It conceives its critique of patriarchal binaries and boy/man distinction by aligning a patriarchal but dysfunctional family unit (John Nixon's) alongside a formally unbalanced but successfully functioning matriarchal unit (D. J. Williams's).

In a novel populated by several comically rendered characters, the text's discursive seriousness in constructing both Williams and John Nixon illuminates the nature of its engagement with gender dynamics. Separated by age, associates, social position and experience they have no reason to come into contact with each other, nor do they. And while the contemplative D. J. Williams is a narrative cynosure, John Nixon appears to exist on its periphery. Indeed, in terms of narrative necessity, there is little reason for his presence at all. However, when the text is read through what Gill Plain calls an 'observation of gender',[47] its typology changes, and a figure who appears marginal in the plot becomes more fully integrated into the novel's ideology when its 'layering of significance' is examined. John Nixon functions as a composite youth, sometimes seemingly in early adolescence, sometimes seemingly older, old enough at least to represent his family at Gwen Evans's funeral. However, as an exemplar of the structural gender model, he incarnates the problematic of the boy-as-embryonic-man, embodying opposing constituents of traditional gender identity – masculine and feminine – which puzzle and trouble him.[48] The challenges he faces of being male attract him, but conflict with his stereotypically feminised characteristics. These are revealed in several ways: temperamentally, in his artistic passivity; somatically, in his 'thin delicate neck like a flower on a stalk' (p. 40); and semiotically, in his habit of tossing his hair like a girl (p. 40). He therefore not only complements the man-as-boy, feminised construction implicit in the conception of D. J. Williams, but his presence furthers the novel's hostility to what Gayle Rubin calls 'the straightjacket of gender'.[49]

The correspondences and differences between Williams and Nixon, as in so much else in the novel, are achieved by insinuations, implications and allusive connections. They are neither signposted by the narrative voice through dialogue, nor probed extensively through interior examination of the character's psychology. However, several significant features emerge that connect the two figures, among the most defining being the relationship each has with his mother, for D. J. Williams is very much his mother's son. Although an adult, he remains 'afraid of plenty' (p. 131), and has experienced no rite of passage where he feels himself comfortably initiated into the status of 'manhood', and its accompanying normative displays. Conspicuously, aside from the shadowy figure of Gerwin Evans's widowed mother, to whom the bachelor Gerwin himself is 'devoted' (p. 21), Ann Williams and Mrs Nixon are the only two women in the text with sons, and they are sons who lack the traditional markers of normative patriarchal masculinity. In what Roland Barthes calls 'a significant absence',[50] Williams senior has no place in the novel, and for the purposes of the narrative it is as though he has never existed. Yet his absence speaks loudly, for this lacuna facilitates the text's construction of an adult male, D. J. Williams, untouched by domestic patriarchal example, emotionally dependent on and consequently feminised by a strong maternal influence, existing within a prevailing industrial and legislative ethos which is male-engendered, male-dominated and therefore alien to him.

It is in the domestic space of the home which his mother has created that he feels secure: 'anchored to the dresser, the corner cupboard, the kitchen table with its red plush cloth and the settle by the fire with a red paisley cushion to match the stockings on the legs of the table' (p. 24). The power of the leading verb and the markedly feminised coding of the furniture, not least in the primness of stockings on the table legs, function as metonyms for his own feminised sensibility, and generate his feeling of a secure selfhood in this feminised space. His desire to withdraw from a world of male agency is represented through his love of poetry, what Frank Lentricchia calls a 'haven for an isolated aesthetic pleasure',[51] an escape from contingent reality into a 'sheltered poetry world' (p. 83). It functions in the text as an intangible corollary to the material objects which anchor him to the home he shares with his mother, an imaginative space in which he feels settled. Notably, the novel explicates the feminising connection between his home, his poetry and his mother when, in the gender-coded space of a quiet kitchen and engaged in writing a poem, 'his mother's presence was for him part of the silence' (p. 160). And when subjected to 'frenzied thoughts' at the scene of the manager's death, he knows that 'only one thing would deliver him – talking to his mother, hearing her sanity. He'd put it all behind him until he got home' (p. 22).

His mother's role as confidante and adviser is exemplified most strongly in an intimate and textually fascinating passage arising from Mr Nixon's death (pp. 110–14) and demonstrates unequivocally how *Strike for a Kingdom* rewards a *scriptible* reading that responds to Barthes's 'layering of significance'. It comes at the close of a series of intimate exchanges between them ranging from Williams's own doubts about his suitability as a magistrate, his disapproval of hanging as a punishment for murder, and his consideration of what it is best to do about Gwen Evans's stillborn baby, whose death Inspector Evans is anxious to treat as foul play. The exchange concludes with a passage that has resonances far beyond its context as another example of mother/son interdependence. Williams is fearful that Nixon's death, occurring, as it has, during a protracted strike, might be misinterpreted by 'people away from Cilhendre who don't know us' (pp. 114–15):

> Some think we are all violent men in the pits, like black savages from Africa, or queer people under the ground like devils or goblins [...]. When I was in Ruskin College I sometimes felt people treating me with an interested kindness and looking at me like a specimen from strange lands, brought over for their scientific curiosity. Made me feel like a thing in a

Wild Beast Show. I wondered whether to talk or growl. Both would surprise them equally. (p. 114)

His mother, referring to him as 'my boy', gently rebukes him for his sensitivity, but this occasion is more than a textual device for identifying his reactive hyper-anxiety as another 'feminised' trait in a Cilhendre male, though it is that too. It is a speech whose implications reverberate because no other voice in *Strike for a Kingdom* speaks with such abstracted authority or with such passion as Williams's, except for the narrative voice. It is a distillation of one of the novel's implied thematic preoccupations: its dissection of anglo-colonial perceptions of and influences on Wales. Of how different cultures, different nations, different peoples perceive each other through systems of exclusion, and, significantly from Williams's perspective, how 'to be different means to be less than'.[52] It touches on Williams's profoundly disturbing personal experience of being 'othered' by those who regarded him 'as a specimen from strange lands'.

As a working-class student at Oxford, Williams is recollecting his experience there as an outsider within an exclusionary English class system. But Williams is Welsh, not English, and the deeper textual resonance here, with his references to 'savages from Africa' and 'Wild Beast Shows', seems not to suggest for him a dismissive social snobbery towards a fellow countryman of a 'lower class', for he was treated with an 'interested kindness'. Instead, he was studied like a 'scientific curiosity', a colonised specimen of a different race of whom his observers knew little and understood less. While class difference might intersect with racial 'otherness', to judge by Williams's discourse the inferior difference he felt on being so observed was not so much social as racial.[53] Ann Williams's gentle censure of her son's sensitivity on this occasion perhaps misses the mark. But the manner in which she steers the conversation back to the death of the manager, and away from her son's particular reflections, and then chides him to 'start tidying up your mind a bit, my boy. Inspector is coming through the gate' (p.114), suggests her awareness that it is not only sensitivity but a profound intellectual disquiet that prompts her son's feelings. The impending visit of an anglicised Welsh police officer is perhaps no unintentional irony.

Spared the intrusive influence of a dominant father, and never growing away from his mother, D. J. Williams has not, in patriarchal terms, achieved masculine autonomy, and therefore has never fully entered the symbolic order of normative manhood that the text criticises in what we learn of Nixon senior and mocks in the police Inspector. The Freudian progression outlined by Michael Kimmel, which requires of a boy the 'devaluing all things feminine – including girls, his mother, femininity, and, of course, *all emotions associated with femininity*'[54] (my italics) – has passed him by. But through what Kimmel calls 'emotions associated with femininity', *Strike for a Kingdom* valorises in D. J. Williams a distinctive form of Valleys' masculinity.

In John Nixon, the text constructs a boy who is temperamentally similar to D. J. Williams, but damaged by the circumstances of his upbringing. As the confused product of a strongly patriarchal paradigm, he seeks an identity that reconciles the competing impulses of his female-coded temperament and his male-coded libido. Whereas D. J. Williams seeks refuge from the world in his poetry, the young John Nixon wonders whether his own irritability can be 'attributed to his artistic temperament' (p. 40). Although he assumes 'a poetic unworldliness' (p. 40), he is not so much a poseur as a young individual experiencing doubts about his identity in his attempt to align his temperamental disposition with his perceived gendered role as a male. At his father's funeral, for instance, he was 'the male lead and did not know his lines' (p. 136). Like D. J. Williams, he is devoted to his mother, but he is problematised by being 'his father's son, fretworked by his mother' (p. 41). Like D. J. Williams, too, his disposition leads him to interpret the world at a remove, through an artistic perspective, either painting, as when his interpretation of the assembled miners is refracted through Rembrandt's 'Night Watch' (p. 49), or when the weeping maids at his father's funeral provoke in him a question from *Hamlet* (p. 137). However, whereas Williams's feminine-coded masculinity is safely anchored in a home without a 'masculine' presence, for John Nixon his father's philandering has offered an enticing model of dominance and pleasure outside the domestic sphere. Within the home, the patriarch's 'beastliness' (p. 41) which repels Mrs Nixon repels her devoted son also, but his father's hegemonic 'othering' and commodifying of women excites him too, as a model of 'true' manhood. For John Nixon, sexuality and gender are not so much 'accomplished in the family', as Kimmel states,[55] as problematised within it, for they bring him into confrontation with two conflicting modes of his own gender development.

Strike for a Kingdom aligns D. J. Williams and John Nixon, then, as two male figures who share temperamental affinities despite their differing ages, but who are the products of differing family trajectories. D. J. Williams has escaped the patriarchal myth of the *Bildungsroman* hero's progression into assured normative masculinity. As for John Nixon, *Strike for a Kingdom* manipulates the compressed time-scheme of the crime novel to suggest that there will be no unproblematic rite of passage into manhood for him. The text leaves him as it leaves Williams, arrested in a moment of time, but whereas for Williams in his quiet kitchen there is at least the possibility that 'It would be alright' (p. 160), John Nixon is not so fortunate. After his attendance at Gwen Evans's funeral where, unlike the 'mumbo-jumbo for his father', he was 'moved almost beyond bearing' (p. 157), the text leaves him arrested in a temporal space, 'furious with his own illogicality' (p. 157), and granted no narrative path to resolution.

Lacking the introspective temperament of D. J. Williams and John Nixon, Inspector Evans cuts a figure at once ridiculous and threatening. With his dislike of the Welsh language, his commitment to the Empire and his anger at the striking miners, some of whom he believes should be shot, Inspector Ernest Evans is an exaggerated incarnation of a patriarchal, anglicised masculinity, detached from the community he polices. As a figure whose presence in the novel benefits from bifocal reading, he is at once a representation of the bombastic male within a diverting whodunnit, and a disturbing example of how institutional status and power featured in the history of Valleys' industrialism. He differs in kind and function from the classical detective, the 'omniscient investigator' who, Gill Plain notes, 'enters an enclosed environment' and exposes the malefactor 'with surgical precision'.[56] Instead, he seems set for comic deflation from his first appearance when, intent on consoling Mrs Nixon on her loss, he arrives clumsily, 'with a noise like falling biscuit tins' and, in a manner reminiscent of Dickens's Mr Bounderby, as 'full as a balloon of his own esteem' (p. 41).[57] As an exaggerated construction of hyper-masculine presence, Evans is positioned in the comic sphere of the persistently self-promoting, self-ignorant subject teetering always on the brink of humiliating exposure. On a straightforward, *lisible* reading, Evans's function appears to rest on the humour to be extracted from how this 'bladder of lard' (p. 118) strives to solve the clue-puzzles and expose the culprit.

Strike for a Kingdom nurtures this impression by constructing him via an intertextual collage of vainglorious comic males, all of them defined by their unmerited but unstaunchable egos. He not only echoes a solipsistic Bounderby, but he incorporates aspects of Kenneth Grahame's pompous Mr Toad, too, in his devotion to his motor car. Like Toad, he is 'not very sure of the gears' (p. 50) and deafens pedestrians when 'playing tunes on the rubber ball of the horn' (p. 78). Later, on losing his dignity when a tree branch dislodges his helmet, he resembles a prickly Oliver Hardy to PC Thomas's hapless Stan Laurel, as he attempts 'to blame Thomas for the mishap' (p. 89) in 'Here's another nice mess you've gotten me into' vein. Later still, he is a conceitedly self-assured Dogberry to PC Thomas's inept Verges. Both Evans and Dogberry make claims regarding their singular prowess that are markedly at odds with their investigative practice, Dogberry that he benefits from the 'Gifts that God Gives',[58] while for Evans the Nixon case 'is serious, but, thank God, I'm in charge' (p. 129).

However, as Gill Plain reminds us, crime novels are 'not quite as straightforward as they might initially appear',[59] and the presence of an overweening senior policeman, 'a representative of the law' (p. 156) disposed to violence in a Welsh novel set during a miners' strike, illustrates the point. The fixed, exaggerated characteristics that construct him as ripe for comic puncturing in one reading, position him also as a grotesquely recognisable agent of state-approved oppression in a Valleys industrial context, where, in his view, all strikers are 'rioters' (p. 116). This, more *scriptible*, reading shifts the animating force behind Evans's construction away from a humorous whodunnit. Instead, Evans emerges as a totemic bully, at once ridiculous and dangerous, embodying Menna Gallie's gendered desire 'to smack down the rugger type' of masculinity. M. Wynn Thomas writes of the Welsh novel: 'One of the ways of re-introducing the nation to its own history is through providing it with conscientiously historical but compelling imaginative fictions.'[60] In this respect, what a mid-century, middle-class English consumer of crime novels in 1959 may read as an untroubling temporal and spatial distancing of transgressive events transported to a 1926 Welsh village becomes, in the context of Valleys' fiction and read through Welsh eyes, a text based on personal recollection investigating a troubled history of extreme social disquiet and the politically mandated power systems that literally policed it.[61] This perspective is present in Evans's insistence that the strike is 'a disgrace', engineered by men whose moral turpitude must be punished because they 'won't do their work properly' (p. 119). Read this way, his reductive orthodoxy places him in the narrative continuum of coercive masculinity performed through institutional, hierarchical office that had already darkened characters like Gwyn Jones's Sir Hugh Thomas in *Times Like These*, and Lewis Jones's Lord Cwmardy. It would reappear later in the century as a continuing element of the Welsh industrial experience in the deviant policeman Elliott Bowles in Roger Granelli's *Dark Edge* (1997), and later still in the silkily machiavellian Adam Smith-Tudor in Kit Habianic's *Until Our Blood is Dry* (2014), for whom striking miners are guilty of moral depravity.

Evans is an interloper into the Cilhendre community. Welsh by birth, he stands in the novel as a colonised agent, interpellated into a hybridised anglo-British identity. This severance enables *Strike for a Kingdom* to mobilise a powerful critique of his narcissistic, authoritarian and alien gendering. Understanding little of the community over which he has jurisdiction – he fails to see why Joe Everynight, the father of twelve children, is so called (pp. 117–18) – he enacts the divergent value systems, prejudices and practices of a dominant and gendered power bloc removed from but controlling of indigenous Cilhendre masculinity. His official role disguises his compulsion to dominate others by clothing itself in the mantle of a civilising economic and moral imperative: 'Think what this strike is costing the country, and our Empire' (p. 129). Appeals by authority figures to an abstract higher cause echo throughout Welsh industrial fiction as a strategic mechanism to secure an existing power balance, and representation of Evans as a mordantly comic figure does not detract from his also being, within the tradition of Valleys' fiction, read as a willing agent of a formalised alien hierarchy, inimical to the collectivised traditions of south Wales.

Evans's obsessive belief that 'What we need is discipline' (p. 129) helps reveal how the power structures of patriarchal authority exploit his proto-fascistic disposition and reciprocate, by legitimizing, his own narcissism. The term 'fascist' requires careful use, but it is a term Menna Gallie deliberately employs in her archive when she denotes the 'inherent fascism' of a particular kind of masculinity that is represented in Evans. For R. W. Connell, fascism promotes debased forms of masculinity based on alterity, irrationality 'and the unrestrained violence of the frontline soldier'.[62] As the novel makes clear, suppression through violence is not incidental to Evans's construction. It permeates his very discourse, leading to an extraordinary confusion of his public role and private sentiments. When the widowed Mrs Nixon, who is chilled by his adversarial impulses, advises him not to antagonise villagers in his investigation, as 'These are difficult times and some of the good people are almost desperate', he replies apoplectically, 'Good people did you say? Damn strikers. We ought to shoot a few of them to show who's boss around here' (p. 47). But Evans's inflammatory comment on shooting striking miners reverberates beyond the crime-puzzle confines of *Strike for a Kingdom* to engage with the larger narrative of industrial relations in Wales, and the violent suppression of dissent. As if for emphasis, the novel has Evans repeat his view later: 'We need the soldiers here to teach a few of them a lesson' (p. 129). Such remarks stir echoes, no matter how ill-founded on fact, of soldiers opening fire on striking Welsh miners in Tonypandy in 1910, and in modern readers anticipate the violent engagement between striking miners and militarised mounted policemen in the 1984–5 miners' strike, as extreme examples of 'othering' those who challenge a dominant orthodoxy. Such a scene in Kit Habianic's *Until Our Blood is Dry,* set during that strike confirms how little had changed in the intervening decades. Writing of such a practice, John Horne argues that 'The positive attributes of national masculine ideals', which Inspector Evans sees himself as embodying, are 'matched by the negative figures of the internal and external enemy – who might be pictured either as female or as a derided or feared type of masculinity'.[63] His phrase referring to an internal enemy bleakly echoes the sentiments of a British Prime Minister regarding striking miners, and embraces Evans's own viewpoint that 'This would be Russia if these colliers had half a chance' (p. 129).

Enclosed within the seemingly safe generic parameters of the whodunnit, Evans's outbursts cited above can be read as examples of his temperamental and comically outrageous irascibility. Within the corpus of south Wales fiction, however, such a representation does not detract from his also being read as a willing agent of a formalised metropolitan hierarchy inimical to the social organisation of the Valleys. *Strike for a Kingdom* deftly makes this point through the fate of a distraught Gerwin Evans, whose crime – the unintentional killing of David Nixon, given that he acted under provocation and a threat of blackmail – was manslaughter, not murder. In an extraordinarily direct paragraph in its closing chapter, *Strike for a Kingdom* passes its own judgement on Inspector Evans, and connects him unequivocally with male-dominated, inhumanely abstract processes of law, compromised as they are between legality and power; common humanity and cultural and racial difference; and justice and revenge. Only 'half satisfied' by Gerwin's suicide:

He was muttering imprecations and meaningless clichés about cheating the hangman, defeating justice, breaking the law, as though he, representing the law, had more claim to Gerwin's poor body than the man had himself. As though in some obscure, obscene way, a bloodless institution, a man-framed body of Government decrees, a tangle of codes and codicils, had become an entity with claims and a will of its own. (p. 156)

Gerwin Evans is accordingly found posthumously guilty of murder. In this way, *Strike for a Kingdom* connects the prejudices of an intemperate, vengeful police Inspector to a 'man-framed body of Government decrees, a tangle of codes and codicils' (p. 156) to subvert a basic principle of the whodunnit: that 'the detective in fiction embodies a promise of individual justice under the law'.[64]

Stephen Knight remarks that 'English reviewers tended to read all post-war Welsh fiction as quaint', and he draws attention to a *Times Literary Supplement* reviewer who found Gallie's *Strike for a Kingdom* 'Fresh and beguiling from the land of her fathers'. It would, the reviewer rhapsodised, 'delight all those [...] who kindle to the elfland music of *bach* and *bachgen i*'. Yet had the reviewer been a little more familiar with the reality rather than the quaintness of Wales, it is possible that he or she would have become acutely aware that *Strike for a Kingdom* kindles more than 'elfland music'. Menna Gallie's Cilhendre is a site where the binary gender definitions and power structures insisted upon by anglophone patriarchy dissolve into a conspectus of indigenous local masculinity founded on gender commonality and social equivalence. Because such commonality embraces children also, the traditionally conceived rite of passage from boyhood to manhood essential to patriarchy is nullified in the figure of D. J. Williams and contested in the figure of John Nixon. The most settled domestic arrangement in the novel is that of a mother and her unmarried son. The birth of a stillborn child from an incestuous but deeply loving relationship passes without condemnation. Where a patriarchal model is presented in the Nixons, the feral masculinity of the father has collided with the bourgeois femininity of the mother, resulting in the son's gender confusion. The reviewer would have noted, too, how the novel brilliantly manipulates a bourgeois literary form to incorporate an implicitly subversive, radically gentler reconfiguring of Valleys' industrial masculinity in which indigenous identities are overlaid and disempowered by the cultural, industrial and legal practices of a male-dominated colonial praxis. The reviewer would then have realised that *Strike for a Kingdom* does not kindle a flame to quicken an anglo-centric delight in Welsh 'elfland' whimsy, so much as a Welsh bonfire of anglo-colonial presumptions. If one asks, 'Whodunnit?', the answer is simple. 'Menna Gallie dunnnit.'

4

Reading Hector Bebb: Masculinity and Mythic Paradigms in So Long, Hector Bebb *(1970)*[1]

Ron Berry's *So Long, Hector Bebb* diverges radically in its form and focus from the three novels so far examined. In this narrative, there are no collieries or miners, traditional Valleys' industries are moribund, and the communality they bred has withered. And while R. W. Connell maintains that for men, 'Marriage, fatherhood and community life often involve extensive compromises with women',[2] this view has little traction in a text where there is no wider community, fatherhood scarcely features and inter-gender relationships are sclerotic. As previous chapters have shown, 'definitions of masculinity were deeply enmeshed in the history of institutions and of economic structures.'[3] By 1970, however, it was not only Valleys' institutions and the economic and patriarchal structures regulating them that were under threat from mine closures and unemployment.[4] So, too, was cultural uncertainty about what masculinity actually was. Second-wave feminism travelled across the Atlantic to challenge further the assumptions of institutional patriarchy and immutable masculinity. And what Lynne Segal perceives as 'the mild domestication of men, represented as more home-based (if not more house-trained)'[5] further contributed to a perceived 'crisis of masculinity'.[6] In that respect, the unambiguously masculine Hector Bebb stands as an expression of defiance against these infusions of cultural change. But Berry's novel is far more than a disgruntled riposte to a contemporary phenomenon. Through the representation of its protagonist it is also an inquiry into hyper-masculinity as an asocial phenomenon. The story of Hector Bebb charts him as a peerless boxer whose career is cut short when he kills his wife's lover in a momentary loss of control, and he escapes to live on a farm with Prince Saddler, and finally is reduced to living wild on the moors until his untimely death, though Berry's narrative method is hardly as straightforward as that summary suggests.

The novel's fourteen narrative voices, unsentimental Valleys' setting and raw, sometimes brutal narrative proved an aesthetic bridge too far for a hapless *Times Literary Supplement* reviewer who judged it to be a 'confusion of voices [...] lacking a clear and credible narrative line'.[7] But as Daryl Leeworthy has remarked, 'the novel would not work that way – it could not work that way. The feral descent of Hector Bebb from local hero to outcast is remarkable in its revelation of the flimsy character of modern civilization ...'[8] Perhaps a similar reviewer, seeking clarity and credibility, would have made a similar judgement of William Faulkner's *As I lay Dying* (1930), which is narrated through fifteen voices, one of whom, Vardaman, declares that his mother is a fish.[9] Despite this, Ron Berry continued to have strong advocates in Wales like Dai Smith and John Pikoulis, and since the reissue of *So Long, Hector Bebb* by Parthian in 2006, at a time when anglophone Welsh writing was acquiring more prominence, it has enjoyed justified critical plaudits. Daniel G. Williams, for example, judges it to be 'the most experimental and successful of all Welsh boxing novels';[10] Craig Austin wonders if it 'may be *the* great Welsh novel' (original italics);[11] and for Niall Griffiths, it is 'one of the greatest novels to come out of the twentieth century'.[12]

The gestation of the novel was long and troubled as it passed through draft after draft before emerging as a sophisticated contrapuntal text. Through its multiple 'voices' (nine male and five female), it comprises fifty-three entries, thirty-six male, seventeen female. Their narratives are presented with no diegetic intervention to validate, explain or modify what they think of themselves or others. Having no panoptic narrator, it is an interlocked series of personal histories which construct competing gender ideologies. Providing the narrative with an organising focus is the *echt* masculinity of Hector Bebb himself. Clarification of details and events given by one character often comes only later through the voice of another, each voice participating in and refracting the narrative's forward movement. The consequence is that while *So Long, Hector Bebb* foregrounds the male body as a site distinguishing man from man and most definitely men from women, it paradoxically does so through a series of interlinked, but disembodied 'voices'. It is a narrative form as fluid as water and as hard as ice.

Yet for all the late acclaim the novel has attracted, little has been written about the composition of its brilliantly conceived central character, the hypertrophic, iconic male Hector Bebb, the text's eponymous focus. In her *Narrative Fiction: Contemporary Poetics*, Shlomith Rimmon-Kenan distinguishes between 'story' and 'text'. She explains that while 'story' is 'a succession of events in chronological order', in the 'text' 'all the items of the narrative content are filtered through some prism or perspective'. In other words, 'the text is what we read'.[13] A gender-oriented reading of 'the text' of *So Long, Hector Bebb* offers just such a prism or perspective into the rich possibilities that constructing Hector Bebb offered a former 'Shoni Tarzan' like Ron Berry.[14] It begins from the premise that Hector Bebb is endowed with male-approved hyper-masculine signifiers at once of his present and the past, his times and earlier times; that he exemplifies a phenomenon Christopher E. Forth calls a 'violent yet rejuvenating alternative to an inauthentic life devoted to politeness, consumption and appearances'.[15] If this were all, it would be achievement enough. But as Dorothy Yamamoto remarks, 'the membrane between humanness and otherness is frighteningly permeable',[16] and for Berry, Hector Bebb also functions as a means of probing the problematic relationship between the male self and the 'other': the male and the female, the animal and the human, the animal in the human, the natural and the civilised, the primitive and the domesticated, especially when that male is a thoroughly hegemonic specimen.

Set in the Rhondda Valleys and the hills above where, as Gareth Jones writes, 'boxing was the sport which most stirred the blood of the locals'[17] like that other iconic Valleys' figure, the miner, the boxer was emblematic of courage, agency, manual skill, dexterity, and pride in the body. Indeed, in Valleys' culture the terms 'boxing' and 'mining' are almost interchangeable for, as Kasia Boddy states, 'To evoke boxing is always to dissociate oneself from the sentimental, the refined, the feminine.'[18] However, boxing is also, crucially, an arena of male definition that celebrates violence as essential to its practice. As Varda Burstyn points out, of all sports it is only boxing where 'lawful sanctioned violence (heroism) is distinguished from unlawful violence (villainy) along rules established by cultural conventions and practised on a large scale by men as a gender'.[19] In the resulting paradox, the controlled violence Hector Bebb displays in the ring is celebrated and rewarded as 'heroism'; a momentary loss of control, when he accidentally kills his wife's lover under considerable provocation, is judged to be 'villainy', and he becomes a fugitive. Submerged within the discourse of the text is Berry's interest in the problematic of how boxing, like warfare, requires the highly trained, potentially lethal male body to act intuitively and violently in one context and with restraint and reflection in another, when in both the very self faces violation.

Even a rudimentary glance through the several drafts of the novel reveals that *So Long, Hector Bebb* hardly arrived fully shaped in Berry's mind. Its form and ethos were drastically refashioned throughout the 1960s from a form of melodramatic social realism into one that fuses verisimilitude with a network of mythic prototypes that enrich its surface narrative. The first complete draft of the novel, undated and handwritten though probably composed in the early 1960s, chronicles through the alternating voices of Hector Bebb and his trainer Sammy John the intertwining fortunes of both figures.[20] Hector begins as an unhappily married patriarch whose wife Ethel is given to drink and religion. His successful career as a boxer allows him to live a life of material comfort, and to place his son Dilwyn, who has polio, in a private school. Various setbacks, including his willingness to engage in match-fixing, leave him needing money to send Dilwyn to Lourdes, and he becomes a minor criminal. His accomplice kills a girl during a bungled robbery and is later hanged. Wanted by the police, Hector flees, and visits each of his three sisters who reject him. He seeks refuge on the moors before Prince Jenkin Saddler discovers him close to death, rescues him and helps him to the extent of arranging plastic surgery in London.[21] Hector returns to work in his locality, is recognised despite his surgery, flees again and falls to his death while being pursued. Neither Jane Evass nor Emlyn Winton, central to the novel's final manifestation, appears in this version.

As may be deduced from the outline above, Hector Bebb was located initially within a sphere of material self-improvement, troubling family relationships, and a sensationalised trajectory, all of which, with the exception of his unsatisfactory marriage, are expunged from later drafts, as the number of voices increases. The minutiae of his home life and the lengthy time span of the action (signified in these drafts by his greying hair) conspire to deny him his legendary status of the final draft, where the turn in his fortunes is compressed and dramatic. Instead of slow decline, there is the abrupt and tragic *peripeteia* of his unintentional killing of his wife Millie's lover, Emlyn Winton, the day after winning the British middleweight title. From being 'One of your Rolls Royce fighters' (p. 21) he becomes a fugitive. From being a compromised failure in an early draft, he is progressively transformed into a mythopoeic tragic hero, an emblematic *figure* of doomed, embodied masculinity.

Boxing offered Berry an ideal practice through which to channel his own interest in the activity and tap it as a resource rich in historical and mythic resonance. Indeed, as Daryl Leeworthy states, 'It is hard to imagine any other sport which allows for such ruminative depth as boxing.'[22] Because it is an activity whose sole purpose is to inflict physical damage on an opponent, it functions in the novel as a metonym for unequivocally hyper-masculine practices and rituals that in their sheer brutality through the ages separate men from other men and, most certainly in the novel, separate men from women. Identifying the peculiar qualities of such masculinity, Joyce Carol Oates observes that they are intensely self-referential and ritualistically dangerous: 'In the brightly lit ring', she writes, 'man is *in extremis*, performing an atavistic rite or *agon*.'[23] In one respect, the entire text of *So Long, Hector Bebb* itself functions as a brightly lit ring. Under its intense spotlight, the reader is invited to observe in Hector Bebb a hyper-masculine presence *in extremis*, performing a sequence of atavistic rites – such as inflicting severe physical and cerebral damage on an opponent in the ring, killing a rival (his wife's lover) by main force, and eventually living wild as a fugitive on the hills – that lead inevitably to his isolation and death. Throughout the text Hector is removed from the systemic patriarchy of the Valleys, though that culture's love of boxing is textually commemorated. Sarah Morse astutely notes that the boxing agent, Abe Pearson, 'occupies a position analogous to that of the exploitative colliery owner, and the boxers echo the position of the colliers',[24] but this is the case principally with boxers like Bump Tanner and Len Jules, over whom Pearson exerts a controlling authority. Although Hector Bebb exists in this culture of exploitative patriarchy, he himself remains largely unblemished by its contingencies. His narrative takes him in a different and more exclusive direction.

In his appreciation of *So Long, Hector Bebb*, Craig Austin comments that 'there are no heroes here'.[25] But it is as a hero, in a paradigmatic, mythopoeic, tragic sense, that Hector Bebb can be read. Ian Watt notes the power of mythic archetypes to embody 'a single-minded pursuit by the protagonist of one of the characteristic desires of Western man'. Such figures, Watt argues, embody 'an *arete* and a *hubris*, an exceptional prowess and a vitiating excess in spheres of action that are particularly important in our culture'.[26] Hector Bebb is such a figure. When an example of elite manhood appears in 'the here and now',

Christopher E. Forth remarks, 'it must bear the residual traces of these other times and places'.[27] And through a form of 'mythic realism',[28] Berry interfuses the verisimilitude of Hector Bebb's construction as a contemporary figure with paradigms, both mythic and legendary, of the male as warrior 'from other times and places'. The result localises but also universalises his 'exceptional prowess and vitiating excess', his *arete* and *hubris* as features of the elite but doomed male.

Within this heroic model, Hector Bebb follows a broad but recognisable mythic trajectory of early neglect, initiation, emergence as an exemplary model of an admired physical manhood followed by exclusion from a social and legal framework to which he cannot be reconciled. In death, his rare distinction attracts continued devotion. The mythic archetypes underpinning the surface narrative of Hector's construction begin with his parentage. Writing on the figure of the hero, Fitzroy Raglan (Lord Raglan) points out that heroes are often conceived in atypical circumstances, sometimes adulterously, sometimes by deception, and sometimes of undetermined paternity.[29] Hector Bebb's parentage is unusual. He is possibly conceived out of wedlock, neglected by his mother and abandoned by his elusive father 'something Bebb' who, in Sammy John's suggestive meteorological trope, 'came and vanished from Cymmer town like a piece of weather' (p. 10).[30] In keeping with Raglan's pattern of heroic development, we are told little of Hector's early childhood. He is taken in and fostered by Sammy and Sue John who, in the text's final draft, have no children of their own. Sammy becomes not only Hector's surrogate father – he 'dotes on him' (p. 104) – but also his mentor. Like the archetypal hero warrior figure, Hector is separated from female influence. Sue John's initially maternal concern for him withers until 'she'd have trampled over Hector in the gutter' (p. 11). Relocated into the space of the boxing gymnasium by Sammy, and animated by its male values of competition, somatic power and aggression, Hector is distinguished from his fellows by his enthusiasm for the disciplines of training, preparation and contest. It quickly becomes evident to Sammy that he incarnates a remarkable form of potent masculinity: 'Pure single-mindedness, fighting his one and only love' (p. 10).

Fundamental to Hector Bebb's pre-eminence is his fusion of ratiocination, intuition and utter self-belief. On an early visit to the White Hart gymnasium, he displays the innate proficiency marking out the hero figure when, after initially taking a beating because of his inexperience, he knocks unconscious with two deadly blows the experienced Len

Jules, who 'sat there like a man sleeping' (p. 15). Almost concurrent with his greatest success, having won the British middleweight title through a feat of controlled aggression, Hector displays 'a vitiating excess', an unusual loss of control, in killing Emlyn Winton, his wife Millie's lover. A prey to chronic claustrophobia, he dreads prison and flees. His expulsion from an enclosed world in which he is pre-eminent echoes Raglan's paradigm that the hero 'loses favour with the gods [...] and is driven from the throne and city'.[31] Hector Bebb finally suffers an early death not, as Raglan accords some heroes, 'at the top of a hill', but from a fatal fall down one, and, like the hero, he is revered by men after his death.[32] While *So Long, Hector Bebb* secularises religious iconography, respect bordering on reverence is inflected through two differing though connected topologies.[33] The first, communicated through Bella Pearson's rebarbative narration, reveals the chasm existing between male and female evaluation of Hector. For Bella, with her aspirations to bourgeois *comme il faut*, Hector is unlamented in death. He was simply uncivilised: 'One of the lowest of the low' (p. 241). Her husband, however, Hector's manager, the invariably unsentimental Abe, feels compelled to undertake a secular pilgrimage to 'take a last look' (p. 241) at Hector's remarkable body. Gathering Hector's associates together, he visits Tosteg, views the body, weeps, and salutes Hector's memory by his uncharacteristic generosity later in Tommy Wills's pub.

In the second topology, communicated through Sammy John, Prince Saddler, a disfigured war veteran devoted to Hector, insists that he and Sammy brave the bitter weather to visit the site where Hector died. Raglan notes that the dead hero 'has one or more holy sepulchres',[34] and Sammy's severely pragmatic approach to the visit contrasts with the quasi-religious experience it is for Prince. The text has already implied Prince's reverential attitude to Hector when he wagers generously on him to win a fight, with the simple words, 'I have faith' (p. 75), and for Prince the visit becomes 'a pilgrimage' (p. 259). Despite Sammy's feeling that it was the most 'futile trip I've ever undertaken' (p. 259), even he needs the support of religious discourse to express his own feelings. Indeed, his vision is even more apocalyptic and reverential than Prince's. He is sure that if the world ends and boxing begins again with strangely mutant contestants, 'some junior monk will tote [Hector's] credit' (p. 259) by carrying a signed photograph of him as a relic that survived the conflagration. The final phrasing of Sammy's reflection is significant, for it underwent delicate modifying in the novel's redrafting. The first draft offers his anaemic assurance that if, after a global calamity, boxing begins again 'from scratch [...] they'll still remember Hector Bebb'.[35] In a later draft, the photograph is added as an iconographic 'relic', and the vague pronoun 'they' is changed to a typewritten 'some fanatic'. Presumably because of its pejorative associations, 'fanatic' is later erased and the handwritten phrase 'junior monk' with its favourable connotations of homage and veneration inserted instead.[36] The eschatological breadth of the image, together with Sammy's view that Prince 'had the look of a man expecting to be saved [...] the look of a rigorous Christian' (p. 259), combine to lodge Hector Bebb securely within the pantheon of heroic figures, the memory of whom carries a redemptive promise.

Within this broad architectural design of the fated hero, the text refines its study of Hector's form of masculine presence through references to more specific *agonistic* iconographies. Varda Burstyn observes that sport bases itself in 'archaic residual values associated with the highly differentiated, ranked gender order of tribal male warrior culture'.[37] By having the veteran soldier Prince Saddler conceive Hector as both a reincarnated 'warrior' and a 'gladiator', someone who, like his own former comrades, 'relished war as the supreme existence' (p. 60), the central sections of the novel create a symbolic and metaphoric pattern aligning him with a 'male warrior culture', where the lethal male body represents the apex of masculine definition. Hector Bebb, Sammy John says, is 'Born for action' (p. 9), a bellicose male for whom somatic passivity is a psychological itch that he can express only through a physiological figure: it 'hurts worse than a pasting' (p. 9). Tommy Wills, by contrast, brings a distinct pragmatism to his career as a boxer. Shackled as he is into a pattern of patriarchal conformity, boxing for him is a means to an end; he fights in order to 'put up the bond' on a pub when he retires (p. 81).

Joyce Carol Oates recognises the alluring but menacing status of the boxer, who inhabits a world where 'Values are reversed, evaginated'. A boxer, she writes, is 'valued not for his humanity but for being a "killer"'.[38] The fictional Sammy John provides a similar insight into the boxer's ambiguous status. When he assesses the young Hector as 'a killer' (p. 11), he is identifying his singular aptitude for conflict in a figurative compliment that becomes a proleptic truth connecting him to his mythical namesake. The veneration of the boxer as an exemplar of warrior manhood, as killer, exists in western culture from antiquity. In Book V of the *Aeneid*, for instance, the Trojan Entellus 'showered volleys of blows, thick as the hailstones which storm-clouds send' on

Dares, nearly killing him.[39] Similarly, in his championship fight with Jesse Markham, Hector is 'unloading as [Markham] tries to smother, over and under his arms, unloading my lot, everything right up the bell' (pp. 84–5). Even his gamesmanship against Mel Carpenter, when he responds to Carpenter's having a strip of wire in his glove by biting him on his shoulder, is legitimised by classical precedent. As Tom Winnifrith remarks, 'There is not in Homer the belief that behaving well somehow wins matches and battles.'[40]

However, Hector Bebb's mythical lineage extends beyond antiquity to interfuse with more recent incarnations of combative masculinity. As part of the novel's intertextual design, several characters, particularly Hector, have names that echo twentieth-century real life or fictional representations of the male as heroic combatant. Clearly, one has to be cautious connecting Hector of Cymmer with Hector of Troy, but in thus naming its protagonist the text incorporates Hector Bebb into the mythical literary tradition of the fated warrior hero, while also associating him through a phonic chiming with the real-life American boxing legend Harry Greb, the world middleweight champion between 1923 and 1926. While Hector Bebb suffers a damaging cut above his eye as the result of a foul blow, Harry Greb actually lost the sight in his right eye for a similar reason. As so often with those who are revered as heroes, Greb's early death, like Hector's, enhanced his iconic renown. A recent article on Greb, for instance, reaches quite naturally for the same combative noun that Prince employs for Hector, when it appraises Greb as 'the most formidable warrior in boxing history'.[41]

But suggestive nominal insinuations in the novel extend beyond Hector Bebb, although they all serve to burnish his reputation. Berry was well read in American fiction, and in Bernard Malamud's novel *The Natural* (1952), the hero Roy Hobbs ousts Bump Baily from his pre-eminent role as the baseball star of the New York Knights. In a piece of intertextual legerdemain, *So Long, Hector Bebb* introduces a parallel that cannot be mere coincidence, when a character called Jerome Wilkinson-Tanner in an early draft acquires a resonating name change into the talented middleweight boxer Bernard Bump Tanner, who is defeated by Hector. And like Bernard Malamud's 'natural' Roy Hobbs, Ron Berry's Hector Bebb is both a fated hero and 'a natural' (p. 12). More prosaically, but also indicative of the novel's intertextual apparatus, is the naming of Tommy Wills, a boxer also defeated by Hector, whose name echoes Harry Wills, the legendary American 'Black Panther'. Even a minor character like the boxer Vic Crane was originally called Soldier Crane, arguably after Ernest Hemingway's boxer Soldier Bartlett.[42] The cumulative significance of such resonances implies a subtle narrative strategy. The figures orbiting Hector Bebb in the novel secure his pre-eminence within a fictional constellation, but they also amplify his allure by their nominal connection to extra-textual embodiments of combative masculinity.

Freely sourcing mythic archetypes and paradigms in assembling Hector Bebb's distinctive alterity, the novel tantalisingly infuses a seemingly prosaic incident with an undercurrent of resonating extra-realism. In preparation for his championship title contest against Jesse Markham, Hector's team employs an odd-job builder, an 'old sioni craftsman, genuine as silver money' (p. 73), to assemble a practice ring for him. The builder, who is not named but is nonetheless endowed with unimpeachable integrity, does not appear in early drafts of the novel, and when he does later, he does not address Hector. But as draft succeeded draft he acquires a strangely seer-like presence, and a significant change in function. In Sammy John's account, the builder comments that Prince Saddler, who is present and of whom he has already heard, is 'Something extra special', but he then turns to address Hector: "though you got a touch of it in you too, boyo". He stroked his hand on Hector's chest then he went bobbing down the lane from Cwmbryn, toolbag humping his back. We never saw him again' (p. 74). His informal judgement and his stroking of Hector's chest – as though tactile contact confers a benediction and confirms an insight – contrasts the shrewdness of his perception with the clumsiness of his gait as he bobs down the lane, leaving without a farewell. The paragraph's closing sentence is at once a factual statement and a teasingly suggestive invitation to read beyond the fact. There is no practical reason why the builder's departure should attract Sammy's comment, but in doing so it generates a suggestive *frisson*, where the realism of the occasion melds with the mythic paradigm of the stranger/seer figure who appears, impresses, pronounces and disappears. It is appropriate that this incident is articulated by Sammy, for he, too, recognises 'something extra special' in Hector beyond his pugilism. Speaking of himself and Sue, he acknowledges that: 'We're like a couple of adverts. No matter what, you've got to find the real, stick by whatever's real. Hector Bebb, he's real' (pp. 11–12). What Sammy recognises in the simulacrum of his own domestic bliss, and what the jobbing builder divines, is that Hector Bebb incarnates a masculinity that cannot accommodate itself within the prescriptions and social nuances of a post-industrial, domesticated, trivialised world. Hector Bebb lives what he is because he can live no other way.

Sammy's distinction between the *ersatz* and the authentic, and the jobbing builder's strangely resonating moment both contribute to Berry's construction of Hector Bebb within the mythos of heroic masculinity, the warrior male living both inside and outside his time. But Berry goes further in substantiating Hector's distinctive alterity through two further attributes: his pre-eminent gifts as a combative male, and his attitude to women. As a boxer, Hector Bebb incorporates two cherished qualities of ultra-masculine definition: a physique and a psychology acutely suited to the rigours of extreme action and performance. A helpful distinction between this fictional representation of physical hegemony and a real-life equivalent is apparent in an interview R. W. Connell conducted with Steve Donoghue, an Australian champion surfer, whose 'job is to be an iron man and to market himself as a sports personality'. Donoghue comments on the enormous personal sacrifices required to achieve and maintain such an exemplary 'iron man' status: 'it is a pretty disciplined sort of life. It's like being in jail.'[43] *So Long, Hector Bebb* constructs Hector on a different model of hegemonic masculinity. Unlike Donoghue, who incarcerates himself in a job as an iron man in order to market himself as a product, Hector Bebb shows little interest in material self-advancement, though Bump Tanner is convinced that 'Hector's mug would sell shirts, socks, beer, anything. You name it, anything for men' (p. 107). Significantly, it also places him outside a constraining system of patriarchal capitalism, for Donoghue's pragmatically functional incarceration contrasts radically with the liberation that boxing gives Hector Bebb for self realisation. For him, a hard-fought contest is 'A great fight. The inside of my smeller like a nutmeg grater. Two shiners. Ears like burnt cobs' (p. 27). Christopher E. Forth writes that boxing 'foregrounds pain and violence as repressed male experiences that are at once cathartic, therapeutic and empowering'.[44] The complex psycho-physiological process Forth describes, where pain experienced through violent action is exhilarating, distinguishes Hector's masculinity from his more pedestrian colleagues, and enables the text to connect him once more to the elite masculinities of the warrior and the gladiator.

Hector's response to pain leads the prosaic Abe Pearson to regard him as a 'high grade machine' (p. 22), an object to be utilised, but to do so is to mechanise his complex natural functioning. Sammy's observation that Hector is 'all fighter, pure and simple as a bird flying' (p. 17), by contrast, emphasises Hector's unfettered integration of form, action and purpose. Virtually every action exhibits his self-actualising through preparation and performance. Millie complains, for example, that he even darted 'his fists across the table during meals, catching flies for boxing practice' (p. 90).[45] In a text where bodily hexis is prominent, Hector's distinguishes him even from other boxers who train at the White Hart. Millie twice refers to him as a 'panther' (pp. 36, 37) in the ring, 'stalking', 'always on the go'. And when Prince Saddler first startles Hector on a training run, Hector 'jinked off like a surprised wolf' (p. 58). The two references define key aspects of his predatory masculinity both in the ring and later on the hills: feline power, sinuous grace and lupine associations with the untamed wilderness. Dai Smith writes that 'the raw edge of boxing can never be completely overcome since it is this which lies at the heart of it',[46] and it is in 'the raw edge' that Hector excels. In a 'scrap' with Bump Tanner which Hector has subtly provoked

> I'm out to put him away. Two short hooks sink in down below. Bump's feet widened for his right-hand swinger. He'll never learn. I felt it dying like a flap of rag against my neck. Then Bump took four hard shots. Three lefts and a right, real hooks sent from the shoulder. (p. 32)

In this compact passage, the text assembles a sequence of signifiers indicating Hector's particular combination of qualities: ruthless determination, technical proficiency, tactical awareness and contempt, as Bump's failed swinger leaves him exposed to the clinical finesse of 'four hard shots'. After the fight, Hector carries on training – 'medicine ball, speedball, skipping' (p. 33). Bump, 'who doesn't look too dandy' (p. 33), is laid off training for ten days. Hector's judgement of Bump – 'He can't ever go where I'm set on reaching in this game' (p. 33) – reveals not only his own exceptional prowess, his *arete*, but a *hubris* that leads to the coming tragic *peripeteia* when he kills Emlyn Winton and becomes a fugitive.

Hector is also distinguished from his fellows by his attitude to women. Christopher E. Forth suggests that 'Bravery, strength, endurance and sexual potency figure prominently in most lists of ideal male bodily attributes',[47] all of which the text confers on Hector Bebb, except for a strong libido. Indeed, the novel goes out of its way to make this clear. Abe Pearson believes him to be 'cool in the goolies' (p. 23), and

Millie compares her 'panther' in the ring to 'a little cock robin' (p. 91) in bed. But in *So Long, Hector Bebb*, sexual potency becomes an attribute directed towards lesser characters, promiscuous users and abusers of women like Vic Crane, Emlyn Winton and Bump Tanner. Sarah Morse suggests that 'Although Hector implies that his masculine energies are directed into his boxing career, the matter of his sexless nature is ambiguous'.[48] But it can also be argued that the text constructs in Hector Bebb a singular version of hegemonic masculinity which is largely detached from sexuality. And what Morse calls 'the question of [Hector's] sexual orientation'[49] is a means of defining rather than questioning this phenomenon. Sammy John's comment that before the fight with Jesse Markham, Hector 'slept like a saint' (p. 74) makes a surprising but illuminating connection between two seemingly conflicting modes of being, the spiritually ordained and the physically embodied. In this regard, Joyce Carol Oates makes the pertinent observation that boxing is 'a unique, closed self-referential world, obliquely akin to those severe religions, in which the individual is both "free" and "determined"'.[50] It is the paradox of freedom achieved through constraint that constructs Hector Bebb's singular mode of being. Obliquely akin to a saint he, too, is engaged in the single-minded expression of unity of self through unity of purpose. It is, as even the severely pragmatic Abe Pearson recognises, 'a gift from on high', making Hector an elite example, one of those who 'don't come often' (p. 24). In contrast, men like Emlyn Winton, the barman and Millie's lover, defined by their personal vanity and sexual predation, do come often. When Millie faithfully records that 'Emlyn reckons [Hector's] a semi-eunuch. Em swears I married a near enough eunuch six years ago' (p. 91), she not only reveals how besotted she is with her lover but exposes the fatuity of Emlyn's preening self-regard. Commenting on Emlyn's 'initialled cuff-links, zebra arm-bands and dickie bow', together with his 'clucks and tishes' and the way he 'wiggled his fingers through his gorgeous locks', Sammy John dismisses him contemptuously as 'a genuine sack of lard' (pp. 45–6).

The novel, however, defines Hector Bebb not through success with women, but through the physical conquest of men. Hector's marriage fails not because he abuses Millie, but because he is unable to appreciate her craving for a man who makes 'a girl melt like butter' (p. 90). He recognises that 'she was left out in the cold a bit' but believes that she 'preferred herself that way' (p. 70). She admits that 'at home there's no danger in him' (p. 37), unlike Abe Pearson, who sadistically stubs out his cigar on his wife's thigh to demonstrate his dominance (p. 134). Hector's difficulty in establishing intimate relationships with women recurs later when his liaison with Doreen Evass also fails. He realises that 'we were as different as salt and sugar. Me and Doreen were foreigners' (p. 167). Within the larger context of the novel, this episode is less an observation of Hector's lukewarm sexuality than another instance of a problematic gender incompatibility that positions women and men as at best achieving a desperate or deluded rapprochement.

The intertextualities of the novel's mythic realism, then, enable a celebration of Hector Bebb as a representative of elite Welsh masculinity located within the pantheon of combative heroes. In its later sections, however, as the narrative accelerates him towards his tragic demise, it focuses more starkly on what Christopher E. Forth calls the 'tensions between polish and primitivity, brawn and brain, and activity and sedentariness'.[51] It is these tensions, present in perceptions of Hector Bebb throughout the text, that are foregrounded in the final third of the novel where Hector as mythopoeic ultra-male becomes Hector as liminal fugitive, existing both physically and psychologically on the fringes of civilisation.

Structurally, the narrative progressively drives Hector Bebb from a social world limited to boxing to a narrower world with Prince Saddler at Bryn Farm and later briefly with Doreen, to a male-defined domain on the hills above Tosteg. In this last space, the novel interrogates what it is that remains of an elite manhood when even the residual complications of social obligation fall away. This final trajectory of Hector Bebb's narrative is both actual and symbolic, and deeply personal to Berry himself. In an undated, unpublished essay, he writes: 'I felt drawn to the wilderness. Extremity manures the soul. The day by day imperatives of being civilised, are less significant when confronted by oneself under a weight of sky.'[52] Whereas in *Times Like These* and *Cwmardy*, green spaces afford recuperation and opportunities for relaxation, *So Long, Hector Bebb* adopts a more ambivalent interpretation of Welsh pastoral, where the hills overlooking the Valleys offer a threat as well as an embrace, an inhospitable otherness 'under a weight of sky' as well as a consoling return to nature. The dialogue with the self, generated by the extremity of the wilderness that Berry refers to, permeates the novel's examination of Hector Bebb's solitary existence on the hills, and through it addresses some of the disturbing complications of the male as predator.

The development marks a change of direction in Hector Bebb's representation. Prior to his forced exile, the amalgam of intertextual mythic archetypes underpinning his construction had been woven implicitly into the texture of the discourse, but these archetypes had not functioned as desired models of self-definition to which Hector Bebb himself aspired. As a peerless primal male Hector himself had not required any. When out shooting with Prince Saddler, for instance, he retrieves a mallard Prince has shot by plunging without hesitation into an icy lake too cold for the retriever. Overcome with admiration, Prince exults in this exemplary exhibition by 'a man matched to his environment' (p. 151). However, when the novel removes Hector Bebb from virtually all human contact on the hills, and turns its lens unsentimentally on his unaccommodated masculinity, it dismisses Prince's easy elision of place and being. Instead, it provokes in Hector a direct confrontation not only with where he is, but who he is. Forced to re-evaluate his own ontological definition, the previously self-focalised Hector finds for the first time that he requires models of liminal masculinity through which to address his own new identity. Significantly, the two mythic models through which the novel constructs him *in extremis* are the American cowboy and, as his prospects become yet more precarious, another liminal male, the wild man.

In an audio interview with Dai Smith, Ron Berry acknowledged that American cultural influences 'were an essential part of my growing up'.[53] It is perhaps no surprise, then, that the text employs the figure of the cowboy as a tool for shaping a subtle but significant modification in Hector Bebb's composition. References to Hector's enthusiasm for Western novels, films and songs are strewn throughout the novel, and serve to align him by association with a culture that, as Jane Tompkins says, 'focuses exclusively on what men do'.[54] But when Hector is cast adrift on the hills, he is for the first time not entirely sure 'what men do'; or more specifically what a man would do in his position. From this point the novel moves into a new sphere of inquiry where primal masculinity intersects with culturally influenced models. To provide himself with a new *modus operandi*, Hector actively and self-consciously constructs himself through the prism of Western archetypes. He imaginatively recontextualises the hills above Pont Fawr as 'Bow and arrow country, [...] as pictured in Western stories' (p. 190). When wet, chilled and disconsolate on his first night alone, he asks himself,

'What would a cowboy or a red Indian do on a night like this?' His response, 'Pull his slicker over himself and stick it out till daylight' (p. 173), gratefully acknowledges not only the cowboy's stoicism, but illustrates the extent of his own imaginative immersion in a cowboy identity through his use of a Western idiom for rainwear.[55] When the rain stops and he finds shelter, he builds a fire, enjoys a meal, and entertains himself with Western tunes like 'Ghost riders in the sky' (p. 173). Hector's masculinity is in no way impaired by this development, for, as Jane Tomkins explains of the cowboy, while 'nature's wildness and hardness test his strength and will and intelligence, they also give him solace and repose'.[56]

Hector's identification with this liminal Western figure offers the same prospect of solace and repose, and it marks a new development in someone previously 'born for action' (p. 9). But in the novel's unsparing scrutiny of an elite masculinity thrust back entirely on its own resources, Berry introduces another, older and more problematic representation of liminal masculinity than the cowboy. Just as the hills in *So Long, Hector Bebb* project a tension between natural wildness, the depleted remains of an industrial past and an encroaching commercialised afforestation, so the novel positions Hector himself as occupying a transitional space between 'nature' and 'civilisation' through the ambiguous figure of the wild man. When Tommy Wills sees a shabby Hector Bebb, whom he does not recognise, begging outside his pub, he associates him with 'the wild man of the woods [...] rotten, all hair, beard down to his chest' (p. 179), hirsuteness being a signifier of the wild man's fallen state.[57] But a little later Tommy also sees him paradoxically as another kind of wild man, 'like a wanderer out of the Bible' (pp. 179–80). The dual optic through which Tommy views Hector both as degenerate sub-human and John-the-Baptist-like itinerant holy man identifies incompatible spheres of being represented by the wild man: the one traditionally a prey to ungovernable passion, the other a calibrated commitment to reflection and separation. Dorothy Yamamoto sees the wild man as a liminal figure who, 'Poised between two worlds [...] brings to a head questions about the dividing line between animals and humans, and the distinctiveness of human identity'.[58] And it is by utilising the manifold possibilities inherent in wild man mythologies that the novel examines through Hector Bebb the complex amalgam of the human and the animal, intuition and intellect, frenzy and cognition, volition and reflection in a physically hegemonic subject when placed *in extremis*.

Throughout the novel, Hector has been 'poised between two worlds', between two incompatible, gendered perceptions by others of his manhood, as 'no more than a trained animal' (p. 65) to Bella Pearson, and 'a single-minded genius' (p. 213) to Sammy John. Having established through Tommy Wills how the wild man generates ambivalent responses to the 'other', the novel further confronts Hector Bebb's masculinity by aligning him with two equally incompatible embodiments of this mythic archetype: the wild man as hunter-gatherer, and the warrior 'ape-man', Tarzan.[59] Both figures encode vastly influential though differing perceptions of hegemonic masculinity through which Hector Bebb's final incarnation is represented. Yamamoto's 'dividing line between humans and animals' becomes a permeable tissue, through which the text interrogates Hector as a figure unable to habituate himself to a feminine-coded vision of 'civilisation', represented in the novel principally through Jane Evass, Bella Pearson and Sue John, but on whom living in the wild has a paradoxically moderating influence.

Both Jane Tompkins writing on the cowboy and Roger Bartra on the wild man reach similar conclusions on the relationship between these liminal figures and the landscape they inhabit that connect them to Hector Bebb. Tompkins notes that although the cowboy's engagement with landscape initially generates fear and uncertainty, 'the landscape has ultimately a domesticating effect',[60] and Bartra contends that the mythical 'European wild man' is also 'the allegory of a domestic life in a wild context'.[61] Significantly, the wild man Bartra is referring to here is not Hector Bebb, but the hunter-gatherer Robinson Crusoe. While the hills above Tosteg have little in common with Crusoe's remote island, key aspects of Defoe's mythic archetype are apparent to a remarkable degree in Berry's also, which point to a domesticating of Hector's virile form of masculinity. Like Crusoe, though in a lower acquisitive register, Hector makes calculated use of the products of civilisation, like a mandrel shaft, a shovel blade, stolen shoes and overcoats, so that the abandoned colliery winding-house on the hills becomes, in a telling moment of self-realisation for Hector, 'my home, funnily enough already my home' (p. 196). Whereas Crusoe finds green limes 'very wholesome' and lays in quantities of grapes and lemons,[62] Hector, acutely aware of his physiological need for roughage, builds up 'a store of veg supplies from allotments' (pp. 219–20). Both figures find humour in their precarious positions. If Crusoe in his goat-skin clothing, 'could not but smile at the notion of my travelling through Yorkshire [...] in such a dress',[63] Hector in his wild man beard 'felt tempted to laugh in

[Tommy Wills's] face' (p. 218) at being unrecognised outside Tommy's pub. And whereas Crusoe records salvaging 'bread, rice, three Dutch cheeses, five pieces of dried goat's flesh',[64] Hector, with an unmarked irony, refers to himself as 'concentrating like a housewife' (p. 196) as he makes a shopping list of the essential goods he needs on a risky visit to Tosteg.

However, although Hector may domestically systematise his life on the hills, he is not, as Crusoe is, the beneficiary of a fruitful landscape supplying his every material need, and violent action becomes a prerequisite of his very survival. Emma Smith suggests that 'incidents where Hector is at one with nature purposely romanticise such savagery',[65] but there is little romanticising when, weak with hunger, he drinks the hot blood of a sheep he has killed. This traumatic episode merits close examination, for it crystallises Berry's study of hyper-masculine behaviour *in extremis*. As Hector prepares his assault on the unsuspecting creature, he once again requires a model of behaviour, and this time chooses Tarzan (p. 193), a figure famous for his dauntingly impressive physical feats. Roger Bartra notes that the figure of Tarzan succeeds in popular culture because it displaces various 'uncomfortable aspects not readily adaptable to the requirements of imperialist culture'.[66] But the 'uncomfortable aspects' of male violence and their place in male identity, and therefore their interface with normative society, are exactly what Berry directly confronts as the episode progresses. As Hector prepares for the attack, Berry, in a moment of textual brilliance, employs a taut figure that risks reducing the entire episode to bathos. When Hector declares that he 'shoved Doreen's bread-knife in my belt like Tarzan' (p. 193), the conjunction is startling, for Tarzan's chosen weapon, we remember, is a long hunting-knife. Within its context, however, the image directs attention to the text's focus on the problematic intersection of violence and restraint, the primitive and the civilised, the hunting-knife and the bread-knife in shaping hyper-masculine definition.

Starving though Hector Bebb is when he first sights the ewe and her lamb, he resists the temptation of a search for birds' eggs. The novel's focus to begin with is on his monochromatic, cerebral self-objectification: '*Think*, Hector, use your wits' (original italics), for the ewe means the deferred gratification of 'a big meal' (p. 194). When the assault comes, however, Berry abruptly switches mode, internalising Hector's own experience to construct more radically how the human and the animal, the cognitive and the instinctive, coalesce and conflict in moments of desperation. In a remarkable rhetorical sequence, Hector's discourse becomes impressionistic: it is allusive here, precise there, subjective and objective, graphic and mundane, a series of internalised sense impressions fusing with fleeting moments of objectified awareness, a blur of kaleidoscopic, ever-shifting data:

> I lost true sight, everything fuzzy and Roman candles firing inside my chest. Strength came in spasms, although I robbed myself, the lamb bleating, bleating, tormenting my mind. Blood splashed over my trousers. Heavy drops of rain began to fall. By and by dead lamb, unconscious ewe, me straddled over her, both of us quite still. She wiggled. I outed her again. (p. 194)

Emma Davies judges this to be 'a fusion of the twin desires of sex and death, reconfigured by Berry as an orgasmic reclamation of (male) self'.[67] However, it is possible to see the experience less as a moment of ecstatic reclamation than a loss of 'true sight', a moment of frightening self-erasure in a figure like Hector for whom self-discipline has been a defining characteristic.

Freud reminds us that 'fright' is different from 'fear' because: '[f]ear requires a definite object of which to be afraid. "Fright", however, is the name we give to the state a person gets into when he has run into danger without being prepared for it; it emphasises the factor of surprise.'[68] Throughout the novel Hector fears nothing, but here, for all his attempted modelling on Tarzan, the 'danger' he runs into is a frightening encounter with an aspect of himself rare in his previous experience. Desperate beyond measure as he is for food, the clinical control he displayed when he dispatched Bump Tanner with 'Three lefts and a right' (p. 32) deserts him. His insight, 'although I robbed myself' becomes an aposiopesis, a curtailed self-evaluation referring not only to the strength he wasted, but to his horrified recognition that his violent paroxysms caused the lamb's terror. From being Prince Saddler's warrior figure, he becomes a contrite violator of innocence. In this critical instance, *So Long, Hector Bebb* distils the instantaneous and dynamic interaction between passion and conscience, action and self-scrutiny in moments of extreme mental activity. When his judgement returns, he feels that he has committed a transgressive act and buries the remains of the lamb – 'poor mite' (p. 196) – in an act of reparation. As a boxer, Hector accepted the need to 'Disregard sentiment' (p. 9). As part of his narrative trajectory, he finds himself surprisingly susceptible to it, but also susceptible to 'fright', a very different 'factor of surprise'.[69]

In this final phase of Hector Bebb's construction, then, the novel inflects his masculinity through representations of the cowboy and the wild man. Together, they illustrate Hector Bebb exhibiting the problematised continuities of elite masculine definition more dramatically than the novel's earlier mythic prototypes had done. But through the figure of the wild man Berry goes much further and pushes Hector Bebb to the very edge of barely functioning cognitive manhood. When, later, he kills a dog for food, 'Under some mad impulse' with 'two bangs against a rock' (p. 219), and later still secretly visits Sammy John and Tommy Wills, the contrast between the celluloid figure of Tarzan and Berry's grimmer fictional reality is shocking. Prince's Hector, who had 'jinked off like a surprised wolf' (p. 58) in his prime, has now become 'a tired fox' (p. 228). He is 'gnawed down in his spirit' (p. 230). As a wanted man, and a wild man unable to reconcile the competing elements of his nature, there can be only one, fatal end to his trajectory. And, therefore, the manner of his going becomes crucial to the curating of his tragic status.

Hector Bebb is both the agent and the victim of his own story, and he faces his death without complaint or fear. As he lies fatally injured from his fall over a sixty-foot cliff, his final monologue becomes a dialogue with himself expressed through stream-of-consciousness. It is not, however, a formless flow of meandering interiority but a structured form of self-representation that characterises Hector as hero:

> It must have been instinct saying 'turn your head there's blood coming out from your mouth take it easy let go a bit at a time just let go slowly this is it this is it let go slowly this is it man let go for Christ's sake let go. Now go.' (pp. 256–7)

The poet and critic Henri-Frédéric Amiel thought himself 'too much of a woman' and nursed a dream 'to be a man just once before death [...] to make my delicateness, my character, my style a bit more *brutal*, to *masculinise* myself and to *virilise* myself',[70] (original italics). Within its strictly gendered dimorphism, *So Long, Hector Bebb* creates in Hector Bebb a figure not needing to '*virilise*' himself, for he naturally embodies an exemplary, though problematic, manhood in all its complex functioning. The implication behind his final instruction, 'Now go', asserts that death will not take him; it is he who has chosen the moment when he commits himself to dying. As when he was a boxer, in confinement he finds freedom. *So Long, Hector Bebb* constructs his passing as the passing of a cherished paradigm of Valleys' hyper-virility, to which the novel itself serves as a memorial, a script insisting that although it has passed it is not forgotten.

Ron Berry's achievement in so skilfully constructing a protagonist at once functioning within acceptable parameters of realism but enriched with mythic patterns and trajectories endows Hector Bebb with iconic status. In the manner of formal tragedy, the narrative ends not with the protagonist's death, but with a judgement upon him. When Sammy John and Prince Saddler visit the place where Hector died, it serves no purpose for the pragmatic Sammy: it is 'Useless offering so-long to Hector. He'll always be with me' (p. 261). For Prince, however, an old warrior himself, only through physical proximity to the place of Hector's death can he express his reverence for, and emotional dependence on, 'the old gladiator' (p. 260). Sammy and Prince close the novel on their mutual incomprehension. Either way, *So Long, Hector Bebb*, with its disarmingly colloquial title but densely textured mythic echoes, serves as a requiem for, and an inquiry into, the passing of a cherished but problematised Valleys' hyper-virility. Cunningly wrought, linguistically dazzling, acutely perceptive and eight years in the writing, it is a novel of its time and for all time.

5

Patriarchy, Power and Politics: Masculinities in Dark Edge *(1997) and* Until Our Blood is Dry *(2014)*[1]

Roger Granelli's *Dark Edge* (1997) and Kit Habianic's *Until Our Blood is Dry* (2014), two novels set in the 1984–5 miners' strike, draw upon and reformulate the representation of masculinities in earlier Valleys' fiction. The principal characters in each novel emerge from a narrative tradition of Valleys' industrial unrest, even as they negotiate the contemporary challenges of a neoliberal government intent on generating a competitive, individualist culture. As Huw Beynon and Peter McMylor explain, the strike was far more than an industrial dispute: 'From the beginning [Margaret] Thatcher had been anxious to break the old consensus [...] The old class compromises were not for her, neither were collective forms of life, and relationships.'[2] This chapter examines how *Dark Edge* and *Until Our Blood is Dry* scrutinise the impact of this form of cultural and economic imperialism on Valleys' male self-definition.

In each novel the strike is presented as a Manichaean struggle between the dark forces of an authoritarian right-wing government and Valleys' men and women fighting to secure their livelihood. *Dark Edge* presents this polarity through its two principal male characters, the 'thuggish, even sociopathic, policeman'[3] Elliott Bowles, whose personal antagonism to his half-brother, the striking miner Edwin, replicates the larger national conflict. *Until Our Blood is Dry* works on a broader canvas of two families, where Gwyn Pritchard, a non-striking colliery overman, seeks to exercise a sternly patriarchal control over his wife Carol, his daughter Helen, and striking miners, while the more cerebral, family-orientated striker Iwan Jones literally embraces his wife Angela and son Simon. Patriarchy, politics and power, both domestic and national, activate the narratives of each text and interfuse to varying degrees in constructing these differing masculinities. Each character constitutes a form of normative masculinity, but each text illustrates that within such an abstraction there are, as Valleys' mining fiction graphically demonstrates, 'ultimately as many varieties of masculinity as there are men'.[4]

Although Elliott Bowles (*Dark Edge*) and Gwyn Pritchard (*Until Our Blood*) inhabit different novels and inscribe different narrative arcs, they are both studies in a deviant form of masculinity intensified, if not initiated, in each novel by the socio-political structures that promise them freedom but deliver insecurity. Christopher Lasch informs us that 'Every age develops its own peculiar forms of pathology',[5] and the peculiar form visited upon Gwyn Pritchard and Elliott Bowles is a narcissistic withdrawal exacerbated by the strike, and expressed through their authoritarian and violent behaviour.[6] There are key structural similarities between these two characters which can profitably be examined at the outset before progressing to scrutinise them separately as differentiated studies of what Bethan Benwell identifies as 'Masculinity as Power Project'.[7] A similar structure is employed in examining Edwin Bowles (*Dark Edge*) and Iwan Jones (*Until Our Blood*). Discussion of their construction begins by identifying points of similarity before moving on to analyse separately their diverging narratives. In *Dark Edge*, the bachelor Edwin inscribes a form of *Bildungsroman* hero for whom the strike leads to radical self-inspection, and the possibility of personal development; while in *Until Our Blood is Dry* the committed husband and father, Iwan, although no 1980s 'new man', positions his relationships with women and children on the basis of mutual respect.

Because *Dark Edge* describes itself as 'a Cain and Abel scenario enacted in a backward Welsh valley' (p. 180) and builds its text on the alternating narratives of Elliott and Edwin Bowles, the closing two sections of this chapter examine masculinities from the more spacious *Until Our Blood is Dry* only. The first of these sections analyses the interplay of power and politics in the professional/managerial roles of the Coal Board's pro-government senior manager Adam Smith-Tudor, and Ystrad's Labour MP, Harry Cross. Adapting Benwell's 'Masculinity as Power Project' to the particularities of these characters, discussion centres on how their individual representations reflect the unequal distribution of power between right-wing and left-wing politics, and government and miners in the strike. Finally, I examine the novel's acute and explicit presentation of a homosexual relationship between Matt Price, a striking miner, and Siggy, a hairdresser. Writing seven years before the miners' strike, Andrew Tolson observed: 'The extent to which definitions of gender interpenetrate attitudes to "work" is not often fully understood.'[8] Through Siggy and Matt, *Until Our Blood is Dry* interrogates not only the coercive interpenetration of gender coding through employment role but goes a step further than Tolson to question the very usefulness of gender coding itself.

The policeman Elliott Bowles in *Dark Edge* and the non-striker Gwyn Pritchard in *Until Our Blood is Dry* present differentiated studies of narcissism as the performance of power, of which neoliberal ideology itself is conceived in each text as an incipiently destructive manifestation. Lynne Segal observes that recourse to violence is often attributable to men's 'threatened loss of dominance, status and privileges',[9] and Gwyn Pritchard and Elliott Bowles respond similarly to differing forms of lost status. Gwyn, the non-striking minor pit official, loses proprietorial influence over 'his lads' (*Until Our Blood*, p. 5) who are on strike, and Elliott, seduced by the neoliberal promise of limitless possibilities, experiences psychic outrage after being rebuffed by his lover, because he believed that 'everything and everyone would fall into his lap' (*Dark Edge*, p. 87). Frustrated in their accustomed roles of authoritarian, entitled males, both characters attempt to recuperate their status through brutality towards their wives. Earlier novels examined in this book had been more circumspect in depicting male-on-female aggression. The hyper-masculine Big Jim Roberts in *Cwmardy*, for instance, likes nothing better than a punch-up involving other men, but is easily quelled at home by Siân; in *Times Like These*, the stern patriarch Oliver Biesty resents his daughter Mary's determination to be her own woman but, unlike Gwyn Pritchard with the feisty Helen, he never resorts to violence; and Elwyn Jeffries in *Strike for a Kingdom* partly blames himself for Jess's adultery. *Dark Edge* and *Until Our Blood is Dry* position their more graphic representation of male coercion within the valences of a brutal power struggle played out on the national stage and replicated in the patriarchal home.

Anthony Giddens writes that in late capitalist individualistic society, 'the erasure of tradition and the emergence of "lifestyle" both contribute to obsessive-compulsive behaviour and poor health, both mental and physical'.[10] *Until Our Blood is Dry* and *Dark Edge* offer striking examples of Giddens's paradigm. For Gwyn Pritchard, the strike, together with the emergence of strong female voices, represents a destabilising threat to a traditional patriarchal hegemony, and, misled by management into believing that his pit has a future, he strives to return other miners to work. Isolated by the insurgent energies of the strike, he finds his authority domestically and socially neutered, with a consequent erosion of his mental stability.[11] Equally damaging, however, is Elliott Bowles's wholesale endorsement of neoliberal values. He regards material acquisition and status as the principal indices of human worth, but the deluded version of self they create in him lead only to the point of psychic breakdown. Both Gwyn Pritchard and Elliott Bowles exist in a transformed political universe where, in George Monbiot's scathing judgement, 'What counts is to win. The rest is collateral damage.'[12] Both figures become part of the collateral damage to which they subscribe. Whether retrospectively patriarchal in Gwyn Pritchard's case, or as an example of the delusional privileged self in Elliott Bowles's, the texts inscribe two narcissistic masculinities predicated on seamless displays of power, control and domination that the strike exposes as inherently precarious and pathologically inclined.

The impact of their childhood on their adult development is pronounced but is exhibited through different narrative techniques. In *Dark Edge*, the unrestrained licence accorded to Elliott's police activity during the strike further distorts a sense of a privileged self that was encouraged as a child by his mother. Any setback to his ego in his private life results in self-justification through intimidation of his wife: 'he sensed [Susan's] fear. He liked it' (*Dark Edge*, p. 159). His narcissism is validated by a figure he regards as his ego-ideal, the Prime Minister, who, like him, 'had no time for losers' (*Dark Edge*, p. 18). Gwyn's narcissism is textually more complex. Brutalised by his father, his inner turmoil is foregrounded so that, as Liz Jones notes, although he is 'destructive and cruel [...] ultimately he is tragic and pathetic'.[13] Like Elliott, he believes in rigid lines of gender demarcation – 'the deal was that Carol [his wife] kept things nice' (*Until Our Blood*, p. 14) – but he is activated by an obstinate sense of social mission, to save the pit, where his affirmation of infallible rightness degenerates into an obsessive-compulsive isolation as the strike deepens. Anthony Giddens writes: 'Under the impact of narcissism, intimate relations as well as broader connections with the social world tend to have inherently destructive aspects',[14] and this is true of Elliott and Gwyn, although their construction differs and benefits from separate treatment.

Dark Edge fashions Elliott Bowles as an authoritarian narcissist positioned in a political arena that exploits such a pathology, but which is itself infected by it. Richard John Evans in his review of *Dark Edge* regards Elliott's construction as artistically flawed and politically compromised because, by making him 'a psychotic thug, the text prevents any real exploration of the role of the police in the strike'.[15] But *Dark Edge* is not a dispassionate representation of government strategy during the strike. Rather, Elliott's narrative may more profitably be framed within the form of a *roman à thèse*, a genre which, Susan Rubin Suleiman says, is 'a novel written in the realistic mode (that is, based on an aesthetic of verisimilitude and representation) which signifies itself to the reader as primarily didactic in intent'.[16] It is, Suleiman continues, one in which 'the "correct" interpretation of the story is inscribed in capital letters, in such a way that there can be no mistaking it'.[17] Reading Elliott Bowles's construction in this way, therefore, requires an awareness of the correspondences between his individual actions and the text's larger, teleological design in constructing his narrative. In his case, it is the correlation between his brutality as a power-obsessed patriarch and the brutality of a government that licenses him, as a law officer, to knock striking miners on the head with impunity. Stripped of textual subtlety, markedly oppositional in its heavy patterning, and animated by hostility to a political philosophy that promises material success but delivers Elliott's mental instability and physical paralysis, Elliott's narrative follows a teleological arc where inevitably he becomes part of Monbiot's 'collateral damage'. In several respects, he stands as a representative figure in Rosi Braidotti's ironic 'Welcome to capitalism as schizophrenia',[18] where the promise of individual self-formation collides with the imperative to commit to commodified consumerism, with disastrous consequences.

Elliott is presented from the outset as an arrogant, psychologically damaged character with an alpha-male body, discovering a pleasing congruity between his own incipient pathology and an atavistic political orthodoxy. By concentrating on Elliott's public role as a policeman, Evans's review sidelines Elliott the patriarch, the husband and father. He not only 'pushes Susan around verbally and physically',[19] as Evans states. He punches her to unconsciousness, cracks her ribs and rapes her. With his 'broad, erect frame tapering to a fit waist and athletic legs' (*Dark Edge*, p. 5), good looks (*Dark Edge*, p. 137) and luxurious moustache, a signifier, as with *Cwmardy*'s Big Jim Roberts, connoting impressive virility, Elliott Bowles is a beneficiary of the physical clichés of iconic masculinity. But the text exposes his '*mucho hombre*'[20] physique as semiotically flattering. Instead of the rugged individualism suggested by such hypertrophy, Elliott is seduced by commodifying surfaces: the 'touch of gel' keeping his swept-back black hair in place (*Dark Edge*, p. 5) implies a consciously wrought objectification, confirmed by his habit of inspecting himself approvingly in mirrors. Through such figures, *Dark Edge* constructs Elliott Bowles as a child of his neoliberal time, obsessed with identity through status enhancement and appearance, and propelled by an insatiable desire to have it all, 'power, money and women' (*Dark Edge*, p. 87).

Elliott's identity is predicated on what Jonathan Rutherford sees as 'the two contradictory forces of the consumer market and the ethic of self realisation',[21] on which neoliberal capitalism itself is predicated. In a political milieu in which 'We are called upon to invent our own identities',[22] Elliott's recently acquired house on a new estate overlooking the valley is the initial step in his self-transformation. But *Dark Edge* pitilessly exposes Elliott's ambition as unthinking commodification, for his house is less an authentic home than a conventional cultural text on which he seeks to write 'his new identity' (*Dark Edge*, p. 7). Mass-produced objects like televisions and videos – he had been 'the first person on the estate to have a video' (*Dark Edge*, p. 7) – function primarily as semiotically charged acquisitions intended to announce a version of his successful 'arrival'. The fake horse brasses and flintlocks hanging over a fireplace without a fire are intended to evoke a stable, patriarchal continuity, but they further manifest his commodification into an *ersatz* lifestyle, while the small garden is itself a derivative 'miniature version of a country estate' (*Dark Edge*, p. 7). Lacking warmth, intimacy, idiosyncrasy or individuality, Elliott's house becomes an objective correlative of his own inauthentic alpha-masculinity. Having 'worked hard to imprint his personality on it' (*Dark Edge*, p. 7), he has merely demonstrated his 'lifestyle' to be a commodification of the self as consumer that is required by the market economy.

In a different context, *Dark Edge* might have cast Elliott as a more sympathetically rendered victim of a deviously exploitative political dogma. However, he is an enthusiastic participant in its promotion, not least in the opportunities it offers for self-gratification through physical brutality. Thankful that 'Thatcher had shown him the way forward [that] opportunities were there to be grasped, if one had the bottle' (*Dark Edge*, p. 18), he becomes a restless series of self-approving signifiers detached from personal or social commitment, where his identity becomes an example of what Judith Butler calls 'an enacted fantasy'.[23]

Locking him into his narcissism, with his 'amazingly inflated idea of his powers' (*Dark Edge*, p. 46), the novel constructs him as a paradigm of the de-centred subject. It is a central feature of the novel that Elliott's 'omnipotent fantasies of the privileged self',[24] are fostered by his role during the strike, where, as an arm of the state, he is 'showered [...] with money' (*Dark Edge*, p. 18). But *Dark Edge* suggests that in the politically endorsed paradigm of winners and losers of which he uncritically approves, Elliott has rather less 'bottle' than he self-deludingly believes. When presented as confronting poorly protected pickets as a member of an aggressive police force, he favours 'the massed actions of strike breaking' where there is safety in superior numbers, over 'one-to-one confrontations' (*Dark Edge*, p. 80), which he strives to avoid. Craving continual affirmation, he narcissistically internalises every corporate success as his own 'personal victory' (*Dark Edge*, p. 12). And lacking the critical inward gaze to a pathological degree, he fails to examine what this signifies, with catastrophic effects on his self-validation.

'The narcissist,' writes Christopher Lasch, 'feels consumed by his own appetites',[25] and *Dark Edge* inscribes Elliott's sense of narcissistic entitlement, and his more limited capacity to satisfy his appetite, through an episode where his swaggering machismo is easily pierced and deflated. Significantly, the incident does not occur on the picket lines, where he can deflect blame onto others, but in a confrontation he seeks with his former lover, Lisa. Outraged by her note daring to end their affair, he is met by Lisa and her new, potentially aggressive partner, Ken. When he is faced one-to-one by 'a powerful, streetwise opponent' (*Dark Edge*, p. 79), Elliott's preening self-belief collapses and his sense of coercive entitlement dissipates. Mocked by Ken, who picks up a gin bottle, thereby showing he clearly has more 'bottle' than Elliott in both senses of the term, and dismissed by Lisa with the advice to 'Get real' (*Dark Edge*, p. 81), he is stripped of his pretensions and humiliated as a 'loser'. Having predicated his identity on abandoning his wife and children, and seamlessly colonising the future with Lisa, Elliott experiences a traumatic affront to his peacock vanity: 'No cow did this to him' (*Dark Edge*, p. 48). Through his response to this setback, *Dark Edge* illustrates his inability to engage in self-assessment. Instead, he externalises the problem and projects himself as victim rather than agent: 'His brother's punch had started off his run of bad luck, since then Lisa had fucked him up and his wife had gone through some weird character change' (*Dark Edge*, p. 115). From this point, his narrative trajectory becomes less one of effortless upward mobility than one of self-justifying recuperation through power of his former patriarchal self.

Dark Edge constructs his humiliation as transformative if not self-illuminating. 'Hegemony', writes Homi K. Bhabha, 'requires iteration and alterity to be effective',[26] and incapable as he is of 'getting real', Elliott becomes a study of pathological rehabilitation through his manic coercion of others, most particularly his wife Susan but also his half-brother Edwin, and all striking miners. As Edwin and the more militant strikers pose a genuine physical challenge to him, Elliott's increasingly threatening behaviour towards a vulnerable Susan is a Freudian displacement of his failure to respond to Lisa's rejection and Ken's aggression. Because he has 'always ruled the roost with her' (*Dark Edge*, p. 115), Susan, as a woman and therefore someone he considers inferior to himself, conveniently embodies every negative against which he can reconstruct his unquestioned gender superiority. The novel illustrates how, in his deluded thinking, the expression of power through violence becomes a constituent of patriarchal rationale, and so when he punches Susan and breaks her rib he justifies his action by telling himself it 'had been necessary' in order to 'get [his] point across' (*Dark Edge*, p. 128). By having Elliott formulate his brutal response towards Susan as a justifiable strategy rather than a brutal impulse, *Dark Edge* connects domestic pathological behaviour to its critique of physical coercion as a legitimate political strategy against the striking miners.

A little later the pattern of violence as permissible repeats itself through two juxtaposed though connected episodes, one committed by an increasingly deranged Elliott in the public arena, the other at his home (*Dark Edge*, pp. 159–61). In the first episode, Elliott is among last-minute reinforcements called on to confront local miners. He does so with clinical efficiency. As he wades into miners from his own village, he is gratified that they 'knew who was knocking them senseless. It was a good way of breaking a few ribs.' The experience is perversely self-affirming and therapeutic, for despite the 'pounding in his head' Elliott becomes convinced that further violence will ease it. This episode merges seamlessly into the second, when he returns home exhilarated and empowered. Enjoying Susan's sense of fear as he pushes past her, he demands food, has a shower and examines his naked body. Christopher E. Forth writes that, 'Muscles have become male fashion accessories in the cult of appearances',[27] and *Dark Edge* once more identifies key features of Elliott's narcissism exhibited through a self-approving somatic scrutiny. Inspecting himself in the full-length mirror, he promises to 'tone up his muscles', but nonetheless 'flexed them and smiled at himself' (*Dark Edge*, p. 159). His vanity restored by his violent punishment of the miners, he seeks to complete his self-validation at home. Through his warning to Susan that 'All that action [has] made me feel randy', the novel explicitly connects patriarchal and political brutality, as he savagely rapes her and gouges her face in a sadistic display of power, correlative to his authorised savagery as an officer of the law.

The novel's lack of subtlety in representing Elliott has led critics like Catherine Merriman to complain that 'Granelli wears his political sympathies far too blatantly on his sleeve', that Elliott is virtually 'flatten[ed] [...] almost permanently to the page'.[28] And it is true that *Dark Edge* is not a text of Jamesian thematic density or forbiddingly polished style, but while this novel's 'flatness' of verbal texture might offend a Forsterian aesthetic, to dismiss Elliott as 'unbelievable'[29] is to situate him in the tradition of classic realism. As Susan Rubin Suleiman comments:

> The realist novel proclaims above all the vocation of rendering the complexity and the density of everyday life; the *roman à thèse*, on the other hand, finds itself before the necessity of simplifying and schematising its representations for the sake of its demonstrative ends.[30]

Reading Elliott's narrative as a *roman à thèse* acknowledges the fictional parameters within which he is constructed, so that there is no room for ambiguity or subtlety. He serves a strand of the novel's ideology, whose teleological purpose is to present a dangerously narcissistic form of masculinity nurtured by and inseparable from the morally defective pragmatics of neoliberalism, a creed that has 'the doubly disastrous effect of reasserting liberal individualism as the unquestionable standard for subject formation while reducing it to consumerism'.[31] When he breaks his back from a fall onto a railway track during a vicious fight with his half-brother, and is rendered tetraplegic, an early death is expected. In the closing paragraphs of Elliott's narrative, the novel makes no connection between his condition and the political ideology he espouses. Perhaps it feels no need. Elliott identified with Mrs Thatcher because 'Like him, she had no time for losers' (*Dark Edge*, p.18). Where there are winners there are also losers, and by a final irony Elliott himself becomes part of neoliberalism's 'collateral damage'.[32]

The social realism of *Until Our Blood is Dry* allows for a more subtle presentation of psychic complexity in Gwyn Pritchard's masculinity than is necessary in *Dark Edge*'s cautionary tale of Elliott Bowles. When asked her reasons for choosing the novel's form, Kit Habianic replied: 'I made no conscious choices. It was all about writing a story that sank into me and wouldn't let go.'[33] Conscious choice or not, *Until Our Blood is Dry* locates itself through its title within a continuum of industrial unrest and political activity in the Valleys,[34] and also skilfully adapts an earlier form of Valleys' fiction described by Raymond Williams as 'the story of a family', or in this case two families at loggerheads with each other.[35] But unlike Elliott Bowles, Gwyn Pritchard is not constructed as an unambiguous antagonist to the other characters. As Liz Jones astutely notes, he is a figure 'trapped in a latter-day Greek tragedy of misplaced loyalties and feuds'.[36] Jones might also have added that he is trapped most destructively within the pathology of his own psyche. Her reference to Greek tragedy is apposite, however, for Gwyn Pritchard embodies in less mythical form emphatic features of destructive, narcissistic compulsion located within a sphere of abnormal familial and civil strife beyond his control, where he is 'helpless to stop loneliness closing in over him' (*Until Our Blood*, p. 250). The novel interrogates through Gwyn the correspondences between his frustrated male agency in the public sphere and his coercive patriarchy at home. But it also problematises his narcissism, for while it propels him to anger, cruelty and self-disgust, the narrative's use of free indirect discourse in his representation draws the reader into his consciousness and reveals a perverse heroism, an insistent attempt to live by his own deluded self-belief, to save the pit and ensure the continuation of the status quo. By regarding the strike as another, though serious, industrial dispute, he entirely misreads the government's ideological motives. By constructing him as a victim of managerial/political expediency and a victim of his own ego, the text interweaves the political with the personal, the communal with the individual, and the strike with the family.

Until Our Blood is Dry connects Gwyn's narcissism to his childhood, though the circumstances generating it are different from Elliott Bowles's. Elliott's indulged childhood left him prey to an inflated sense of his own entitlement. Gwyn's narcissism springs from a pledge that after being beaten by a drunken father, 'no-one would make him powerless again' (*Until Our Blood*, p. 196). The novel examines how this resolution is internalised into a potentially clinical need to dominate others. 'The libido that has been withdrawn from the external world has been directed to the ego', writes Freud, 'and thus gives rise to an attitude which may be called narcissism.'[37] Gwyn myopically positions himself as the reference point on which exterior phenomena converge, a point where egoism melds with possessiveness. Structurally, the text presents his failure to negotiate his self-definition by critiquing two typologies of his patriarchal mindset: Gwyn as domestic patriarch, and Gwyn as colliery overman demanding compliance from 'his men' (*Until Our Blood*, p. 4). Both position him in a dominant role, a role to which he feels entitled by gender, custom and experience. As Anthony Giddens notes, 'Narcissism relates outside events to the needs and desires of the self, asking only "what this means to me".'[38] For Gwyn, miners are 'his lads'; the pit is 'his pit'; and when the men vote to strike, they do so for no other reason than 'to spite me' (*Until Our Blood*, p. 55). Like Connell's representative authoritarian male, when he is at home Gwyn is unable to empathise with his wife and daughter.[39] For him, keeping them both at an emotional remove is a demonstration of his inviolate, hegemonic self. He thus denies them individuality, consigning them instead to gender categories by addressing them through antonomasia, so that his wife Carol is merely 'woman' and his daughter Helen is invariably 'that girl'.

Stephen Whitehead observes that 'what appears to be a subordinated masculinity in one site always has the potential to be a hegemonic masculinity in another',[40] and *Until Our Blood is Dry* examines in Gwyn Pritchard the psychic collision of his subaltern position, as a factotum used by Adam Smith-Tudor to help break the strike, and his empowered authoritarianism as colliery overman and domestic patriarch. These conflicting roles at a time of momentous social and political upheaval enable the text to critique traditional patriarchy and expose as a fiction male autonomy within a capitalist patriarchal structure. Under such a polity, Anthony Giddens argues, 'the individual experiences feelings of powerlessness in relation to a diverse and large-scale social universe.'[41] In Gwyn's case, by becoming a strike-breaker, he cedes control to dominant senior management in the form of Adam Smith-Tudor, who regards him as no more than a dispensable functionary in a ruthless contest for power. Short-term submission to Smith-Tudor, Gwyn feels, offers the prospect of long-term security for the pit, and a small but craved status enhancement of a desk job: 'as dreams went that wasn't much to ask' (*Until Our Blood*, p. 23). The narrative reveals the ruinous psychic energy released by this *quid pro quo* most dramatically in the dissolution of his family.

Representing a model of patriarchy on the brink of obsolescence, overwhelmed by generational and cultural changes, Gwyn adheres to a strict paradigm of gender binaries in which expressions of affection are regarded as feminine. Emotional intimacy is out of the question. His instrumental patriarchy is posited on the assumption that Carol should be the grateful beneficiary of his largesse, but should never forget that she is a subordinate possession: '*This* is my house, *that* is my money, *you* are my wife' (*Until Our Blood*, p. 242, original italics). When she violates the conditions of her status by neglecting housework, she 'needed telling again' (*Until Our Blood*, p. 14), and when she dares to intervene with questions about his life at work he is contemptuous: 'She was clueless, his wife' (*Until Our Blood*, p. 23). Initially, he exhibits only oral contempt for her. That has been the paradigm of their marriage until the strike exposes the fragility of his apparent ego equilibrium. When this happens, 'human powers are experienced as forces emanating from an objectified social environment',[42] and Gwyn constructs himself as the lone representative of order, propriety and sanity in an otherwise dysfunctional world.

Although the novel discloses how he attempts to combat his increasing impotence by retreating further into a sequestered self-righteousness, it refuses to demonise him. Instead, it clinically exposes how the challenges to his gender-legitimised authority provoke an unremitting stubbornness he defines as principle. His view that 'the country's females' are getting 'too assertive by half' (*Until Our Blood*, p. 160) is similar to Elliott Bowles's, and like Elliott, Gwyn's cruelty is an exercise in displaced frustration. His daughter Helen realises, even as he beats her, that this 'wasn't about her, not really, but about everything else that had riled her dad these last few months' (*Until Our Blood*, p. 106). Instead, like Elliott, too, he persistently exonerates himself from responsibility for his actions by displacing the blame onto others. This feature extends across a spectrum from the relatively trivial to the unjustifiable as his pathology becomes more pronounced. When he forgets Carol's birthday, it is her fault for not reminding him (*Until Our Blood*, p. 195). More disturbingly, in a furious quarrel with her, when 'Rage crashed through him in waves', and he is powerless to stop himself hitting 'her again and again', it was 'Her fault for pushing him to the limit' (*Until Our Blood*, p. 243).

In his review of *Until Our Blood is Dry*, Dylan Moore argues that he finds it difficult to care for Gwyn.[43] But surely the novel does not invite such an unambiguous response to him. Despite his narcissism, emotional distance from his wife and child, and susceptibility to violence he is not constructed as a crude exemplar of brutal masculinity. Instead, he is presented as a site of competing psychological tensions, a magnified form of what Peter Middleton calls 'discrete islands of subjectivity',[44] and particularly so after he is diagnosed as suffering from progressive massive fibrosis – black lung. His terminal illness precipitates his need to be reconciled to Helen, yet the narrative discloses the unbridgeable gulf between his conflicting selves: 'A man had his pride. It fell to the girl to meet him half way' (*Until Our Blood*, p. 236). Male narcissism and paternal love are here separated in the subjectivity of Middleton's discrete islands and render Gwyn tragically impotent. Intractably self-righteousness, remote from his wife and child, and product and victim himself of a warped patriarchy, he is killed by Dai Dumbells who heaves a headstone from a cemetery onto a minibus in which he is travelling to continue his work as a strike-breaker. Gwyn Pritchard is resolute to the point of mania in believing that he is an inviolate agent. The workings of his psychological necessity are shaped by a childhood over which he had no control, and determine his future as he comes into conflict with his community, which is itself in conflict with a macroeconomic system intent on destroying it. As the principal markers of his repressive masculinity, his authority and status, are progressively stripped away, his narcissistic self-righteousness remains his abiding identifying principle and eventually undoes him. While the novel exposes the destructive potency of his ego, it also seeks to understand his pathology and to locate it within cultural and political determinants beyond his control. He is no tragic hero of the kind that has a flawed grandeur reaching a moment of self-illumination. But from a gender-focused reading he emerges as both a tragic victim of circumstances beyond his control, and a product of a patriarchal model that accords men pre-eminence while denying them integration of self and the means of critical self-evaluation.

Gwyn Pritchard and Elliott Bowles are both products of dysfunctional patriarchies and themselves replicate that dysfunction in their own families. Their limited empathy for others is revealed as a pathology expressing itself through aggression which, as Lacan notes, is 'the correlative tendency of a mode of identification that we call narcissistic'.[45] Their recourse to domestic violence expresses their contempt for women when their axiomatic status as men is challenged by them. Within *Dark Edge*'s schema of the *roman à thèse*, Elliott's crippling injuries from the fight he provokes with Edwin, and his anticipated early death signify the neurotic impulse behind the fabled emancipation of self that is promised by neoliberalism. In Gramscian terms, Elliott has served a hegemonic body that 'not only formulates directives which will become the norm of conduct for the others, but at the same time creates the instruments by means of which the directives themselves will be "imposed"'.[46] He is just such an 'instrument'. Gwyn's death has a different significance, though he too may be seen as an 'instrument' utilised by a hegemonic body. In his review of the novel, Dylan Moore argues that *Until Our Blood is Dry* is 'light on metaphorical and symbolic significance',[47] but Gwyn's death surely resonates with suggestive power. With the strike lost and the pit, like him, under terminal threat, it inscribes the passing narrative of a Welsh masculinity based on the cultural assumptions of conservative patriarchy. And it inscribes through Gwyn Pritchard how industrial patriarchy in the Valleys, with its asymmetrical gendering, produced a form of masculinity requiring constant replication through performance that denied the individual integration of self.

Structurally, each novel counterbalances its representation of a pathological masculinity by the presence in *Dark Edge* of a self-aware but frustrated miner in Edwin Bowles, and by the stabilising presence of Iwan Jones in *Until Our Blood is Dry*. Their divergent narrative biographies require separate analysis and will be discussed later, but one striking feature of their gender definition connects them not only with each other, but with a recurring constituent in earlier Valleys' novels: the figure of the cerebral, literate, unionised miner. Reading confers competences of insight, judgement and evaluation as union officials on both figures, but importantly it also operates as a metonym for a more self-disciplined form of gender coding. Rather like Menna Gallie's D. J. Williams, Edwin is a self-effacing 'reader' (*Dark Edge*, p. 35), and the 'bookish' Iwan (*Until Our Blood*, p. 9) copes with his wife Angela's tempestuous outbursts without regarding them as assaults on his masculinity. From the outset, he displays a stable self-definition, fearing that the strike is doomed, but bound by loyalty to his kind. Edwin's identity is more problematised. The strike breaks a routine into which he had fallen, making him dissatisfied with himself but unfitted to envision a compelling future. Until the arrival of Kathryn Peters, a London academic engaged in studying women's roles in the strike, he hovers between loyalty to what he considers an unsustainable future, and an incapacity to translate his intellectual frustration into purposeful agency.

Whereas Gwyn Pritchard and Elliott Bowles's narcissism locks them into immovable pathologies exacerbated by the strike, and Iwan Jones's textual function is to embody an equipoise already achieved, Edwin is the only male in either text to offer the promise of emergent personal development in response to fundamental socio-historical change. *Dark Edge* transcribes his particular progression through a subdivision of the *Bildungsroman* genre, one that Mikhail Bakhtin considers 'the most significant' of them all. Such a genre, Bakhtin argues, illustrates how 'man's individual emergence is inseparably linked to historical emergence'; that is, the world in which the protagonist emerges into selfhood is not 'the immobile background of the world, ready-made and basically quite stable'.[48] Instead, the *Bildungsroman* hero is no longer within an epoch, but at a transition point where 'it is as though the very *foundations* of the world are changing'[49] (original italics). *Dark Edge* positions Edwin precisely at a stage of Welsh history where the epoch of postwar welfare capitalism recedes before the onset of neoliberal individualism. Within a Bakhtinian paradigm, his response to this radical change determines his identity as a *Bildungsroman* protagonist. The text thus addresses through him how recurring motifs of patriarchy in Valleys' fiction, impinging on hybrid identity and nationhood, communal versus individual value systems, and industrial versus natural landscape, are contextualised and challenged.

Shy like Len Roberts in *Cwmardy* and withdrawn like D. J. Williams in *Strike for a Kingdom*, Edwin exists initially in a liminal space between dutiful community engagement and bookish withdrawal. In a mining culture where normative masculinity is equated with agency in the public arena, Edwin initially seeks a ready-made identity in the exclusively male NUM, whose collectivist values he internalises 'like a catechism and believed them' (*Dark Edge*, p. 20). Channelled thus into a life of pre-ordained, hegemonically gendered activities and outcomes, he finds himself constrained by the very collectivism that gave him an identity. Doubting the strike's success but committed to the struggle as a union official, he 'assumed his delegate role' (*Dark Edge*, p. 20) by articulating reassuring mantras he no longer believes in but is emotionally reluctant to abandon. Prior to Kathryn Peters's arrival from London, *Dark Edge* manoeuvres Edwin through a series of episodes demonstrating his existential stasis. Most significantly, he commits himself to action on behalf of his fated union where the oppressive continuities of performative masculinity expected of union activists at first mobilise and then confine him. Tactically astute, he has the idea of occupying cranes at Port Talbot to prevent imported coal being unloaded and distributed, but in taking action he is hampered by his acrophobia and his fear that 'all external weaknesses were pounced on by miners' (*Dark Edge*, p. 83). *Dark Edge* emphasises here the constraining nature of performative masculinity which requires a seamless exhibition of self-control and self-expression. Submitting to his acrophobia, Edwin is violently sick, much to the satisfaction of Ronnie Jenkins, a manifestation of posturing masculinity who regards Edwin's cerebral and strategic approach to industrial conflict as weakness. But the text also inscribes a subtler representation of Edwin's difference from his fellows. When the sympathetic Tom Davies comments that the autumn weather is striking chill on top of the cranes, Edwin responds by quoting from Keats's 'To Autumn': 'Season of mists and mellow fruitfulness' (*Dark Edge*, p. 86). As with D. J. Williams, poetry offers him a fleeting escape from contingent reality and an engagement with a continuum of human experience in which that reality is contextualised. Anxious to avoid embarrassment to a puzzled Tom and also to himself, however, Edwin passes off his remark as a simple wish that he had access to some fruit.

Dark Edge redirects Edwin's demonstrable failure as a potent strike leader by calibrating his possible emergence into a more progressive form of masculinity, and fashions this *Bildung* within the space of two significant walks he takes on the hills above his village. Within the text's strategic organisation, the walks serve key formal and *chronotopic* functions in Edwin's self-expansion.[50] The first (*Dark Edge*, pp. 104–5), which is, significantly, taken the day before Kathryn Peters arrives, formally prefigures his final walk on the hills (*Dark Edge*, pp. 184–6) after her departure, when he decides to learn Welsh, to travel to London to study and, perhaps, advance his tentative hope of a closer friendship with her. Striding along 'the spine of the ridge' (*Dark Edge*, p. 104) and later 'stepping over the backbone of his land' (*Dark Edge*, p. 185), Edwin reconnects with his sense of nationhood. On the hills, he experiences time as visible in space, and space as a repository of time and cultural history. As Kirsti Bohata notes, Welsh culture invests 'familiar landscape with enormous emotional and, often, political importance',[51] and in Edwin's development from existential stasis to a promise of evolution which yet honours the past, the hills act as *chronotopes* of a Welsh history and identity, immune to, and chronologically more spacious than, the temporalities of the strike and the politics behind it.

By the close of the narrative, the hills have acquired resonances for him significantly beyond the 'affinity' (*Dark Edge*, p. 105) he felt earlier. Homi K. Bhabha reminds us that remembering 'is a painful re-membering, a putting together of the dismembered past to make sense of the trauma of the present'.[52] Edwin's dis-membered past incorporates the trauma of a 'war which had encompassed his family, politics and creed of living' (*Dark Edge*, p. 185). On the hills Edwin is able to remember his past and contextualise his present, to 're-member' the constituent features of his subjectivity and construct a possible future. The text expresses his *chronotopic* engagement with Wales, quickened by the Englishwoman Kathryn, as a quasi-religious communion with 'his land': 'All its tortured history lay under his feet. He wanted to take the solitude of the hillside into his hands, crumple it into a ball and eat it. Such was his addiction and sense of oneness with the spirit of the place' (*Dark Edge*, p. 185).[53] And 'the place' is 'Wales, not just "the valley"' (*Dark Edge*, p. 185). Investing landscape with a numinous quality, *Dark Edge* addresses in Edwin an emergent form of Welsh identity. It will acknowledge its hybridity by recommunion with Wales's enduring history symbolised by the hills, but it will be characterised unapologetically by confident national affiliation (Edwin intends to learn Welsh), not provincial nostalgia (he will travel to study in London). In *Times Like These* (1936), the strong-minded Mary Biesty is anxious to slough off her Welshness when she moves to London, and her former boss Broddam notes approvingly when he meets her that 'her accent was already *better*' (*Times Like These*, p. 254, my italics). By contrast, in what Homi K. Bhabha calls 'the importance of the hybrid moment',[54] Edwin Bowles will attempt to 'broaden his horizons without denying his roots' (*Dark Edge*, p. 186).

Form and narration coalesce here. Bakhtin writes that in the *Bildungsroman* the emerging man 'enters into a completely new, *spatial* sphere of historical existence'[55] (original italics). In projecting a post-industrial Welsh identity through Edwin, *Dark Edge* constructs a narrative where spatial borders both metaphorical and literal, personal and social are crossed and recrossed. Whereas James A. Davies feels that Edwin's intention merely 'gestures at Welsh and Welshness',[56] Jane Aaron and M. Wynn Thomas see him as 'Energised by this nationalistic conscious-raising'.[57] Given the *Bildungsroman*'s focus on individual development, *Dark Edge* cannot offer a general prescription for a new form of Valleys' social organisation. Its aim is more limited. And in any case, after the trauma the Valleys have suffered, any prescription at this stage is inevitably an inchoate blend of hope, anticipation and anxiety. However, as with Keith in Christopher Meredith's *Shifts* (1988), space/ place, history, nationality and language combine in Edwin as markers combining a past with a future. Significantly, *Dark Edge* does not echo Luke Biesty's despairing nihilism that 'Everything do seem so useless, somehow', which closes *Times Like These* (p. 319), and on which James A. Davies believes there has been no advance in subsequent anglophone Welsh mining novels.[58] Implicit in *Dark Edge*'s construction of Edwin is the possibility of a reconfigured model of Valleys' masculinity. His 'hybrid moment' on the hills conceives an empowered identity at once indisputably Welsh and transcultural, a dynamic of emergence that is in 'a continual process of border crossing [that] allows for a recognition of multiple points of identification'.[59] *Strike for a Kingdom* (1959), like *Dark Edge*, concludes with a bachelor miner poised at a moment of creation. But whereas for D. J. Williams, the text trails his poem away into ambiguous stasis, Edwin Bowles's regeneration, realised symbolically on the hills, energises him as he strides towards a horizon open to possibilities, 'Looking forward to Christmas' (*Dark Edge*, p. 186).

Until Our Blood is Dry constructs a different trajectory for Iwan Jones. His unwavering involvement as a committed strike activist consolidates his masculine credentials, but it is through his representation as a stable husband and father that the text encodes a manifest development in Valleys' mining fiction. Stephen Whitehead has commented that in late modern society, 'men can and do experience family life in ways that are far removed from [...] those experienced by their fathers and grandfathers'[60], and Iwan Jones's construction is an engagement by a female narrative voice with contemporary cultural discourses impinging on the representation of 'masculine' men. Because this engagement is woven into the text's discursive fabric rather than being foregrounded through any self-conscious stance on Iwan's part, its Machereyan 'silence' has the effect of naturalising Iwan's representation rather than flagging it as a polemical declaration.[61]

Marriage in the novels examined so far, whether Luke Biesty's placid adoration of Olive in *Times Like These* or the dysfunctional patriarchy in marriages present in *Strike for a Kingdom*, has assumed dualistic gendered role definition. In late modernity, Anthony Giddens declares, marriage, 'unlike its traditional predecessor, depends on enduring voluntary commitment' because, 'The social environment in which marital relationships are formed and sustained has become disturbing and unsettling'.[62] Iwan and Angela's marriage is positioned within such a social environment. *Until Our Blood is Dry* does not dissolve their gender differences but repositions them within the dynamics of a complex relationship where traditional boundaries are crossed, and antagonisms are contained within a tacit, if sometimes exasperated, mutual commitment. To facilitate this representation, the novel incorporates into Iwan attributes associated with the 'new man' which became a feature of the cultural discourse of the 1980s when the novel is set. Rosalind Gill sees the 'new man' as a figure who is 'generally characterised as sensitive, emotionally aware, respectful of women, and egalitarian in its outlook'.[63] However, Gill suggests that the emergence of the 'new man' in the 1980s was as much a result of 'discourses or cultural repertoires' as of fundamental changes in masculinity.[64] But *Until Our Blood is Dry* does not construct Iwan as a self-consciously aware representative of such a phenomenon, and demonstrably avoids the narcissism that Gill associates with some definitions of 'the new man'.[65] Gill's brief taxonomy, however, offers insights useful for an analysis of Iwan's domestic relationships where he occupies a different fictional space from the paranoid, emotionally suppressed patriarchy of Gwyn Pritchard.

Whereas Gwyn Pritchard subsists on takeaway meals when his wife leaves him, Iwan prepares a family meal and discusses the simple ingredients enthusiastically with his astonished daughter-in-law Helen, Gwyn's daughter (*Until Our Blood*, p. 168). And in contrast to Gwyn's contempt for women, Iwan works alongside the women's support group gathering garden produce (*Until Our Blood*, pp. 176–7). Most significantly, whereas Carol Pritchard vainly attempts to accommodate to Gwyn's temper, in Iwan's marriage to the volatile Welsh-Italian Angela it is he who accommodates to hers. Yet he is not constructed as a *tabula rasa* on which Angela imprints her formidable identity. Instead, *Until Our Blood is Dry* incorporates his domestic activities as a feature of his secure masculinity, through which it challenges the 'universalising framework' of traditional binary constructions.[66] The novel facilitates this examination of a committed but sometimes argumentative relationship by constructing Angela as both an entrepreneurial café owner, and a wife and mother dedicated to her family. A skilled businesswoman, she is a shrewd negotiator, supplementing the family's limited income by supplying home-made pasta to a Cardiff restaurant owner, securing a deal where 'she'd undercut his regular supplier' (*Until Our*

Blood, p. 267). The text therefore provides Angela with an extra-domestic view of reality, where financial pragmatics govern her decisions. As such, she has a status, a rationale and a voice to which Iwan must respond, and it is through the nature of his response that the text examines his masculinity.

Although their marriage broadly subscribes to the theoretical parameters of traditional gender difference, the text subverts them within the practicalities of a singular but deeply committed relationship. As Giddens states, 'Intimacy has its own reflexivity and its own forms of internally referential order.'[67] The internally referential order in *Until Our Blood is Dry* centres on the conflict between Iwan's 'male' allegiance to abstract political principle embodied by the strike – he had 'never crossed a picket line in [his] life' (*Until Our Blood* p. 41) – and Angela's 'female' emphasis on the practicalities of domestic survival: 'Is gonna ruin the family, the strike' (*Until Our Blood*, p. 109). Angela's protestations lead to furious disagreement and arguments, but Iwan never questions her right to protest, still less threatens violence. The text implies a relationship where he and Angela exchange roles, however disputatious, as *primus inter pares*. Angela sometimes dominates, as when she calls 'a family summit' to announce her unilateral decision to close the café because the strike has rendered it uneconomic (*Until Our Blood*, pp. 208–9). Iwan's protestations that they wait until spring are brushed aside: 'Short of a fucking miracle, Iwan Simon Peter Jones, is what will be different, come the spring?' Later, when Iwan refuses the management bribe to go back early to work in return for a bonus (*Until Our Blood*, p. 213), the positions are reversed. Her impatient outburst causes his eyes to harden: 'Angela had pushed him too far now' (*Until Our Blood*, p. 211), and it is he who brooks no challenge.

When provoked by women, figures like Gwyn Pritchard and Elliott Bowles are quickly pushed too far, in what Lynne Segal describes as 'their attempt to shore up a sense of masculine identity'. Significantly, she continues, 'Others, however, may not.'[68] In the furious argument between Angela and Iwan that follows his refusal to accept the bribe, *Until Our Blood is Dry* takes Segal's view a stage further to a significant reversal of traditional gender roles, when a frustrated Angela hits Iwan. Simon hears 'the sound of flesh striking flesh' and knows enough to explain to Helen, 'It's not dad did the hitting' (*Until Our Blood*, p. 213). By closing the chapter on this striking remark, without a laboured explanation of why Simon immediately knows who is hitting whom, the novel neatly closes the episode. But when Helen later glimpses

Iwan and Angela, they are wrapped lovingly in each other's arms (*Until Our Blood*, p. 287). Demonstrations of tender physical affection between men and women are rare in the Valleys' novels so far examined, and so the significance of Helen's fleeting glance is crucial in framing Iwan's and Angela's relationship, and in confirming Iwan's assured form of masculinity. Anthony Clare writes that the demands of work remain 'impervious to demands for family-friendly policies that would enable the more personal and domestic aspects of being male to flourish'.[69] Iwan Jones emerges as a remarkable counter to this view. What Helen sees is that Angela's volatility is an aspect of her temperament that Iwan understands and accommodates within the context of a deep regard for her. If Angela is a new form of woman in her entrepreneurial independence, Iwan is a form of new man, for whom the exercise of crude patriarchal power has no place in a marriage. It is an example of his emotional intelligence that enables him to adopt the role of confidant and adviser to his son.

The close relationship between Iwan and Simon is constructed inferentially. Simon follows Iwan in his left-wing politics and in his engagement with serious reading: Iwan reads 'his tall, pink newspaper or some tome from the library' (*Until Our Blood*, p. 307), and Simon reads Camus's *The Plague* (*Until Our Blood*, p. 67).[70] But the novel extends their relationship beyond the shaping influence Iwan has had upon his son. Stephen Whitehead is of the view that:

> given the rigidly masculinist conditions of family life that have historically underpinned Western societies, one might conclude that many men are creating, through negotiation with children and partners, new and more positive ways of relating to families and fatherhood.[71]

Gwyn Pritchard and Elliott Bowles represent obvious fictional deviations from Whitehead's provisional model, but it is the characterisation of Oliver Biesty in *Times Like These* (1936) that provides a more revealing contrast to Iwan, for Oliver, too, is a caring, dutiful father to his son, Luke. However, their discursive relationship is based on predominantly factual and denotative exchanges. They speak of work, the strike, and employment prospects thereafter, but both maintain an emotional distance, and seldom look 'squarely into each other's eyes' (*Times*, p. 20). When a bereft Luke leaves the hospital after his wife Olive has died, a distraught Oliver is portrayed as a victim of his own emotional repression, and can only mutter an inadequate, 'All right! All right! Come on now, boyo' (*Times*, p. 307) by way of consolation. The chapter closes almost immediately, as though to save him further embarrassment. Peter Middleton observes that men hide their feelings for fear of others gaining power over them,[72] but the point here is that Oliver, bound as he is within the rigidly masculinist conditions of his culture, has no discourse of paternal intimacy available to him. *Until Our Blood is Dry* situates Iwan in a different social context where, as a paternal 'father' rather than a patriarchal 'father-figure', he is able to engage in a less formal bond with his son than Oliver can with Luke.

This generational and cultural shift is implied in moments of intimacy between Iwan and Simon ('Scrapper'). As the two prepare for Simon's marriage to Helen, for example, Iwan's closeness to Simon is the unstated motor activating the scene. Simon's complaint that he 'Can't be doing wi' this bloody tie, Dad' (*Until Our Blood*, p. 120), is a coded expression of anxiety reaching beyond the merely practical. Recognising that Simon's comment is less about the intricacies of knotting a tie than nerves about his forthcoming marriage to Helen, Iwan immediately offers support by identifying jokingly with his son: 'You and me both, lad […] A badge of slavery, the tie', where the constrictions of the tie encode the time-honoured male complaint that marriage is 'a badge of slavery'. But he proceeds to knot his son's tie for him, before modulating the tone. As with so much in the portrait of this relationship, narrative significance lies in discursive undertones. Unlike an Oliver Biesty, Iwan has no hesitation in making eye-contact. Fixing Simon with his 'ice-grey eyes', he asks:

> 'You sure you're ready for this, son?'
> Scrapper remembered Debbie's wet hair and slick brown skin and shook himself.
> 'Course.'
> Iwan gripped his shoulders. 'You get to do this once in your life, lad.'
> 'But Mam said' —.
> 'To hell with what your mam said. The girl's young. You both are.' (*Until Our Blood*, p. 120)

Iwan's opening question is no conventional platitude, nor does it represent hostility to marriage. It intimates a backstory of which he is fully aware, and which Simon's sensual memories of Debbie, a former lover, confirm for the reader. Iwan's response implies that he has immediately read the meaning of Simon's bodily reaction. Informal intimacy has progressed into paternal responsibility as he makes physical contact with his son. Facing him squarely, he issues what is at once a warning and implied support should Simon decide to go no further. Dismissing

Angela's insistence on marriage so brusquely is untypical of Iwan, but in promoting principle over financial expedience – Angela argues that 'If they marry the DHSS'll give Simon £9.20 a week' (*Until Our Blood*, p. 109) – it replicates his principled refusal of a bribe to return to work, while also offering Simon the emotional support of a father.

While Iwan Jones and Edwin Bowles share similar functions in their respective texts – to contrast with deviant forms of masculinity expressed through coercion – they also encode commonalities in their gender definition echoing earlier socio-fictive tropes. Cerebral rather than demonstratively physical, together they celebrate a Valleys' mining masculinity, embodied in characters like Len Roberts and D. J. Williams, that diverges from the 'macho' image outlined by Deirdre Beddoe.[73] But Edwin's cerebral individualism and Iwan's intellectual collectivism, qualities emphasised at the close of each text, construct two different futures as Valleys' mining becomes a historical not a living narrative. Edwin once believed that 'the affairs of his workmates could be enough' (*Dark Edge*, p. 185), but discovers they are not. Unmarried, he seeks a future both Welsh and cosmopolitan, where his masculinity is not defined solely against the accretions of a collectivist mining culture. Iwan, conversely, is positioned within such a marginalised cultural domain. Homi K. Bhabha asks: 'Is there a poetics of the "interstitial" community? How does it name itself, author its agency?'[74] It does so for Iwan through an act of private integrity and determined intent. When the strike fails, he authors his own agency by marching back to work 'with his butties, stoic in his donkey jacket and helmet' (*Until Our Blood*, p. 333). His integration of self within a *genuine* community is a political act of passive resistance to a cynical neoliberal paradigm, promoting 'the homogeneity of the *imagined* community of the nation'[75] (my italics). The text sets his stoicism against a bleak future, signified graphically by crows blackening the sky as they leave the valley and fly towards the sun. To an outward view his return to work might suggest submission, but his loyalty to a localised collectivist principle signifies a rejection of what Bhabha calls 'the grand globalising narrative of capital' as represented by an unprincipled figure like the Coal Board's Adam Smith-Tudor.[76]

The 1980s style of management has been characterised as 'masculine, abrasive and highly autocratic'.[77] *Until Our Blood is Dry* positions Iwan Jones's probity and collectivist identity against such forms of masculinity existing in a sphere of professional management activity, where power, politics, narcissistic vanity and ambition are the signifiers of their gendered definition. In the novel, they comprise principally Adam Smith-Tudor, 'the Coal Board's most senior man in South Wales' (p. 324), and the flatulent Labour MP Harry Cross, who confers to his own advantage with the pro-government journalist James Hackett, but has 'not spoken to the men in twelve months' (p. 331). The contrast between Smith-Tudor's ideologically purposeful masculinity and Cross's conflicted ineffectual posturing replicates at the level of individual representation the larger dynamic of powerful government versus compromised opposition in an industrial dispute which is the site of a radical socio-economic experiment. Sympathetic to this political *zeitgeist*, Smith-Tudor constructs a coherent if limited and narcissistic identity; Cross, as a representative of a moribund opposition, flounders in self-contradiction. Two bureaucrats from London, Henshall and Turnbull, who arrive armed with documents and 'dressed like undertakers in fine dark wool suits' (p. 278) to pronounce on the future of Blackthorn Colliery, further the text's exposure of the powerful and depersonalising forces facing the striking miners.

None of these is a principal character in the narrative, but they cumulatively project identities through a form of discourse consigning its practitioners, especially Smith-Tudor and Cross, to respective hegemonic or subordinate masculine definition. Norman Fairclough has pointed out that, as part of its political practice, neoliberal thinkers 'problematised and de-constructed the discourse of their political opponents and attempted to impose their own re-structuring'.[78] Through its portrayal of Cross and Smith-Tudor, *Until Our Blood is Dry* examines how such colonising of discourse 'naturalised' a politically freighted ideology as universal. To do so, it appropriates a form of discourse Ross Poole defines as 'instrumental rationality', which selects from a range of possible actions 'that action which on the best evidence available is most likely to achieve a given end'.[79] Significantly, with regard to *Until Our Blood is Dry*, instrumental rationality is concerned 'above all with efficiency', and is most clearly represented in the male-dominated 'marketplace, the labour process and capitalist accounting procedures'.[80] In *Until Our Blood is Dry,* it functions as a strategic practice of 'othering' the miners as incoherent zealots driven by prejudice.

The novel critiques each of these characters by confining him within his own self-advancing, professional space. Constructing them as functionaries does not reduce them to clumsily conceived caricatures, however. Instead, it further exposes the reductive impetus of an economic paradigm that sidelines the human complexity explored elsewhere in the narrative. Denied any subjective depth by the text, these characters are activated by a monolithic ideology where identity is formulated through a public display of dominance. And so, none of them is seen in other than a publicly constituted role where, in the pursuit of self-realisation, they practise what Ross Poole describes as 'separation from particular individuals, relationships and activities',[81] a form of narcissism. In a speech to government supporters, Smith-Tudor, intoxicated by his own rhetoric, 'seemed to gaze right through the assembled men' (p. 97); for James Hackett, the television journalist, the strike is merely an opportunity 'to make a name for himself' (p. 40). And Henshall and Turnbull, the Coal Board's money men, reveal the convoluted interpenetrations of prejudice, contempt, power and sadism of their hegemonic masculinities by applying such abstractions as Poole's 'capitalist accounting procedures' to the future of Blackthorn colliery (pp. 278–82). None of them is portrayed at leisure and, in a significant Machereyan silence, the text never mentions their families.

Poole contends that 'The internal constraint on instrumental action is the voice of morality',[82] but as these characters are discursively perceived as ambitious constructions, serving or responding to an amoral political discourse, none of them is given an ethical dimension. Instead, they function in spheres of expedient representation where ends justify means, and where, in Ross Poole's terms, they are 'concerned with profit maximisation'.[83] Christopher Lasch identifies the need in such figures, 'to promote and defend the system of corporate capitalism from which they – the managers and professionals who operate the system – derive most of the benefits'.[84] And so Smith-Tudor, for whom the discourse of power is the ultimate gender signifier, manipulates and betrays Gwyn Pritchard over the future of Blackthorn colliery, and then abandons him 'with a jaunty bounce to his gait' (p. 282).

But while Smith-Tudor exhibits the '"macho" management style' of the 1980s[85] – for example, he publicly humiliates Albright, Blackthorn's manager, by sarcastically addressing him as 'sonny' (p. 280) – he is far more than an abrasive, two-dimensional bully. While the text never inscribes a thumbnail sketch of his distinguishing features, the resonating effect of unmarked signifiers constructs him as a potent masculinity attuned to the callous *zeitgeist,* but not crudely defined by it. He shares his first two names, for example, with the eighteenth-century theorist of free-market economics, and his hyphenated and hybrid Anglo-Welsh surname implies a secure bourgeois lineage, as do his 'fruity baritone' (p. 65) and social élan. Sometimes autocratic, he is capable of projecting a softer form of power when occasion demands. In the company of 'key players' hostile to the strike, for example he: 'navigate[s] the room, a galleon in full sail. Approached each man in turn, addressed him by name. A smile, a lofty pat on the shoulder and off he sailed to his next target' (pp. 97–8). While the text makes no overt comparison between the two characters, the accountant Turnbull's showy 'platinum cufflinks [and] outsized platinum watch' (p. 278) act as metonyms of an easily identified neoliberal arriviste against the more spacious, and therefore more dangerous, range of discursive accomplishments it grants Smith-Tudor.

Prominent among these accomplishments is his ability to articulate a version of the strike where political ideology is transformed, through what Norman Fairclough calls the 'hidden power' of discourse,[86] into an incontrovertible representation of a totalised rationale. It occurs in a speech Smith-Tudor gives (pp. 96–7) that rewards close examination, not least because it communicates how his dominant masculinity and the government's hegemonic discourse function symbiotically, each reflecting favourably upon the other. The text's strategy in constructing his speech is to allow the assumptions, contradictions and partisan ideology implicit in his discourse to pass unmarked, in keeping with its practice elsewhere, so that assertion, prejudice and connotative attribution are successfully manicured into universalised ethical 'fact'.

Adopting a stance of instrumental rationality, where he represents what Raymond Williams describes as the 'apparently disinterested criteria' of management,[87] Smith-Tudor positions the government as the custodian of national stability and moral integrity confronting apocalyptic forces whose intent is to 'destroy the coal industry and sabotage Britain's manufacturing base' (p. 96). It is through such discourse that fear is generated, ideology is more widely disseminated as fact, and power more deeply entrenched. As if the miners' behaviour is not irresponsible enough by their striking, warns Smith-Tudor, they are also utterly devoid of civic responsibility, for they are recklessly 'causing violence and criminal damage [so that] we are hovering on the edge of anarchy'. Because 'These people will stop at nothing to get their way', they must be stopped, 'By whatever means' (p. 96) including, it would paradoxically appear, a more powerful but entirely acceptable form of violence.

Much of Smith-Tudor's hyperbole criticising the miners, the kind Frank Lentricchia calls 'rhetoricopolitical activity', is ironically equally applicable to the government on whose behalf he speaks.[88] While they 'will stop at nothing', neither will he. And his claim that the miners' leaders are 'dangerous agitators whose agenda has nothing to do with coal' (p. 96), when lifted from its context, could be attributed to a government for whom the strike is a tactic in its larger strategic agenda of radical social reformulation. But, as Smith-Tudor's speech demonstrates, by controlling context, 'discourse types actually appear to lose their ideological character' and become naturalised,[89] so that aggressive action coordinated by the dominant power through a well-armed police force is framed as an example of instrumental efficiency, whereas collective action by unionised labour is a riotous assembly.

It is the harmonious coexistence of self with a 'structure of understandings that successfully claims normative status' that facilitates Smith-Tudor's performative hegemony.[90] In his case, the dance and the dancer fuse into a seamless whole through which the text projects the unified power of state apparatus. Smith-Tudor thus becomes the text's discursive complement to the clinical dominance unleashed on the miners by a well-resourced police force. Alongside him, the local Labour MP Harry Cross emerges in a few brief episodes as a diminished masculinity, a simulacrum of Smith-Tudor's effortless performativity. Cross presents a paradox where his insatiable desire to construct himself as a charismatic figure conflicts with his lack of rhetorical or behavioural substantiality, and so he attracts only ridicule and opprobrium: he is 'old Double-Cross' (p. 331) to Smith-Tudor's 'Winston bloody Churchill' (p. 97). Rhetorically, his televised speech on the day the defeated miners return to work is an amalgam of casuistry and blather: it is 'a slap in the face for the Tory government [...] a triumph for common sense [...] a moral victory...' (p. 331), requiring the activist Helen Jones to restrain a friend from physically assaulting him. It is the closest the narrative comes to bitter satire.

The text ruthlessly deconstructs his pretensions to be regarded as a significant performer in the political arena. David Howell has criticised the policy of miners' representatives in the strike and the lexis through which the policy was transmitted: 'Hostages [were] given to prevailing sentiments about strikes, about pickets and police, about the proper scope for political agitation. Definitions [were] accepted which disadvantage[d] a socialist cause.'[91]

In his café tête-à-tête with the pro-government journalist James Hackett, the symbolic order into which the text incorporates Cross is virtually indistinguishable from Smith-Tudor's. He does not so much accept definitions damaging to the miners' cause as couch them in the sophistry of the ideological right. Attempting to demonstrate a finely tuned political *nous*, he approvingly, and wrongly, depicts Helen as a member of the struggling *petits bourgeois*: she is one of 'The little people. The small hardworking businesses that the unions threaten to destroy' (p. 154), casually abandoning the unionised miners he represents. Cross's fear of the consequences if Labour's 'hard left' (p. 154) triumphs in the strike compounds his political equivocation, for he is myopically unconcerned by the prospect of a triumphalist 'hard right' government if it does not. In a revealing moment later in the novel, Henshall, a London-based NCB bureaucrat, expresses delight that the 'union is buckling', and he uses the term 'loony left' (p. 282) as a universal nominator. The text makes no overt connection between the similarity of their views, but Cross's language confirms his supine acceptance of a dominant political discourse: what Bakhtin regards as 'language conceived as ideologically saturated, as a world view, even as a concrete opinion'.[92]

Wendy Holloway has argued that 'depending on their anxieties, defences and statuses men project parts of themselves on to others of different categories in order to present themselves as living up to a masculine ideal'.[93] Cross has strenuously appropriated distinguishing features like 'a snooty tilt to his large square head' (p. 153), a well-fed body and a context-specific, managerial double-breasted suit (p. 331),[94] to separate himself from his poorly clothed, ill-nourished constituents. However, with particular regard to male 'anxieties, defences and statuses', Holloway continues: 'The main recipient of these projections is "woman".'[95] To complete its demolition of Cross, the novel dismisses him as 'a right sleaze' (p. 153), with Helen, a young woman several years his junior, as the less than impressed recipient of his projected masculinity. At work in the café, when she asks what she can get him, his response is lubriciously suggestive: '"Hmm", his eyes travelled along her legs. "How about a coffee. To start with"' (p. 153). Later, mistaking prurience for charisma, he addresses her as 'sweetheart' and grabs her hand tightly between 'two damp palms' (p. 154).

In Cross's construction, the combination of sweaty nympholepsy, political charlatanism and personal vanity resists any alternative reading of his illegitimacy as a miners' representative. Whereas *Until Our Blood is Dry* portrays Smith-Tudor as heartless, it acknowledges the impressive range of discourses he brings to his manipulation of others. Ross Poole's view that instrumental rationality treats 'all desires as having a right to gratification' and is concerned 'above all with efficiency',[96] neatly illustrates the difference between the two characters. While Smith-Tudor has successfully mastered the various codes of discourse through which neoliberal ideology can efficiently be disseminated as rationally disinterested, the text portrays Cross as having barely learnt to read them, still less offer a rebuttal.

In their respective texts, the cerebral Iwan Jones and Edwin Bowles represent diversions rather than subversions of 'heroic' mining masculinity, for they both are unambiguously built on heterosexual models. By introducing a homosexual relationship between Matt Price, a miner, and Siggy, a hairdresser, *Until Our Blood is Dry* extends its gendered repertoire into an area previously unexplored so directly in Valleys' mining fiction. John Sam Jones in *Welsh Boys Too* (2000) had already examined the male gay scene in Wales, but his short fictions are located largely in non-industrial settings.[97] In an essay written before the publication of *Until Our Blood is Dry*, Jane Aaron and M. Wynn Thomas applaud such confident post-devolution literary representations as Jones's of a 'minority culture previously cocooned in […] heterosexual space', which has led to 'differences in sexual […] orientation […] being more openly acknowledged in a more heterogeneous Welsh culture'.[98] However, in *Until Our Blood is Dry,* set in a mining community in 1984–5, the implications behind such differences are not so much openly acknowledged as not even thought to exist there. Helen's response, for instance, when she stumbles upon Matt and Siggy *in flagrante*, is one of incredulity: 'Two men together? In Ystrad? Was that possible?' (p. 287). Siggy's and Matt's voices are therefore the voices of a marginality in a community already economically marginalised by the strike.

Ian M. Harris observes that 'Male behaviour is strongly influenced by gender role messages men receive from their social environments',[99] and the differing social environments of Matt and Siggy as miner and hairdresser are fundamental to their perceived gender construction. *Until Our Blood is Dry* inspects their representation through their differing occupations, particularly Matt Price's, and the larger assumptions regarding distinct and unequivocal gender binaries associated with those occupations. As Terry Threadgold argues, 'What is valued in patriarchy is not masculinity (gender) but male masculinity. The issue is not gender, but sexual difference.'[100] In the patriarchal Ystrad of the text, hairdressing and mining lie at two ends of a cultural spectrum of masculinity, in which hairdressing is a 'feminised' occupation stereotypically attractive to gay men, and mining is the epitome of a working-class 'male masculinity'. And so, when Gwyn Pritchard sees Matt leave Siggy's flat early one morning, he concludes immediately and correctly that Matt is gay because he associates with Siggy, who must be gay by virtue of his occupation (p. 75). To Gwyn's mind, there can be no other reason for their connection.

Male hairdressers, research suggests, are no more likely to be gay than men in many other occupations.[101] However, constructing Siggy as a gay hairdresser enables *Until Our Blood is Dry* to interrogate the relationships between gender and sexual orientation, and between occupation and gender stereotyping, and to expose normatively constructed gender formations as being, in Butler's terms, 'the illusion of symmetrical difference'.[102] In their study of the male hairdresser, Victoria Robinson, Alexandra Hall and Jenny Hockey note that in the predominantly female world of male hairdressers there is a '"hairdressing culture" [which] might have manifested itself in personal styles of dress and hair'.[103] Siggy, with his carefully styled hair and iconoclastic wardrobe, has acquired several signifiers identifying him as part of such a culture, and therefore as being feminised in Ystrad's closed system of gender thought. As Lynne Segal points out, however, 'gay sexuality offers further confirmation of the ambiguity, even ultimately the unintelligibility, of the mapping of active/passive onto masculine/ feminine',[104] and on Siggy's first appearance the text deftly illustrates the limitations of oppositional gendered descriptors. The complementary toning of his scarf and eye colour, his dark blond hair 'with highlighted curls' and the careful draping of his scarf, evident when at work in his salon, semiotically accord with a stereotyped effeminacy (p. 185).[105] Yet the text dispels such easy categorising, for traditional gender coding through the body is reversed. It is Siggy who is physically 'strapping' (p. 287), while Matt is 'Ferrety' (p. 287). And whereas Matt avoids violence, it is Siggy who is potentially aggressive. When Helen surprises him as she stumbles clumsily into his salon and he is momentarily unaware of her gender, his instinctive response is to turn and raise his scissors 'like a weapon' (p. 185). Later in the scene, his 'stern gaze trawling from her boots to her hair' indicates cool evaluation, authority, and an assured sense of self. In melding traditionally coded masculine and feminine attributes, Siggy heralds in Welsh mining fiction a subversion of the trope where the confident expression of self is a feature of the confident heterosexual male.

However, subversion of traditional gender roles in the figure of Siggy extends beyond his appearance and manner into his non-hierarchical, non-possessive love of Matt. Michael Kimmel's argument that 'gay relationships are more egalitarian'[106] is apparent in an exchange Siggy has with Helen. Believing that her husband Simon is unfaithful, she asks Siggy what he would do in her place. His responses illuminate the text's interrogation of a system of associations regarding power and heterosexual, hegemonic masculinity:

> 'Who cares if it is just sex.'
> 'But if he loved you, why go somewhere else?'
> 'Women,' he sighed. 'I hear the same thing, all day long. '*If he loved me, he would. If he loved me, he wouldn't.* Men are simple creatures, *schatzi*. It is never as complicated as you think.' (p. 309, original italics)

Siggy's macaronic response simultaneously disrupts the Gwyn Pritchard patriarchal, power-based model of marriage, and also presents an alternative to the more nuanced model represented through Iwan Jones, where fidelity is a *sine qua non* of a close marital relationship. The text further problematises conventional gendering by having Siggy downgrade men to the status of 'simple creatures' while nonetheless sighing patronisingly over women's delusions of romantic love, itself a male construct. Siggy, therefore, occupies a space where he confidently creates a hybridised allo-identity, combining culturally feminised signifiers like waxed, highlighted hair and eyebrows, with a donkey jacket like Iwan's, and a flying helmet: 'Part fighter pilot; part ghost of miners past' (p. 307). Paradoxically, it is a site where he exercises a form of male hegemony over women by working for them. But as he is freed from the homosocialising constraints of mining masculinity unlike Matt, macho performativity is not expected of him.

Matt Price's sexual orientation is discursively more problematic. His occupation enables the text to decouple conventionally perceived associations of gayness and femininity,[107] but being a gay miner represents for him an irreconcilable hybridity. Kevin Devaney, a former miner himself, provides a valuable insight into a dilemma like Matt's when he writes: 'Homosexuality is not acknowledged in mining.' It is not acknowledged, he suggests, not because miners are homophobic, but because in their cultural ambience heterosexuality is simply assumed.[108] *Until Our Blood is Dry*, therefore, places Matt in a cruel double bind when it confronts him with two potentially destructive choices generated by the strike: either he maintains his gendered pretence by acceding to Gwyn Pritchard's blackmail and therefore definitively betrays his community by strike-breaking; or he accepts the uncertain consequences of what exposure might bring. By placing him in this impossible position, the text demonstrates the coercive power of gendered expectation within an occupational paradigm. His desperate attempt to maintain the pretence of gender 'integrity' and conceal his difference from 'the boys' (p. 179) supersedes everything. In doing so, he condemns himself simultaneously to ostracism as a traitor, and to continuing personal fracture.

In constructing this fracture, the text employs a different narrative methodology from that used in the figure of Gwyn Pritchard. Whereas Gwyn is often examined through free indirect style, so that the narrative voice is, in Bakhtin's terms, 'simultaneously represented and representing',[109] the narrative voice removes itself from Matt's subjectivity, making him an object of detached scrutiny. By distributing details of his biography throughout the narrative, but declining to clarify them, by withholding information that may or may not relate to his homosexuality, and by denying the reader access to his consciousness, *Until Our Blood is Dry* both creates and replicates the challenge of subjective incoherence Matt faces in accepting the semiotics of his own gendering. Faced with such lacunae and textual indirection, the task of comprehending his troubled masculinity requires that, in Macherey's words, 'we investigate the silence'[110] once more. Matt is recently divorced, for example (p. 28), but though no reasons are disclosed, the fact resonates with significance alongside other biographical data. And when he arrives late at Simon's wedding, shamefaced and shaken, having been beaten up, there is 'something shifty, something more than guilt about losing the ring' (p. 130) about him, but the text colludes with his mumbled reticence beyond his claim that the 'Fella didn't give a name' (p. 127). Yet within the context of Matt's representation, such incidents echo through the text to construct a picture of personal anguish, confusion, fear and difference. It is Siggy, given a choric function, who offers a terse clarification of Matt's predicament: 'Matthew does not tell the truth about himself' (p. 309). The implied reason is clear. As the text demonstrates, the weight of a culture resting on the patriarchally sustained myth of the macho miner presupposes heterosexuality.

Through Matt's construction, the text exposes as oppressive the conventions of a social ethos in which heterosexuality has been naturalised as normative. Pierre Macherey's question on the meaning of the textually unspoken – 'to what extent is dissimulation a way of speaking?'[111] – can be modified in Matt's case to examine his public display as a defensive shield designed to deflect attention. Living a perpetual lie, Matt camouflages his sexual orientation in a performance of exaggerated heterosexual promiscuity. The text reveals it to be a continuous dissimulation speaking of his unshakeable dread of exposure. Claiming to have 'conquests from Monmouth to Milford Haven' (p. 29), his construction utilises pronounced masculinised discourse that sexually objectifies women: 'It's St David's Day soon', he says. 'I'm off to find myself a nice young lady. Gonna drag her up the allotments, show her my leek' (pp. 33–4). And when young women join the picket line, it is he who is the most demonstratively sexist: 'Quick chorus of *Get Yer Tits Out*, eh, lads?' (p. 90). Because, as Devaney says, homosexuality is largely unacknowledged by miners, Matt's scripted display of extravagant heterosexuality raises no suspicion among his workmates; the text thereby reveals the extent to which the objectifying of women is normative in Ystrad's male culture. It is a woman, Debbie Power, who speculates whether, in Macherey's terms, the 'speech' of Matt's rampant sexism is, in fact, 'dissimulation'. Briefly puzzled by his offensive comments, she remarks that 'For a bloke reckons he's a ladies' man, he don't like women at all' (p. 90), but in the activity of the picket the significance of her comment is lost on her associates, though not on the implied reader.

Discursive presentation of Matt extends beyond his own existential dilemma to deconstruct one of the pillars of hegemonic masculine definition: that gayness is 'the repository of whatever is expelled from hegemonic masculinity'.[112] As a gay miner, Matt is discursively used to expose the masculine semiotics to which he appears to subscribe as culturally defined codes rather than transcendent signifiers. As Berthold Schoene-Harwood argues, 'closeted gay men's performative expertise in maintaining their straight camouflage indirectly draws attention to traditional masculinity as an artificial, author(is)ed script.'[113] There is, of course, a risk that the repetition of such scripts underwrites them rather than exposes their artificiality. However, in constructing Matt Price through his occupation, *Until Our Blood is Dry* at least extends Schoene-Harwood's paradigm by overlaying the construction of Matt as *faux*-heterosexual with Matt as a valid member of an occupation defined by rugged masculinity facing quotidian danger. Ian M. Harris avers that 'in general [gay men] fit the same characteristics as other men',[114] and this is clearly implied in the narrative. Prior to the opening of the novel,

Matt and Simon have narrowly escaped a fall underground which killed a fellow miner. The text communicates the traumatic experience as recalled by Simon: 'the warning creak of the rocks, the eerie silence that filled the chamber before the roof caved in, the memory of rubble biting his skin as he scrabbled to free himself and Matt' (p. 29). And referencing Matt's expertise in this most 'manly' of occupations, the text further questions the artificial scripts of masculinity: 'Everything [Simon] knew about mining he had learned from Matt Price: the difference between the moaning of rocks settling into position and the rumble of rocks about to drop. How to hold a pickaxe and hold his drink' (p. 172).

Except for his sexual orientation, then, Matt demonstrates qualities that are associated with heteronormative masculinity and valorised in his culture. To adapt Katie Gramich's Whitmanesque phrase, he is 'both in and out of the game'.[115] Through his construction, the text addresses, by implication rather than direct confrontation, both the ambiguities and inadequacies of ingrained gender semiotics, and the oppressive power of Threadgold's 'male masculinity' which has him 'scared to tell the truth about himself' (p. 333). *Until Our Blood is Dry* presents Matt as a double victim of the strike: he is not only a tragic casualty of an industrial dispute like the other figures in the text, but a casualty also of what Terry Threadgold calls 'the persistencies of malestream knowledges'[116] regarding gender practices.

The 'heterogeneous Welsh culture'[117] that Aaron and Wynn Thomas argue has emerged in post-devolution Wales is yet to appear in the public consciousness of Ystrad, but the text implicitly suggests that Ystrad is potentially more pluralistic than Matt thinks. There is no mention of homophobic attitudes to Siggy. Helen is surprised when she stumbles on Matt and Siggy together, but she is not judgemental and feels no need to disseminate the information; and when Simon pleads with Matt to return to work, his assurance that 'every last one of the boys would welcome you back with open arms' (p. 173) appears unconditional. They are small but significant details in a text whose indirect narrative method confers significance on just such details. However, they are too small to register on Matt's consciousness, and he and Siggy leave Ystrad to go somewhere 'no-one knows us' (p. 333). Through their trajectory, *Until Our Blood is Dry* inscribes a new development in the theme of migration in the Welsh novel. Unlike Ben Fisher, Mary Biesty and Edwin Bowles, who seek either financial reward or personal development or both by leaving their valley, Matt and Siggy simply wish for anonymity.

One of the problems of examining masculinity, Rosalind Gill tells us, is 'the tendency to think in rather static terms, with a kind of one-size-fits-all notion of masculine identity'.[118] Writing in 1996 of the effect the 1984-5 miners' strike had on south Wales, Ned Thomas provided an example of what she meant, when he observed that, among other things, it created 'a crisis of identity for those whose self-image was based on the industrial culture of the mining areas'.[119] Using the interplay of patriarchy, politics and power as a structural model, this chapter has shown that within the fictional spaces of *Dark Edge* and *Until Our Blood is Dry* there is no composite, uniform 'crisis of identity'. In both narratives, an abstract term becomes a particular, individual reality in the bullying Elliott Bowles, the tormented authoritarian Gwyn Pritchard, the slippery politician Harry Cross and the gay miner Matt Price. And it is a challenge that is met and overcome in figures as diverse as the rejuvenated Edwin Bowles, the collectivist Iwan Jones and the gay hairdresser Siggy.

The diverging masculinities of Edwin and Elliott Bowles in *Dark Edge* are presented through a hybridised novel in which Elliott's decline into psychic disorder is transmitted through a form of *roman à thèse*, and Edwin's emergent self through a form of Bakhtinian *Bildungsroman*. The mutual antagonism of the half-brothers, one a policeman, the other a striking miner, mirrors the larger antipathies of the strike itself. *Until Our Blood is Dry* constructs Gwyn Pritchard and Iwan Jones as two radically contrasting forms of masculinity, each responding to challenges both personal and ideological. The performance of masculinity as power-based narcissism in Elliott Bowles and Gwyn Pritchard, and the probity of Edwin Bowles and Iwan Jones across the two texts are as striking as the individualised contrasts between the pairs of characters within their respective narratives. While the effect is to generate an overarching impression of Valleys' masculinity under threat, their particular biographies elucidate how profound social disruption affects different individuals in different ways.

The wider narrative space of *Until Our Blood is Dry* mobilises interrogations of two other arenas of male construction. Focusing on politics and power in the confident hegemony of Adam Smith-Tudor, the novel demonstrates how a power/knowledge nexus enables government representatives to colonise and normalise a form of rhetoric suited to their own strategies. By contrast, although the politically compromised Labour MP Harry Cross appropriates the dress, manner and lexis of the self-assured managerial male, they serve only to define him as derivatively subaltern. The breadth of masculine study in *Until Our Blood is Dry* is considerably enhanced by the gay relationship between the miner Matt Price and the hairdresser Siggy. It recalls a strikingly provocative question John MacInnes asks regarding gender: 'under what historical conditions did men and women come to believe that masculinity exists?'[120] In Matt and Siggy, gender is coded through an employment status that is itself a product of cultural manipulation and historical validation. Like MacInnes, in its representation of Matt and Siggy, *Until Our Blood is Dry* ponders the same existential question.

Conclusion

This book opened with Deirdre Beddoe's observation in 1986 that Wales was imagined as a collective of 'male and mass [and...] macho' coal miners, choristers and rugby players.[1] She was not alone in attributing to miners the features of an elite masculinity that separated men from women, or miners from most other men. Fifty years earlier, George Orwell had also collectivised miners. For him, they were notable for having bodies like 'hammered iron statues', with 'arms and belly muscles of steel'.[2] Yet, intriguingly, when seeking a figure to fix a miner's body as impenetrably statuesque and undeniably masculine, he described it as 'a sort of caryatid'.[3] Orwell presented his miners as impermeably male, and then through a sculpted female form combining physical grace with effortless strength that supports a dependent 'other'. His reference, whether intentional or not, implies that there is rather more to gender than patriarchally conceived binary distinctions suggest. This book has devoted itself to just such an inquiry.

By looking behind the image that Beddoe identified, and examining the representation of individual characters, gender-specific readings of these novels have questioned the 'hammered iron' versions of 'real men'. Mythic icons of working-class masculinity sustain egos, presume that the virile body encodes inherent qualities that are peculiarly male, help define a culture and promote self-respect by elevating the routinely mundane into the insistently heroic. Every nation needs its Hector Bebbs, whatever form – or gender – they take, but this book has argued that Hector's potent and irreducible masculinity is sourced from mythic archetypes rather than the activities and experiences of quotidian Valleys' life. By contrast, the achievement of five of these novels lies elsewhere. Emerging from the cultures in which they were written, they engage with the psyches, the insecurities, the performativities, the differences of bodily form, and the individualities of a male working class that inhabits those bodies. The novels challenge, as has this book, the collectively general by scrutinising the individually particular. Not

Conclusion

even the repeated allusions to Jim Roberts's 'magnificent body' tell all there is of him. Individually and collectively, the novels expose the industrially enshrined axioms of patriarchal masculinity to be culturally generated fictions. It is a view of masculinity that wrote gender instability into the Valleys' male psyche. Promulgating gender as binary and men as hegemonic, patriarchal masculinity posited a theoretically pleasing congruity between a male-formulated, hierarchical model of industrial patriarchy and a male-formulated hierarchical model of familial authority. What it actually created was a template where instability at the macro-level of socio-economic organisation was replicated in the micro-level of individual male identity, as men were required to square a vexing existential circle. In reality, they were subordinated, dispensable and dependent figures within the power/knowledge nexus of industrial capitalism. In theory, they were alchemically transformed into authoritative, stable patriarchs behind the front doors of their terrace houses. The consequent disruption, disaffection, violence, and immiseration – both individual and collective – this flawed model produced has featured in all five of the mining novels examined.

With the notable exception of Hector Bebb, none of these novels represents masculinity as either innate or monolithic, but as culturally constructed and pluralistic. Both individually and collectively, they illustrate how core practices attributed to 'true' masculinity engendered by and distributed through patriarchal power structures discriminate against men as well as women. Taken together, the novels comprise an impressive examination of masculine representation over a significant period of time within a topographically confined space. They are all, in a sense, historical novels filtered through the empirical perspectives of the authors. None of them is strictly autobiographical, yet each novel is a personal recollection of and a memorial to each writer's own lived-through times created as a historicised narrative moment. To this perspective of the viewpoint from which they were written may be added another: the viewpoint from which they may be read. One of the features of this book, when the texts are read in diachronic sequence, has been to note how acutely they speak to a development of masculine representation throughout the twentieth century, where culturally driven perceptions of contemporary Welsh masculinity coexist with enduring and recurring characteristics that bind the novels into a distinctively Valleys' canon. The effect is that the connection between an examination of masculinity and the passing of time can appear complex and disjointed. Iterative tropes, such as the cerebral miner, the bachelor, the political activist, the eastward migrant, the ruthless manager, the compromised patriarch, and, more structurally, the dysfunctional marriage, the immiserated household and the pervading hostility to institutional authority, have spoken to the recognition of a shared history and a communal network of cultural practices and values. But the diachronic overview of the book has also disclosed representations of Valleys' masculinities responding to shifting inter-gender dynamics consequent on changing social patterns, especially feminism in *Strike for a Kingdom*, *Dark Edge* and *Until Our Blood is Dry*.

A diachronic reading of the novels has additionally revealed how narratives either neglected or safely categorised as 'industrial novels', or as the most 'successful of all Welsh boxing novels'[4] in the case of *So Long, Hector Bebb*, and therefore not considered 'proper literature' at all, connect to transnational inscriptions of masculinity. Parochial as these novels might appear to the jaded metropolitan eye, they are parochial only in a topographical sense. 'Literary space', as Pascale Casanova points out, 'is not an immutable structure, fixed once and for all in its hierarchies and power relations',[5] and anglophone Welsh novels like the six examined here nudge for a literary space so that their representations of a distinctive topography and culture may be noted. While it would be perverse not to acknowledge the influence of England on hybridised Welsh masculine identity, of which the residual anglo-imperialism of Big Jim Roberts in *Cwmardy* and Inspector Evans of *Strike for a Kingdom* are notable examples, Valleys' fiction draws sustenance from sources far beyond England's occluding shadow. The rugged masculinities of the American west offered a fantasy of liberation from the class-based fetters of English colonialism to the Valleys' miner Jim Roberts. Gwyn Jones's biophiliac Welsh working-class masculinities – his exuberant young swimmers, for example – are overtly positioned within a tradition of classical and neoclassical pastoral models, while his heartless exploiters of labour would not be out of place in the work of American social realists like Upton Sinclair and Theodore Dreiser. Ron Berry adapts William Faulkner's multi-voiced structure of *As I Lay Dying* (1930) to construct an iconic Welsh masculinity in Hector Bebb through embedded references to mythic paradigms from the Old World to the New World, from antiquity to modernity, and positions his narrative within a contrapuntal text that is carried by the stream of European intertextual modernism. And elements of Greek tragedy are perceptible in *Until Our Blood is Dry*, where Gwyn Pritchard, isolated by his own narcissism in a blighted landscape, is a doomed character with no possibility of redemption, confronted by his own mortality and a plaything of an Olympian Adam Smith-Tudor.

However, the principal energies of this book have gone into the synchronic examination of masculinities in individual texts. Apart from *Cwmardy* and *So Long, Hector Bebb*, none of them has attracted close, sustained study, let alone theorised readings of masculine representation. This book has attempted to add fresh impetus to critical inspections of the two novels that have, and to demonstrate that the other four novels together present a remarkable breadth of masculine representation, each one of them offering a fruitful source of critical inquiry. The methodology of this study has accordingly been intentionally eclectic. Central to its approach has been the work of Stephen Knight, Katie Gramich, M. Wynn Thomas, Jane Aaron, Kirsti Bohata and Dai Smith and others in contextualising anglophone Welsh fiction as a distinctive body of work. Gender theorists, especially R. W. Connell, whose argument that 'hegemonic masculinity' seeks to address 'the problem of the legitimacy of patriarchy',[6] and Judith Butler's gender as 'the stylised repetition of acts',[7] helped formulate a theorised approach to masculinity through which that body of work has been read. Raymond Williams's vast expertise in so many fields of cultural study, and Pierre Macherey's 'establishing that absence around which a real complexity is knit',[8] both contributed enormously to the methods by which this book examined how masculinity is transmitted through these novels.

Macherey's contention that the 'the fallacy of rules'[9] can establish preconceptions regarding literary achievement has been apparent in the critical reception of Gwyn Jones's neglected *Times Like These*. Generally located within the orbit of the industrial novel, and as a consequence judged as at best lacking the requisite political passion of *Cwmardy*, and at worst afflicted by ideological incoherence, the novel has been read from a different perspective in this book. Adapting Raymond Williams's tripartite schema of 'dominant', 'residual' and 'emergent' energies in social process, this book has read masculinities in *Times Like These* as offering fascinating studies of performative identity inflected through a historicised perspective in which Gwyn Jones himself was implicated. Focusing on the construction of its two principal characters rather than the political mobilisation of the community in *Cwmardy*, chapter 2 examined how the coercive paradigms of patriarchal masculinity in the novel fragment both the debilitatingly sensitive Len Roberts and his physically robust, though emotionally suppressed father, Jim. The following chapter examined how Menna Gallie's whodunnit *Strike for a Kingdom* manipulates a traditionally patriarchal subgenre to feminise and juvenalise Welsh miners, thereby challenging both the gendering and genre of earlier male-authored industrial novels. Diverging from examining masculinity as a cultural construct, chapter 4 proposed that in Ron Berry's *So Long, Hector Bebb*, Hector is an intertextual celebration of heroic, mythical characteristics whose lineage extends back to antiquity, who also becomes a study of the conflict between self and 'other', reason and passion, the civilised and the primitive in the elite male. The final chapter considered how, in *Dark Edge* and *Until Our Blood is Dry*, the 1984–5 miners' strike subjected Welsh masculinities to fundamental challenges of self-identity when confronted by a politically engaged feminism and a government intent on radical social and economic reformulation through high unemployment. Although the critical field devoted to studying masculine representations in the Valleys is expanding, it remains relatively small. With the passing of the mining industry, a whole tranche of Welsh literary history is threatened with elision from public consciousness, or incorporation into a mythical retrospective of stabilised masculinity predicated on unassailable patriarchal hegemony. As the preceding chapters have attempted to illustrate, a gender specific reading of these texts exposes 'masculinity' as being an elusive concept, as capable of incarcerating men in a patriarchal code of practice as of liberating them.

Even though the Valleys are among the most densely populated and socially hybridised areas of Wales and are arguably the one area instantly recognised nationally and internationally by a single noun, the study of masculine representation in its fictions is still an emerging line of inquiry. This book can make no claims to comprehensive authority. Rhys Davies, Alun Richards and Gwyn Thomas, for instance – who have already attracted significant critical attention elsewhere – have made way for less well-known writers of the Valleys' industrial experiences. But by focusing its attention on the Valleys' narrow channels, represented through six anglophone novels over a distinctive, even convulsive, period of time, it has approached and responded to two matters. Synchronically, how each novel, of itself, addresses the destabilising paradoxes behind a Valleys' masculinity predicated on the patriarchal performance of power. And diachronically, when read as a corpus, how culturally embedded patterns of masculine definition recur in the novels over time, and the extent to which the 'disembedding mechanisms' of social change throughout this period result in modifications of masculine behaviour and self-perception.[10] As such, they act as custodians of a distinctive history imaginatively recreated through a literary medium. Masculine representations in these six novels are a small but significant strand of that continuing narrative. They tell an extraordinary story of exploitation, fortitude, resilience, resistance and humanity, one that deserves to be recognised, read and celebrated in Wales and beyond.

Notes

Introduction

1. Writing on gender difference, Michael S. Kimmel, for instance, remarks that, 'Biological arguments reassure us that what *is* is what should be, that the social is natural' (original italics): *The Gendered Society* (Oxford: Oxford University Press, 2000), p. 22.
2. Kimmel, *The Gendered Society*, p. 21.
3. Rosi Braidotti, *Nomadic Theory*, in *The Portable Rosi Braidotti* (New York: Columbia University Press, 2011), p. 211.
4. Deirdre Beddoe, 'Images of Welsh Women', in *Wales, The Imagined Nation: Essays in Cultural and National Identity*, ed. Tony Curtis (Bridgend: Poetry Wales Press, 1986), pp. 227–38 (p. 227).
5. Beddoe, 'Images of Welsh Women', p. 227.
6. Two rare examples are: Aidan Byrne's 'Constructions of masculinity in four 1930s Welsh novels in English: Lewis Jones's *Cwmardy* and *We Live*, Richard Llewellyn's *How Green Was My Valley*, and Gwyn Thomas's *Sorrow For Thy Sons* (unpublished doctoral thesis, University of Wolverhampton, 2007) and Emma Smith's, *Masculinity in Welsh Writing in English: The Cases of Lewis Jones, Glyn Jones, Gwyn Thomas and Ron Berry* (Saarbrücken: VDM, 2009).
7. Beddoe, 'Images of Welsh Women', p. 227.
8. Stephen Whitehead, *Men and Masculinities* (Cambridge: Polity Press, 2002), p, 127.
9. Antonio Gramsci, *Selections from 'The Prison Notebooks'*, ed. and trans. Quintin Hoare and Geoffrey Nowell-Smith (London: Lawrence and Wishart, 1991), p. 266.
10. R. W. Connell, *Gender and Power* (Cambridge: Polity Press, 1987, repr. 1996), p. 183.
11. Connell, *Gender and Power*, p. 184.
12. R. W. Connell *Masculinities* (Cambridge: Polity Press, 2005), p. 77.
13. Whitehead, *Men and Masculinities*, p. 90.
14. Whitehead, *Men and Masculinities*, p. 90.
15. In Kit Habianic's *Until Our Blood is Dry* (2014), Adam Smith-Tudor is the Coal Board's senior man in south Wales during the 1984–5 miners' strike. In

the early part of Ron Berry's *So Long, Hector Bebb* (1970), Bebb is a peerless boxer.

[16] Judith Butler, *Gender Trouble: Feminism and the Subversion of Identity* [1990] (Abingdon: Routledge, 2006), p. 33.

[17] John Tosh, 'Hegemonic masculinity and the history of gender', in *Masculinities in Politics and War: Gendering Modern History*, ed. Stefan Dudink, Karen Hagemann and John Tosh (Manchester: Manchester University Press, 2004), pp. 41–62 (p. 41).

[18] See also Michael Ward, 'The performance of young working-class masculinities in the south Wales Valleys' (unpublished doctoral thesis, Cardiff University, 2013), pp. 27–30.

[19] In the first decade of the twentieth century, immigration into industrialised south Wales was pro rata second only to that of the United States. See Daniel G. Williams, *Black Skin, Blue Books: African Americans and Wales 1845–1945* (Cardiff: University of Wales Press, 2012), p. 192. Kenneth O. Morgan estimates that between 1921 and 1931 about 430,000 people moved out of Wales, most of them permanently: *Rebirth of a Nation* (Cardiff: University of Wales Press, 2002), p. 231. Tony Bianchi writes that 'Between 1976 and 1986 over one million people – 36% of the population – moved in or out of Wales': 'Aztecs in Troedrhiwgwair: recent fictions in Wales', in *Peripheral Visions*, ed. Ian A. Bell (Cardiff: University of Wales Press, 1995), pp. 44–76 (p. 45).

[20] Stephen Knight writes that 'The *gwerin* ideal, still alive in Cymraeg Wales, was an image of a community which, while it recognised differences of status and income, rejected class difference': *A Hundred Years of Fiction* (Cardiff: University of Wales Press, 2004), p. 5.

[21] M. Wynn Thomas, *Internal Difference: Twentieth-Century Writing in Wales* (Cardiff: University of Wales Press, 1992), p. 26.

[22] Nigel Edley and Margaret Wetherell, *Men in Perspective: Practice, Power and Identity* (Hemel Hempstead: Prentice Hall/Harvester Wheatsheaf, 1995), p. 128.

[23] This book broadly follows John Tosh's definition of patriarchy as 'descriptively to indicate those areas where men's power over women and children constitutes a significant form of stratification': John Tosh, *Maleness and Masculinities in Nineteenth-Century Britain* (Harlow: Pearson, 2005), p. 53.

[24] Steffan Courtney-Morgan, 'Masculinity and the miners' strike in south Wales 1984–85' (unpublished doctoral dissertation, University of Swansea, 2008), 71.

[25] Braidotti, *Nomadic Theory*, p. 280.

[26] Connell, *Masculinities*, p. 77.

[27] Raymond Williams regards *Times Like These* as 'a memorable example of this form' [of industrial novel], in 'The Welsh Industrial Novel', in *Who Speaks for Wales? Nation, Culture and Identity*, ed. Daniel Williams (Cardiff University of Wales Press, 2003), pp. 95–111 (p. 105).

[28] James A. Davies, 'Kinds of Relating: Gwyn Thomas (Jack Jones, Lewis Jones, Gwyn Jones) and the Welsh Industrial Experience', *The Anglo-Welsh Review*, 86 (1987), 73–86 (p. 74).
[29] Knight, *A Hundred Years of Fiction*, p. 84.
[30] Raymond Williams, *Marxism and Literature* (Oxford: Oxford University Press, 1977), p. 121.
[31] Williams, *Marxism and Literature*, p. 122.
[32] Williams, *Marxism and Literature*, p. 122.
[33] Braidotti, *Nomadic Theory*, p. 30.
[34] Katie Gramich, '"Those Blue Remembered Hills": Gender in Twentieth-century Welsh Border Writing by Men', in *Gendering Border Studies*, ed. Jane Aaron, Henrice Altink and Chris Weedon (Cardiff: University of Wales Press, 2010), pp. 142–62 (p. 145).
[35] See Homi K. Bhabha, *The Location of Culture* (London: Routledge, 1993), pp. 85–92.
[36] Stephen Knight, 'Anarcho-Syndicalism in Welsh Fiction in English', in *To Hell with Culture*, ed. H. Gustav Klaus and Stephen Knight (Cardiff: University of Wales Press, 2005), pp. 51–65 (p. 57).
[37] Knight, 'Anarcho-Syndicalism in Welsh Fiction in English', p. 57.
[38] Braidotti, *Nomadic Theory*, p. 29.
[39] It is a feature that re-emerges in Roger Granelli's construction of Elliott Bowles in *Dark Edge* (1997).
[40] Bhabha, *The Location of Culture*, p. 93.
[41] Bhabha, *The Location of Culture*, p. 93.
[42] Gayle Rubin, 'Traffic in Women: Notes on the "Political Economy" of Sex', in *Toward an Anthropology of Women*, ed. Rayna R. Reiter (New York: Monthly Review Press, 1975), pp. 157–210 (p. 179).
[43] Raymond Williams, *Culture and Society 1780–1950* (London: Penguin Books, repr. 1982), p. 18.
[44] See John Scaggs, *Crime Fiction* (London and New York: Routledge, 2005), p. 45.
[45] Paul O'Leary writes of the strike as, 'an event which at the time appeared to represent continuity in the traditions of mining communities but, in reality, marked the end of a particular social formation and resulted in the destabilising of traditional relations between the sexes in these communities': 'Masculine Histories: Gender and the Social History of Modern Wales', *The Welsh History Review*, 22/2 (December 2004), 252–3.
[46] Susan Rubin Suleiman, *Authoritarian Fictions: The Ideological Novel as a Literary Genre* (New York: Columbia University Press, 1983), pp. 200–1.
[47] 'Chronotope' is a term coined by Bakhtin for 'the intrinsic connectedness of temporal and spatial relationships that are artistically expressed in literature': M. M. Bakhtin, *The Dialogic Imagination*, ed. Michael Holquist, trans. Caryl Emerson and Michael Holquist (Austin: University of Texas Press, 1998), p. 85.

Notes

⁴⁸ John Docker, *Postmodernism and Popular Culture: A Cultural History* (Cambridge: Cambridge University Press, 1994), p. 221.
⁴⁹ Docker, *Postmodernism and Popular Culture*, p. xvii.
⁵⁰ Thomas, *Internal Difference*, p. 44.
⁵¹ Katy Shaw, *Mining the Meaning: Cultural Representations of the UK 1984–85 Miners' Strike* (Newcastle upon Tyne: Cambridge Scholars, 2012), p. 2.
⁵² Christopher Meredith, *Shifts* (Bridgend: Seren, 1998).
⁵³ Dai Smith, *Dream On* (Cardigan: Parthian, 2013).
⁵⁴ Dai Smith, 'Author's Notes', *Wales Online*, www.walesonline.co.uk (10 August 2013), n.p.
⁵⁵ Nigel Jarrett, *Miners at the Quarry Pool* (Cardigan: Parthian, 2013).
⁵⁶ Owen Sheers, *The Green Hollow* (London: Faber and Faber, 2016).
⁵⁷ Louise Walsh, *Black River* (Llanrwst: Gwasg Carreg Gwalch, 2016).
⁵⁸ Dai Smith, *The Crossing* (Cardigan: Parthian, 2020).

Chapter 1

¹ Gwyn Jones, *Times Like These* (London: Victor Gollancz, 1936; reissued 1979). All future references are to the 1979 edition.
² As mentioned in the Introduction, Glyn Jones and Raymond Williams are rare in their unqualified advocacy.
³ Gwyn Jones, 'Anglo-Welsh Literature, 1934–1946: A Personal View', in *Transactions of the Honourable Society of Cymmrodorion* (London: Issued by the Society, 1987), 184.
⁴ Stephen Knight, '"A New Enormous Music": Industrial Fiction in Wales', in *A Guide to Welsh Literature*, vol. VII: *Welsh Writing in English*, ed. M. Wynn Thomas (Cardiff: University of Wales Press, 2003), pp. 47–90 (p. 72), and 'A collective challenge to constraining forces', *New Welsh Review*, 47 (1999), 28–31 (p. 28).
⁵ Stephen Knight, 'Industrial Fiction', in *The Cambridge History of Welsh Literature*, ed. Geraint Evans and Helen Fulton (Cambridge: Cambridge University Press, 2019), p. 396.
⁶ Dai Smith, 'A Novel History', in *Wales – The Imagined Nation: Essays in Cultural and National Identity*, ed. Tony Curtis (Bridgend: Seren, 1991), pp. 129–58 (p. 141).
⁷ Katie Gramich, 'Both In and Out of the Game: Welsh Writers in the British Dimension', in *Welsh Writing in English*, ed. M. Wynn Thomas (Cardiff: University of Wales Press, 2003), pp. 255–77 (p. 256).
⁸ James A. Davies, 'Kinds of Relating', p. 76.
⁹ Williams, *Marxism and Literature*, p. 122.
¹⁰ Williams, *Marxism and Literature*, p. 122.
¹¹ Williams, *Marxism and Literature*, p. 123.

[12] A mining agent was a senior manager in charge of a group of collieries.
[13] Writing of the Georgian period, John Brewer observes that 'the aim of politeness was to reach an accommodation with the complexities of modern life and to replace political zeal and religious bigotry with mutual tolerance and understanding'. It was, he states, a civilising moral concept which, 'spoke for the generality of mankind – "the blanks of society" – seeking not to impose uniformity on society but to understand and celebrate its variety': *The Pleasures of the Imagination: English Culture in the Eighteenth Century* (London: HarperCollins, 1997), pp. 103, 102. In *Times Like These*, the humane Shelton finds himself locked into a role predicated on a socio-economic practice that has little time for 'the blanks of society'.
[14] Williams, *Marxism and Literature*, p. 126.
[15] Macherey, *A Theory of Literary Production*, p. 53.
[16] 'The tonal uncertainty' that James A. Davies identifies in Jones's novel is certainly there. The discourse of the novel stretches from the highly formal, with terms like 'canaille', 'objurations', 'simulacrum', references to 'Sisyphus' and the 'Virgins of the Masters', quotations from *King Lear*, and so on to the use of south Walian demotic. When Snooker Kelch's right eye 'put the shutters' in his fight with Ben Fisher, 'despite having bellows to mend' he 'drives a grunter' into Ben's ribs. While this polyphonic effect may damage the aesthetics of the novel and compromise its thematic unity, more interestingly, perhaps, it reveals how Gwyn Jones himself was engaged in the same dynamic of social process and individual development that features in *Times Like These*. He becomes part of the process of which he writes. Terry Eagleton observes of Raymond Williams that 'he features as a character within his own drama'. Perhaps the same may be said of Gwyn Jones: Terry Eagleton, *Criticism and Ideology: A Study in Marxist Literary Theory* (London: Verso Books, 1992), p. 23.
[17] Macherey, *A Theory of Literary Production*, p. 53.
[18] David L. Collinson and Jeff Hearn, 'Breaking the Silence: On Men, Masculinities and Managements', in *Men as Managers, Managers as Men*, ed. David L. Collinson and Jeff Hearn (London: SAGE, 1996), pp. 1–24 (p. 14).
[19] Andrew Tolson, *The Limits of Masculinity* (London: Tavistock, 1977), p. 58.
[20] David Leverenz, *Manhood and the American Renaissance* (Ithaca and London: Cornell University Press, 1989), p. 4.
[21] Herbert Spencer (1820–1903) popularised Darwin's theory of evolution by natural selection by finding an analogy with what happened in the world of business, commerce, industry and social organisation generally. The theory made a great impression on American writers like Theodore Dreiser (1871–1945), Hamlin Garland (1860–1940) and Jack London (1876–1916), but also influenced Thomas Hardy and George Eliot: see Nancy L. Paxton, *George Eliot and Herbert Spencer: Feminism, Evolutionism and the Reconstruction of Gender* (Princeton: Princeton University Press, 1991).

Notes

22. Stefan Collini, *Public Moralists: Political Thought and Intellectual Life in Britain 1850–1930* (Oxford: Clarendon Press, 1999), p. 100.
23. Gwyn Jones's father was sacked in the same manner as Oliver Biesty, and never worked underground again. Cecil Price records that Gwyn Jones told him how he hated 'the coal owners for what they had done to his father and grandfather': Cecil Price, *Gwyn Jones* (Cardiff: University of Wales Press, 1976), pp. 9–10.
24. Judith Butler, *Excitable Speech: The Politics of the Performative* (New York and London: Routledge, 1997), p. 49.
25. Berthold Schoene-Harwood, *Writing Men* (Edinburgh: Edinburgh University Press, 2000), p. 56.
26. Chris Hopkins, *English Fiction in the 1930s: Language, Genre, History* (London: Continuum, 2006), p. 63.
27. Andrew V. Ettin, *Literature and the Pastoral* (New Haven and London: Yale University Press, 1984), p. 146.
28. Hopkins, *English Fiction in the 1930s*, p. 66
29. David James and Philip Tew, *New Versions of Pastoral: Post-Romantic, Modern and Contemporary Responses to the Tradition* (Madison, WI: Fairleigh Dickinson University Press, 2009), p. 14.
30. Michael Kimmel, 'Masculinity as Homophobia: Fear, Shame and Silence in the Construction of Gender Identity', in *The Masculinities Reader*, ed. Stephen M. Whitehead and Frank J. Barrett (Cambridge: Polity Press, 2006), pp. 266–87 (p. 275).
31. Peter V. Marinelli, *Pastoral* (London: Macmillan, 1971), p. 17.
32. Hywel Francis and David Smith observe that in the 1930s and earlier as a result of the intrusion of mining, 'the unnatural state of South Wales was stressed ("natural" was Welsh neo-pastoral)': *The Fed* (London: Lawrence and Wishart, 1980), p. 39.
33. Hopkins, *English Fiction in the 1930s*, p. 63.
34. Ettin, *Literature and the Pastoral*, p. 166.
35. Davies, 'Kinds of Relating', pp. 75–6.
36. Stephen Knight, *A Hundred Years of Fiction* (Cardiff: University of Wales Press, 2004), p. 84.
37. From an anonymous late seventeenth-century poem cited by Raymond Williams in *The Country and the City* (Oxford: Oxford University Press, 1973), p. 24.
38. For a full discussion of this aspect of pastoral, see Terry Gifford's *Pastoral* (London: Routledge, 1999, pp. 47–117).
39. John Milton, 'L'Allegro', in *John Milton: Poems*, ed. B. A. Wright (London: J. M. Dent, 1962), p. 31, line 83.
40. Andrew Marvell, 'The Picture of Little T. C. in a Prospect of Flowers', in *The Poems of Andrew Marvell*, ed. Hugh MacDonald (London: Routledge and Kegan Paul, 1963), p. 36, line 36.

41 Matthew Arnold, 'Thyrsis', in *The Oxford Book of English Verse 1250–1918*, ed. Sir Arthur Quiller-Couch, [1900, new edition 1939] (Oxford: Oxford University Press, repr. 1979), p. 915, lines 33–5.
42 Terry Gifford, *Pastoral*, p. 82.
43 Marinelli, *Pastoral*, p. 53.
44 James and Tew, *New Versions of Pastoral*, p. 14.
45 Anthony Easthope, *What a Man's Gotta Do* (London: Routledge, 1990), p. 88.
46 Gwyn Jones draws on his own childhood experience here. Cecil Price records Jones telling him that as a youngster he enjoyed swimming with other boys in the Horse Pond where they swam 'naked as newts and noisy as starlings': Price, *Gwyn Jones*, p. 7.
47 Davies, 'Kinds of Relating', p. 76.
48 Patrick Cullen, *Spenser, Marvell and Renaissance Pastoral* (Cambridge, MA: Harvard University Press, 1970), p. 2.
49 See, for example, Theocritus, *Idylls*: 'The Reapers', Idyll X: 'Good workmen think of nothing but their job'; and the unsentimental 'Idyll XXI': 'It is poverty alone breeds craftsmanship, / Diophantus; she teaches men to work': *Greek Pastoral Poetry*, trans. Anthony Holden (London: Penguin, 1974), pp. 85, 118.
50 Butler, *Excitable Speech: A Politics of the Performative*, p. 51.
51 Theocritus here both participates in the experience as a character and constructs for the reader what William Empson in *Some Versions of Pastoral* described as 'a double standard of the artist to the worker, the complex man to the simple one ("I am in one way better, in another not so good")'. See Stefan Collini, *The Nostalgic Imagination: History in English Criticism* (Oxford: Oxford University Press, 2019), p. 113.
52 Easthope, *What A Man's Gotta Do*, p. 87.
53 See, for example, Theocritus, *Idylls*: 'The Singing Match', Idyll VI; 'The Second Singing Match', Idyll VIII; 'The Third Singing Match', Idyll IX: Anthony Holden, in *Greek Pastoral Poetry*, pp. 71–3; 78–82; 83–4.
54 Karl Marx, 'Economic and Philosophical Manuscripts', in Erich Fromm, *Marx's Concept of Man* (New York: Frederick Ungar, 1961), p. 98.
55 Williams, *Marxism and Literature*, p. 122.
56 Knight, *A Hundred Years of Fiction*, p. 83.
57 Williams, *Marxism and Literature*, p. 122.
58 Gramich, 'Both In and Out of the Game: Welsh Writers in the British Dimension', p. 256.
59 Helen Yallop, *Age and Identity in Eighteenth-Century England* (Abingdon: Routledge, 2013), p. 108.
60 Michael Bunce, *The Countryside Ideal: Anglo-American Images of Landscape* (London: Routledge, 1994), p. 50.
61 Bunce, *The Countryside Ideal*, p. 53.

[62] Bunce, *The Countryside Ideal*, p. 53. Bunce notes that *In Search of England* (1927) by H. V. Morton, 'a rural myth-maker of the first order', ran to twelve editions by 1936. He notes, too, the popularity of a romanticised view of country life in novels of the time by writers like Sheila Kaye-Smith, Hugh Walpole and Mary Webb.

[63] Stefan Collini, *Public Moralists*, p. 186. In his Introduction, Collini notes that with very few exceptions, his study 'includes no women, and the use of a male pseudonym by one of these [George Eliot] and the "correct" married form by the other [Mrs Humphry Ward] may hint at some reasons for this' (p. 3). It is, he suggests, another example of the male-as-norm.

[64] The re-emergence of residual 'Victorian values' in the late twentieth century after the post-war, one-nation consensus is a modern instance of Raymond Williams's point that 'dominant' cultures incorporate 'residual' values where they suit their ideological purpose.

[65] John Brewer, *The Pleasures of the Imagination: English Culture in the Eighteenth Century* (London: Routledge, 2013), p. 114.

[66] Brewer, *The Pleasures of the Imagination*, p. 103.

[67] Brewer, *The Pleasures of the Imagination*, p. 41.

[68] The colliery agent Adam Smith-Tudor in *Until Our Blood is Dry* is similarly presented only at work, as is the ambitious miners' representative Ceri Griffiths in *Dark Edge*. Denying them any degree of intimacy features as an implied critique of their hegemonic masculinities, where their identities are defined by hierarchy, power and agency.

[69] Collini, *Public Moralists*, p. 105.

[70] See Brewer: coffee houses, for instance, became 'key places in creating new cultural communities', *The Pleasures of the Imagination*, p. 3.

[71] Another autobiographical reference creeps in here. Near to where Jones lived in his early years in Blackwood, Monmouthshire, was an open space called the Tip, which is similar to the Tip where Ben and Snooker fight.

[72] Knights, *Writing Masculinities*, p. 127.

[73] Brewer, *The Pleasures of the Imagination*, p. 100.

[74] Raymond Williams, *The Country and the City* (Oxford: Oxford University Press, 1973), p. 176.

[75] Davies, 'Kinds of Relating', p. 95.

[76] Knight, *A Hundred Years of Fiction*, p. 83.

[77] Tony Brown, 'Separate, different, individual', *New Welsh Review*, 48 (2000), 20–2 (p. 22).

[78] Williams, *The Country and the City*, p. 117.

[79] In an intriguing gender reversal *Times Like These* imbues Mary Biesty with several of the signifiers generally associated with men. Unlike her brother Luke, she is ambitious, adventurous, materialistic and self-focused.

[80] The term 'people' in Caradoc Evans's *My People* (1915) signifies a collective with shared cultural assumptions and practices. It was also an English

upper-class colloquialism for family, as Broddam clearly uses it here. See also John Mortimer, *Paradise Postponed* (London: Viking, 1985), p. 107.
81 Williams, *Marxism and Literature*, p. 124.
82 Anthony Giddens, *Modernity and Self-Identity* (Cambridge: Polity Press, 1991), p. 48.
83 Giddens, *Modernity and Self-Identity*, p. 188.
84 Brewer, *The Pleasures of the Imagination*, p. 117.
85 John Mortimer, *Paradise Postponed*, p. 107.
86 Mortimer, *Paradise Postponed*, pp. 106–9, for example.
87 Giddens, *Modernity and Self-Identity*, p. 185.
88 Norman Fairclough, *Language and Power*, third edn (Abingdon: Routledge, 2015), p. 90.
89 Williams, *Marxism and Literature*, p. 125.
90 Erich Fromm, *The Fear of Freedom* (London: Routledge, 1960), p. 160: quoted by Anthony Giddens, *Modernity and Self-Identity*, p. 191.
91 Butler, *Gender Trouble*, p. 200.
92 Davies, 'Kinds of Relating', p. 74.
93 Macherey, *A Theory of Literary Production*, p. 53.
94 *The Oxford Companion to the Literature of Wales*, compiled and edited by Meic Stephens (Oxford: Oxford University Press, 1986), p. 589.
95 Williams, *Marxism and Literature*, p. 121.
96 Knight, *A Hundred Years of Fiction*, p. 84.

Chapter 2

1 Lewis Jones, *Cwmardy* [1937] (London: Lawrence and Wishart, 1978). All future references, unless otherwise stated, are to the 1978 edition.
2 Carole Snee, 'Working-Class Literature or Proletarian Writing?', in *Culture and Crisis in Britain in the 1930s*, ed. Jon Clark, Margot Heinemann and David Margolies (London: Lawrence and Wishart, 1974), p. 182.
3 Jane Tompkins, *West of Everything* (Oxford: Oxford University Press, 1992), p. 4.
4 R. S. Thomas, 'Cynddylan on a Tractor', in *Selected Poems*, ed. Anthony Thwaite (London: J. M. Dent, 1996), p. 23.
5 Steve Bodington, 'The Political Morality of Work', in *The Achilles Heel Reader: Men, Sexual Politics and Socialism*, ed. Victor J. Seidler (London: Routledge, 1991), pp. 176–82 (p. 178).
6 George Orwell, *The Road to Wigan Pier* [1937] (London: Penguin, 1986), pp. 18–31 (p. 18).
7 Raymond Williams, *Culture and Society 1780–1950* (London: Penguin, 1961), pp. 289–90.
8 *Cwmardy*, for David Smith, reveals the external pressure on a community because it focuses 'so sharply on the local, on individuals and on the detail

of their lives': *Lewis Jones* (Cardiff: University of Wales Press on behalf of the Welsh Arts Council, 1982), p. 42.
9. Alyce von Rothkirch, for example, tentatively suggests that 'its quality as literature is [...] difficult to answer': 'Liberty and the Party-Line: "Novelising" Working-class History in Lewis Jones's *Cwmardy* and *We Live* (1937 and 1939)', in *Mapping the Territory: Critical Approaches to Welsh Fiction in English*, ed. Katie Gramich (Cardigan: Parthian, 2010), pp. 81–101 (p. 84).
10. David Bell, *Ardent Propaganda: Miners' Novels and Class Conflict 1929–1939* (Uppsala: Swedish Science Press, 1995), p. 96.
11. Byrne,'Constructions of masculinity in four 1930s Welsh novels in English: Lewis Jones's *Cwmardy* and *We Live*, Richard Llewellyn's *How Green Was My Valley* and Gwyn Thomas's *Sorrow For Thy Sons*', p. 107.
12. Gramsci, *Selections from 'The Prison Notebooks'*, p. 266.
13. Snee, 'Working-Class Literature or Proletarian Writing?', p. 183.
14. Macherey, *A Theory of Literary Production*, p. 41.
15. Braidotti, *Nomadic Theory*, p. 29.
16. *Cwmardy*, 'Foreword', n.p.
17. Macherey, *A Theory of Literary Production*, p. 101.
18. Rolf Meyn, 'Lewis Jones's *Cwmardy* and *We Live*: Two Welsh Proletarian Novels in Transatlantic Perspective', in *British Industrial Fictions*, ed. H. Gustav Klaus and Stephen Knight (Cardiff: University of Wales Press, 2000), pp. 124–36 (p. 128). Bert Coombes's *These Poor Hands: The Autobiography of a Miner Working in South Wales* is probably the best-known example of fictionalised autobiography emerging from the inter-war south Wales coalfield (London: Victor Gollancz, 1939; repr. Cardiff: University of Wales Press, 2011). See also Bill Jones and Chris Williams, *B. L. Coombes* (Cardiff: University of Wales Press, 1999), especially pp. 47–8.
19. Meyn, 'Lewis Jones's *Cwmardy* and *We Live*', p. 128.
20. Stephen Knight, *A Hundred Years of Fiction*, p. 86. William Abraham (1842–1922), known by his bardic name 'Mabon', was a prominent miners' leader. Noah Rees was a member of the Cambrian Combine Committee, whch led the miners in their 1910–11 strikes against the Cambrian group of collieries.
21. Connell, *Masculinities*, p. 12.
22. John Pikoulis, 'Lewis Jones', *Anglo-Welsh Review*, 74 (1983), 62–71 (p. 66).
23. Hywel Francis, 'Foreword', in *Cwmardy* and *We Live*, Library of Wales series (Cardigan: Parthian, 2006): Jones, 'enjoyed the company of men and women', unpaginated.
24. Pikoulis, 'Lewis Jones', 63.
25. A tantalisingly suggestive diary entry for 1930, for instance, records how he 'Went on Randy': Lewis Jones's diary entry, 1930, microfiche, South Wales Miners' Library, University of Swansea.

26. Ross Poole, for instance, argues that to be a masculine subject requires an intent 'to aspire to the norms of rational thought and action': 'Modernity, Rationality and "the Masculine"', in *Feminine/Masculine and Representation*, ed. Terry Threadgold and Anne Cranny-Francis (London: Unwin Hyman, 1990), pp. 48–60 (p. 48).
27. Billy Griffiths, interview with Hywel Francis, 1969, South Wales Miners' Library, unpublished archive. Francis includes a longer section of the interview in his Foreword to the omnibus Library of Wales edition of *Cwmardy* and *We Live* (Cardigan: Parthian, 2006), n.p.
28. Pikoulis, 'Lewis Jones', 66.
29. Steve Bodington, 'The Political Morality of Work', p. 178.
30. Suleiman, *Authoritarian Fictions: The Ideological Novel as a Literary Genre*, p. 65.
31. Meyn, 'Lewis Jones's *Cwmardy* and *We Live*', p. 129.
32. Émile Zola, *Germinal*, trans. Leonard Tancock (London: Penguin, 1954; repr. 1983), p. 495.
33. M. M. Bakhtin, *Speech Genres and Other Late Essays*, trans. Vern W. McGee (Austin: University of Texas Press, 1986), p. 24.
34. Bell, *Ardent Propaganda*, p. 93.
35. Bell, Abstract, *Ardent Propaganda*, n.p.
36. Emma Smith, *Masculinity in Welsh Writing in English*, pp. 25–6.
37. Suleiman, *Authoritarian Fictions*, p. 43.
38. Bell, *Ardent Propaganda*, p. 93. See also pp. 149–50.
39. See Pikoulis, 'The Wounded Bard', 23.
40. See Peter Middleton, *The Inward Gaze: Masculinity and Subjectivity in Modern Culture* (London: Routledge, 1992), p. 3.
41. The inability of male characters to engage with their emotions is a recurring trope in Welsh industrial fiction. In *So Long, Hector Bebb*, Prince Saddler has no means of articulating his love of Hector, except vicariously through the language of comradeship in battle; and in *Until Our Blood is Dry*, Gwyn Pritchard's pride in his own rationalism disables any ability to understand his true feelings for his daughter.
42. Middleton, *The Inward Gaze*, p. 116.
43. Tolson, *The Limits of Masculinity*, pp. 12–13.
44. Pikoulis, 'The Wounded Bard', 24.
45. David Bell, by contrast, focuses on how 'Len's political education begins when he starts work', through which he emerges as 'a mature character': *Ardent Propaganda*, p. 98.
46. Butler, *Gender Trouble*, p. 19.
47. See Nigel Edley and Margaret Wetherell, *Men in Perspective*: 'Work [for a boy] thus becomes seen as a privilege, an instantiation of masculinity' (p. 103).
48. Tolson, *The Limits of Masculinity*, p. 43.

Notes

49 Byrne, 'Constructions of masculinity in four 1930s Welsh novels in English: Lewis Jones's *Cwmardy* and *We Live*, Richard Llewellyn's *How Green Was My Valley* and Gwyn Thomas's *Sorrow For Thy Sons*', p. 120.
50 Ron Berry's Hector Bebb also kills a sheep for food but, unlike Will, even he 'lost true sight, everything fuzzy and Roman candles firing inside my chest': *So Long, Hector Bebb*, p. 194.
51 Berthold Schoene-Harwood, *Writing Men*, p. 3.
52 Schoene-Harwood, *Writing Men*, p. 3.
53 See Middleton, *The Inward Gaze*, p. 120.
54 Kevin Devaney, 'Mining – A World Apart', in *The Achilles Heel Reader*, ed. Victor J. Seidler, pp. 151–60 (p. 154).
55 Middleton, *The Inward Gaze*, p. 122.
56 Graham Dawson, 'The Blond Bedouin', in *Manful Assertions: Masculinities in Britain since 1800*, ed. Michael Roper and John Tosh (London: Routledge, 1991), pp. 113–44 (p. 119).
57 Knights, *Writing Masculinities* (Basingstoke: Macmillan, 1999), p. 5.
58 David Lodge, *After Bakhtin: Essays on Fiction and Criticism* (London: Routledge, 1990), p. 26.
59 Aidan Byrne makes a powerful case for reading Len from a humanistic perspective: 'Constructions of masculinity in four 1930s Welsh novels in English: Lewis Jones's *Cwmardy* and *We Live*, Richard Llewellyn's *How Green Was My Valley* and Gwyn Thomas's *Sorrow For Thy Sons*', pp. 119–26.
60 Emma Smith, *Masculinity in Welsh Writing in English*, p. 26, and David Bell, *Ardent Propaganda*, p. 94, for example.
61 Bell, following Orwell, notes the middle-class reductive classification of the working class as 'a source of humour, and therefore harmless, or a potential threat to the status of the middle-class, and therefore dangerous': *Ardent Propaganda*, p. 72.
62 Snee, 'Working-Class Literature or Proletarian Writing?', p. 167.
63 See, for example, Bell: 'The primary feature of a *roman à thèse* is that the role of the reader is strongly programmed': *Ardent Propaganda*, p. 35.
64 Suresh Srivastva and Frank J. Barrett, 'The Transforming Nature of Metaphors in Group Development', *Human Relations*, 41/1 (1988), 31–64 (p. 36).
65 Srivastva and Barrett, 'The Transforming Nature of Metaphors in Group Development', p. 36.
66 Srivastva and Barrett, 'The Transforming Nature of Metaphors in Group Development', pp. 60–1.
67 Middleton, *The Inward Gaze*, p. 230.
68 After Jane's death, when Len dreams that she is still alive and he kisses her only to find he is actually kissing Evan the Overman's son, his rival, 'His body quivered with disgust' (p. 62).

[69] Siân is given the name Shane in the 1937 and 1978 editions of *Cwmardy* in an attempt to anglicise her name for a wider readership. The 2006 Parthian omnibus edition of *Cwmardy* and *We Live* restores her name to its proper Welsh form. This book uses the 1978 text for general reference but follows the 2006 edition in spelling her name. Transgressive desire is a recurring theme in Valleys' industrial fiction. It is implied again in *Cwmardy* in Ezra's feelings towards his daughter Mary; it results in the birth of a child in *Strike for a Kingdom*, and propels Gwyn Pritchard in *Until Our Blood is Dry* to seek sex from a girl no older than his daughter from whom he is estranged.
[70] Knights, *Writing Masculinities*, pp. 28–9.
[71] Katie Gramich, 'Mountains and Mirrors', *Planet*, 128 (1998), 70–5 (p. 70). Emma Smith makes a similar point with special reference to Jane in *Masculinity in Welsh Writing in English*, p. 36.
[72] Connell, *Masculinities*, p. 164. See also Nigel Edley and Margaret Wetherell, *Men in Perspective*, p. 157.
[73] Marianne DeKoven, *Rich and Strange: Gender, History, Modernism* (Princeton: Princeton University Press, 1991), p. 32. In a note, she writes 'There are, of course, exceptions – Poseidon comes readily to mind. Generally, bodies of water on earth, particularly oceans, lakes or ponds [...] lend themselves most readily to use as feminine iconography, rain to masculine' (p. 224).
[74] Emma Davies, '"He was a queer lad for his age ...": The Crisis of Masculinity in Lewis Jones's *Cwmardy*', in *Welsh Writing in English: A Yearbook of Critical Essays*, ed. Tony Brown, Vol. 8 (2003), 29–45 (p. 43).
[75] Graham Holderness, 'Miners and the novel, from bourgeois to proletarian', in *The British Working-Class Novel in the Twentieth Century*, ed. J. M. Hawthorn (London: Edward Arnold, 1984), pp. 19–31 (p. 28).
[76] Schoene-Harwood, *Writing Men*, p. 4.
[77] Stephen Greenblatt, *Renaissance Self-Fashioning* (Chicago: University of Chicago Press, 1984), p. 256.
[78] Snee, 'Working-Class Literature or Proletarian Writing?', p. 183.
[79] Knight, *A Hundred Years of Fiction*, p. 86.
[80] Smith, *Lewis Jones*, p. 44.
[81] Sung by the American entertainer Jimmy Dean.
[82] Valentine Cunningham, *British Writers of the Thirties* (Oxford: Oxford University Press, 1988), pp. 310–11.
[83] Macherey, *A Theory of Literary Production*, p. 84.
[84] Michael E. McGill, *The McGill Report on Male Intimacy* (New York: Harper and Row, 1985), p. 185. Cited in Middleton, *The Inward Gaze*, p. 121.
[85] Cunningham, *British Writers of the Thirties*, p. 310.
[86] Tompkins, *West of Everything*, p. 56.
[87] Middleton, *The Inward Gaze*, p. 121.

88 David Smith notes that the ages of Len and his sister do not tally with Big Jim's fighting in the Boer War: *Lewis Jones*, p. 42.
89 John Tosh, 'Domesticity and Manliness', in *Manful Assertions: Masculinities in Britain since 1800* (London: Routledge, 1991), pp. 44 73 (p. 67).
90 Dawson, 'The Blond Bedouin', p. 120.
91 Tosh, 'Hegemonic Masculinity and the History of Gender', p. 49.
92 Butler, *Gender Trouble*, p. 189.
93 Piers Brendon, *The Decline and Fall of the British Empire 1781–1997* (London: Vintage, 2008), p. 124.
94 John Horne, 'The Age of Nation States and World Wars', in *Masculinities in Politics and War: Gendering Modern History*, ed. Stefan Dudink, Karen Hornemann and John Tosh (Manchester: Manchester University Press, 2004), pp. 22–39 (p. 31).
95 *Dictionary of the American West*, ed. Winfred Blevins (Ware: Wordsworth, 1995), p. 118. *The Hard Hombre*, for instance, was a 1931 Western, and the term still functioned as a descriptor in Paul Newman's *Hombre* in 1967.
96 Tompkins, *West of Everything*, p. 4.
97 The freedom and rugged masculinity associated with the American west is a recurring trope in Welsh writing in English. For example, it is there in *So Long, Hector Bebb* (1970), and occurs throughout Duncan Bush's *Glass Shot* (1991), where Stew Boyle dresses like a cowboy and considers his hair to be black like an Apache (London: Martin Secker and Warburg, 1991), p. 41 The influence of the American west on the Welsh popular imagination can scarcely be exaggerated. Buffalo Bill Cody, for instance, brought his Wild West show twice to Cardiff (1891 and 1903) and to the Valleys' towns of Aberdare and Ebbw Vale in 1903, among several other Welsh locations. America continues to fascinate the Valleys. As the character Ellie Evans says of the Valleys in Rachel Trezise's, *Sixteen Shades of Crazy*: 'America's already in the blood' (London: Blue Door, 2010), p. 211.
98 Greenblatt, *Renaissance Self-Fashioning*, p. 256.
99 Marx, 'Economic and Philosophical Manuscripts', p. 98.
100 Emma Smith has a fine paragraph on this story: *Masculinity in Welsh Writing in English*, p. 30.
101 David Smith, *Lewis Jones*, p. 27.
102 Billy Griffiths on Lewis Jones, from his interview with Hywel Francis, 1969.

Chapter 3

1 Menna Gallie, *Strike for a Kingdom* [1959] (Dinas Powys: Honno, Welsh Women's Classics, 2003 and 2011). All future references are to the Honno, 2011 edition. Gallie's works other than *Strike for a Kingdom* are: *Man's*

Desiring (London: Gollancz, 1960); *The Small Mine* (London: Gollancz, 1962; repr. Honno, 2000); *Travels with a Duchess* (London: Gollancz, 1966; repr. Honno, 2011); *You're Welcome to Ulster* (London: Gollancz, 1970; repr. Honno, 2010); *In These Promiscuous Parts* (New York: St Martin's Press, 1986). Her final novel, was published in America, but not in the UK. In a letter to Angela V. John, Gallie recommended that it had 'a tidy burial and forget it ever happened': Angela V. John, *Rocking the Boat: Welsh Women who Championed Equality 1840–1990* (Cardigan: Parthian, 2018), p. 281. In 1973, Gallie's translation of Caradog Pritchard's *Un Nos ola leuad* (1961) was published by Hodder and Stoughton (London) under the title *Full Moon.*

[2] Raymond Stephens, 'The Novelist in the Community: Menna Gallie', in *Anglo-Welsh Review*, 14/34 (1964–5), 52–63 was one of the first.

[3] Gill Plain, *Twentieth-Century Crime Fiction: Gender, Sexuality and the Body* (Edinburgh: Edinburgh University Press, 2001), p. 8.

[4] From a *Sunday Times* review, 1959; cited in the frontispiece of Gallie's *Man's Desiring* (London: Victor Gollancz, 1960).

[5] Stephen Knight, 'The Golden Age', in the *Cambridge Companion to Crime Fiction,* ed. Martin Priestman (Cambridge: Cambridge University Press, 2003), pp. 77–94 (p. 77). The term 'Golden Age' is attributed broadly to whodunnits written between the wars, though as Stephen Knight and others comment, the form remained popular and influential long after.

[6] See Stephen Knight, *Crime Fiction, 1800–2000: Detection, Death, Diversity* (Basingstoke: Palgrave Macmillan, 2004), p. 91.

[7] Julian Symons, *Bloody Murder* (Harmondsworth: Viking, 1985), p. 96.

[8] Roland Barthes, *The Pleasure of the Text*, trans. Richard Miller (New York: Hill and Wang, 1975), p. 12.

[9] Plain, *Twentieth-Century Crime Fiction*, p. 90.

[10] Menna Gallie Archive, undated Address to Swansea Writers' Group, National Library of Wales, Aberystwyth, L1/16.

[11] Menna Gallie Archive, Address to Swansea Writers' Group, L1/16.

[12] Sophie Hannah, 'It's no mystery that crime is the biggest-selling genre in books', *Guardian*, 12 April 2018, *www.theguardian.com* (accessed 12 April 2018).

[13] Plain, *Twentieth-Century Crime Fiction,* p. 89.

[14] John Scaggs, *Crime Fiction* (London: Routledge, 2005), p. 45.

[15] How radically different from the depictions of heroic, hypertrophic miners can be seen by contrasting their portrayal with George Orwell's miners, whose masculinity resides in their bodies like 'hammered iron statues' and 'arms and belly muscles of steel': George Orwell, *The Road to Wigan Pier* [1937] (London: Penguin, 1986), pp. 18–31 (pp. 18, 31).

[16] Dennis Porter, T*he Pursuit of Crime: Art and Ideology in Detective Fiction* (New Haven and London: Yale University Press, 1981), p. 125.

[17] Plain, *Twentieth-Century Crime Fiction*, p. 247.

Notes

[18] Menna Gallie Archive, Address to Swansea Writers' Group, L1/16.
[19] Menna Gallie Archive, Address to Neath Townswomen's Guild, L1/16.
[20] Menna Gallie Archive, Address to Swansea Writers' Group, L1/16.
[21] Menna Gallie Archive, Address to Swansea Writers' Group, L1/16.
[22] Menna Gallie Archive, Address to Swansea Writers' Group, L1/16.
[23] Menna Gallie Archive, Address to Swansea Writers' Group, L1/16.
[24] Menna Gallie Archive, Address to Swansea Writers' Group, L1/16.
[25] See Idris Davies, 'Gwalia Deserta XV', in *The Collected Poems of Idris Davies*, ed. Islwyn Jenkins (Llandysul: Gomer Press, 1990), pp. 34–5.
[26] In Kit Habianic's *Until Our Blood is Dry*, the politically committed striker Iwan Jones is described as reading his 'tall pink newspaper', possibly *The Morning Star*.
[27] Menna Gallie Archive, Address to Swansea Women Graduates, undated but probably given in the early 1970s, L1/16.
[28] Menna Gallie, 'For God's sake hold your tongue and let me love', *Cambridge Review*, 92/2199 (1970), 49–50 (p. 50).
[29] 'For God's sake hold your tongue and let me love', p. 50.
[30] See also Stephen Knight, 'Welsh Industrial Fiction by Women', in *British Industrial Fictions*, ed. H. Gustav Klaus and Stephen Knight (Cardiff: University of Wales Press, 2000), pp. 163–80 (p. 169); and Virgilia Peterson's review, in *Herald Tribune*, 7 February 1960; Gerwin, 'her too-loving brother': Menna Gallie Archive, L4/1.
[31] Angela V. John, *Strike for a Kingdom*, 'Introduction', p. xii.
[32] John Beynon, for example, notes how 'British (and in particular "English") masculinity was generally held to be superior to other "races"': *Masculinities and Culture* (Buckingham: Open University Press, 2002), p. 29.
[33] David Glover and Cora Kaplan, *Genders* (London: Routledge, 2000), p. 3. As the footnote immediately above illustrates, Glover and Kaplan would not be alone in arguably conflating the terms British and 'Anglo-Saxon' in gender studies.
[34] Lynne Segal notes that in Britain: 'Women learned the traits of nurturance, gentleness and the fear of success; men learned to be ambitious, rational and competitive': *Slow Motion: Changing Masculinities, Changing Men* (London: Virago, 1990), p. 65.
[35] Glover and Kaplan, *Genders*, p. 5.
[36] Susan Rowland, *From Agatha Christie to Ruth Rendell* (Basingstoke: Palgrave, 2001), p. 16.
[37] See Louis Althusser, *Lenin and Philosophy and Other Essays*, trans. Ben Brewster (New York: Monthly Review Press, 1972), pp. 144–6.
[38] G. G. Bolich, *Cross-dressing in Context*, vol. 4 (Raleigh, NC: Psyche's Press, 2008), p. 117.
[39] Judith Butler, 'Performative Acts and Gender Constitution: An Essay in Phenomenology and Feminist Theory', in *Performing Feminisms: Feminist*

Critical Theory and Theatre, ed. Sue-Ellen Chase (Baltimore and London: Johns Hopkins University Press, 1990), pp. 270–82 (p. 282).

[40] Gayle Rubin, 'The Traffic in Women: Notes on the "Political Economy" of Sex', in *Toward an Anthropology of Women*, ed. Rayna R. Reiter (New York and London: Monthly Review Press, 1975), pp. 157–210 (pp. 179–80).

[41] Stephen Knight, *A Hundred Years of Fiction*, p. 28. Leslie A. Fielder has noted the way 'the "boyish" theme recurs with especial regularity in American fiction', although he associates it, as in James Fenimore Cooper's 'Leatherstocking Tales', with escape and adventure: *Love and Death in the American Novel*, second edn (London: Penguin, 1984), pp. 181–2.

[42] David S. Gutterman, 'Postmodernism and the Interrogation of Masculinity', in *The Masculinities Reader*, ed. Stephen M. Whitehead and Frank J. Barrett (Cambridge: Polity Press, 2006), pp. 56–71 (p. 59).

[43] Jonathan Rutherford, *Forever England: Reflections on Masculinity and Empire* (London: Lawrence and Wishart, 1997), p. 21.

[44] *Strike for a Kingdom* is anticipating events here, for the Cow and Gate royal baby slogan did not appear until 1930.

[45] Macherey, *A Theory of Literary Production*, p. 99.

[46] Todd W. Reeser, *Masculinities in Theory: An Introduction* (Chichester: Wiley-Blackwell, 2010), p. 13.

[47] Plain, *Twentieth-Century Crime Fiction*, p. 90.

[48] Katie Gramich has an interesting paragraph on the interstitial gendering of boyhood in Rhys Davies's short stories where, '"the boy" may represent that third gender possibility which has continually fascinated writers as diverse as Théophile Gautier and Jeanette Winterson': 'The Masquerade of Gender in the Stories of Rhys Davies', in *Decoding the Hare*, ed. Meic Stephens (Cardiff: University of Wales Press 2001), pp. 204–15 (p. 209).

[49] Rubin, 'The Traffic in Women', p. 200.

[50] Roland Barthes, *Elements of Semiology*, trans. Annette Lavers and Colin Smith (New York: Hill and Wang, 1986), p. 77.

[51] Frank Lentricchia, *Criticism and Social Change* (Chicago and London: University of Chicago Press, 1983), p. 25.

[52] Braidotti, *Nomadic Theory*, p. 17.

[53] It is possible to interpret Williams's comments as arising from a class rather than a colonial difference, though his language suggests the latter. In his *Neighbours from Hell?* Mike Parker includes a photograph of the head and scarf-covered throat of a Welsh miner from an Edwardian postcard held by the National Library of Wales. It is mockingly headed: 'Daio Jenkins from the Rhondda Look You'. The miner's dusky appearance and physiognomy certainly suggest a racially inferior difference from the prototypical English male: Mike Parker, *Neighbours from Hell?* (Talybont: Y Lolfa, 2007), p. 18. This feeling of racial otherness, with its implied inferiority, was not peculiar to Williams. The racist writer Arthur Tysilio Johnson (1873–1956), for example, advised the Welsh in his polemical *The Perfidious Welshman*

(1910): 'Anglicise yourself as speedily as you can. It will never be possible for you to be equal to an Englishman': Parker, *Neighbours from Hell?*, pp. 18–19.
54   Kimmel, *The Gendered Society*, p. 76.
55   Kimmel, *The Gendered Society*, p. 69.
56   Plain, *Twentieth-Century Crime Fiction*, p. 4.
57   Bounderby is 'A man with a pervading appearance on him of being inflated like a balloon and ready to start': Charles Dickens, *Hard Times* [1854], ed. Kate Flint (London: Penguin, 2003), p. 20.
58   *Much Ado About Nothing*, in *The Arden Shakespeare*, ed. A. R. Humphreys (London: Methuen, 1981), III.v.41.
59   Plain, *Twentieth-Century Crime Fiction*, p. 90.
60   M. Wynn Thomas, 'Afterword' to Emyr Humphreys's *A Toy Epic* (Bridgend: Poetry of Wales Press, 1989), p. 144.
61   Though young herself during the 1926 strike, Gallie records that she was 'seared' by it. Prevented from joining the communal school meal for children of striking miners because her father was not a miner, she states that in *Strike for a Kingdom* she was 'trying to rid my conscience of both my father's guiltless guilt and my own': Menna Gallie Archive, Address to Swansea Writers' Group, L1/16, p. 7.
62   Connell, *Masculinities*, p. 193.
63   John Horne, 'The Age of Nation States and World Wars', in *Masculinities in Politics and War: Gendering Modern History*, ed. Stefan Dudink, Karen Hornemann and John Tosh (Manchester: Manchester University Press, 2004), pp. 22–39 (p. 29).
64   Rowland, *From Agatha Christie to Ruth Rendell*, p. 46.

Chapter 4

1   *So Long, Hector Bebb* [1970] (Cardigan: Parthian, 2006). All future references are to the Parthian edition.
2   Connell, *Masculinities*, p. 79.
3   Connell, *Masculinities*, p. 29.
4   In 1960, there were 106,000 south Wales miners; by 1970 there were 60,000.
5   Lynne Segal, *Slow Motion*, p. 13.
6   Anthony Clare, for example, believes that 'phallic man, authoritative, dominant, assertive – man in control not merely of himself but of woman – is starting to die, and now the question is whether a new man will emerge phoenix-like in his place or whether man himself will become largely redundant': Anthony Clare, *On Men: Masculinity in Crisis* (London: Chatto and Windus, 2000), p. 9.
7   *Times Literary Supplement* (1 January 1971), p. 5. Cited by Sarah Morse, '"Maimed Individuals": The Significance of the Body in *So Long, Hector*

Bebb (1970)', in *Mapping the Territory: Critical Approaches to Welsh Fiction in English*, ed. Katie Gramich (Cardigan: Parthian, 2010), pp. 271–87 (p. 272).

8 Daryl Leeworthy, 'The Full-Time Amateur: Sport in Ron Berry's South Walian Imagination', in *Fight and Flight: Essays on Ron Berry*, ed. Georgia Burdett and Sarah Morse (Cardiff: University of Wales Press, 2020), pp. 69–89 (p. 79).

9 William Faulkner, *As I Lay Dying* [1930] (London: Penguin, 1963), p. 67.

10 Daniel. G. Williams, *Wales Unchained: Literature, Politics and Identity in the American Century* (Cardiff: University of Wales Press, 2015), p. 45.

11 Craig Austin, 'Great Welsh Novels Revisited: So Long, Hector Bebb', *Wales Arts Review*, www.wales arts review (10 November 2016).

12 Niall Griffiths, 'Foreword' in *So Long, Hector Bebb*, p. xiii.

13 Shlomith Rimmon-Kenan, *Narrative Fiction: Contemporary Poetics* (London: Routledge, 1994), pp. 2, 3.

14 John Pikoulis records that, 'As a young man Berry was what he calls a "Shoni Tarzan"': 'Word-of-mouth cultures cease in cemeteries', *New Welsh Review*, 34 (Autumn 1996), 9–15 (p. 9).

15 Christopher E. Forth, *Masculinity in the Modern West: Gender, Civilisation and the Body* (Basingstoke: Palgrave Macmillan, 2008), p. 229.

16 Dorothy Yamamoto, *The Boundaries of the Human in Medieval English Literature* (Oxford: Oxford University Press, 2000), p. 10.

17 Gareth Jones, *The Boxers of Wales: Rhondda* (Cardiff: St David's Press, 2012), p. vi.

18 Kasia Boddy, *Boxing: A Cultural History* (London: Reaktion, 2009), p. 391.

19 Varda Burstyn, *The Rites of Men: Manhood, Politics and the Culture of Sport* (Toronto and London: University of Toronto Press, 1999), p. 166.

20 Ron Berry Archive, WWE/1/1/3/1, University of Swansea. The archive contains six drafts of the text, the last draft, WWE/1/1/3/6, being very close to the final version with a few corrections and additions.

21 In this draft, WWE/1/1/3/1, Prince Saddler's lover, Mrs Mainwaring, gives £100 towards Hector's surgery. She is removed from later drafts and Prince's more complex relationship with Jane Evass begins to emerge.

22 Leeworthy, 'The Full-Time Amateur', p. 82.

23 Joyce Carol Oates, *On Boxing* (London: Bloomsbury, 1987), p. 75.

24 Sarah Morse, '"Maimed Individuals": The Significance of the Body in *So Long, Hector Bebb* (1970)', p. 276.

25 Austin, 'Great Welsh Novels Revisited: *So Long, Hector Bebb*'.

26 Ian Watt, *The Rise of the Novel* (Harmondsworth: Penguin, 1963), pp. 88–9.

27 Forth, *Masculinity in the Modern West*, p. 10.

28 A term M. Wynn Thomas uses when writing of Emyr Humphreys, in which myth enriches and suggests a deep-rooted continuity of human experience in an otherwise realistic text. In Berry's novel, the term indicates how Hector Bebb is at once a gifted Valleys boxer and a lineal descendant of

heroic masculinities: 'The Relentlessness of Emyr Humphreys', *New Welsh Review*, 13 (1991), 37–40 (p. 39).

29 Lord Raglan, *The Hero: A Study in Tradition, Myth and Drama* (London: Methuen, 1936), p. 179.

30 Through Sammy's meteorological simile, the text teasingly hints at an extra-real agency fathering Hector. Zeus, we remember, came to Danaë as 'a piece of weather', a golden rain shower, and fathered Perseus, the slayer of monsters, on her.

31 Raglan, *The Hero*, p. 180.

32 Raglan, *The Hero*, p. 180.

33 Barbara Prys-Williams detects a similar elegiac and reverential quality in Berry's autobiography, *History is What You Live*, which she regards as 'a secular requiem': *Twentieth-Century Autobiography: Writing Wales in English* (Cardiff: University of Wales Press, 2004), p. 82.

34 Raglan, *The Hero*, p. 180.

35 Ron Berry Archive, WWE/1/1/3/1.

36 Ron Berry Archive, WWE/1/1/3/4.

37 Burstyn, *The Rites of Men*, p. 32.

38 Oates, *On Boxing*, p. 74.

39 Virgil, *The Aeneid*, Book V, trans. W. F. Jackson Knight (Harmondsworth: Penguin Classics, 1963), p. 133.

40 Tom Winnifrith, 'Funeral Games in Homer and Virgil', in *Leisure in Art and Literature*, ed. Michael Mallett (Basingstoke: Macmillan, 1992), pp. 14–26 (p. 16)

41 Bob Mee, 'Harry Greb dished out one of boxing history's most savage beatings', *Boxing News*, boxingnewsonline.net (22 October 2016), n.p.

42 See Ernest Hemingway's short story 'Fifty Grand', in *Men Without Women* (London: Jonathan Cape, 1975), pp. 114–56.

43 R. W. Connell, 'An Iron Man: The Body and Some Contradictions of Hegemonic Masculinity', in *Sport, Men and the Gender Order*, ed. Michael A. Messner and Donald F. Sabo (Champaign, IL: Human Kinetic Books, 1990), pp. 83–95 (p. 85).

44 Forth, *Masculinity in the Modern West*, p. 230.

45 A likely reference to a scene from the Western *The Magnificent Seven*, dir. John Sturges (1960), where the gunfighter Lee (Robert Vaughn) tests his reaction time by snatching at flies on a table.

46 Dai Smith, 'Focal Heroes: A Welsh Fighting Class', in *Sport and the Working Class in Modern Britain*, ed. Richard Holt (Manchester: Manchester University Press, 1990), pp.198–217 (p. 200).

47 Forth, *Masculinity in the Modern West*, p. 8.

48 Morse, 'Maimed Individuals', pp. 281–2.

49 Morse, 'Maimed Individuals', p. 282.

50 Oates, *On Boxing*, p. 13. Writing of the heavyweight boxer Rocky Marciano, she observes that he 'trained with the most monastic devotion', focusing

unremittingly on his opponent 'as the cloistered monk or nun chooses by an act of fanatical will to "see" only God' (pp. 28–9).

[51] Forth, *Masculinity in The Modern West*, p. 219.

[52] Ron Berry, 'A Necessary Kind of Love', unpublished essay, a copy of which was given to me by his daughter, Dr Lesley Berry.

[53] Ron Berry, undated audiotape interview with Dai Smith: 'My influences were American authors, English authors', University of Swansea Miners' Library; my transcription. See also Mark Glancy, who suggests that it was through the Western that 'generations of Britons became acquainted with American folklore, history and myth': *Hollywood and the Americanisation of Britain: from the 1920s to the Present* (London: I. B. Tauris, 2014), p. 212.

[54] Tompkins, *West of Everything*, p. 41.

[55] *Shorter Oxford English Dictionary*, third edn (Oxford: Clarendon Press, 1964), vol. II, p. 2018: 'U.S., a waterproof coat, 1884'.

[56] Tompkins, *West of Everything*, p. 81.

[57] Roger Bartra, *Wild Men in the Looking Glass*, trans. Carl T. Berrisford (Ann Arbor: University of Michigan Press, 1994). Bartra sees the wild man as 'white, bearded, with an abundant head of hair' (p. 88).

[58] Dorothy Yamamoto, *The Boundaries of the Human in Medieval English Literature* (Oxford: Oxford University Press, 2000), p. 144.

[59] Forth writes that Tarzan 'experienced a resurgence in popularity in the early 1960s', the decade when *So Long, Hector Bebb* was written: *Masculinity in the Modern West*, p. 219.

[60] Tompkins, *West of Everything*, p. 81.

[61] Roger Bartra, *The Artificial Savage: Modern Myths of the Wild Man*, trans. Christopher Follett (Ann Arbor: University of Michigan Press, 1997). Bartra distinguishes between the 'European wild man' and the 'savage': 'The former belongs to a Western myth with a long history; the latter is used for people "discovered" and colonised by modern Europe', pp. 165, 164.

[62] Daniel Defoe, *Robinson Crusoe* [1729] (London: Penguin, 2012), p. 97.

[63] Defoe, *Robinson Crusoe*, p. 145.

[64] Defoe, *Robinson Crusoe*, p. 45.

[65] Emma Smith, *Masculinity in Welsh Writing in English*, p. 143.

[66] Bartra, *The Artificial Savage*, p. 268.

[67] Emma Davies, '"Manufacturing men": literary masculinities in industrial Welsh writing in English' (unpublished MA thesis, University of Swansea, 2001), p. 34.

[68] Sigmund Freud, 'Beyond the Pleasure Principle', The Penguin Freud Library, trans. James Strachey, ed. Angela Richards (London: Penguin, 1984), vol. 11, pp. 275–338 (p. 282).

[69] Freud, 'Beyond the Pleasure Principle', p. 282.

[70] Henri-Frédéric Amiel (1821–81), cited by Christopher E. Forth, *Masculinity and the Modern West*, p. 141.

Chapter 5

1. Roger Granelli, *Dark Edge* (Bridgend: Seren, 1997); Kit Habianic, *Until Our Blood is Dry* (Cardigan: Parthian, 2014). All future references are to these editions.
2. Huw Beynon and Peter McMylor, 'Decisive Power: The New Tory State against the Miners', in *Digging Deeper*, ed. Huw Beynon (London: Verso, 1985), pp. 29–45 (p. 33).
3. Knight, 'A New Enormous Music', p. 84.
4. John MacInnes, 'The Crisis of Masculinity and the Politics of Identity', in *The Masculinities Reader*, ed. Stephen M. Whitehead and Frank J. Barrett (Cambridge: Polity Press, 2001), pp. 311–29 (p. 324).
5. Christopher Lasch, *The Culture of Narcissism* (New York and London: W. W. Norton, 1979), p. 41.
6. Narcissism as a disorder is defined by Anthony Giddens as 'a preoccupation with the self which prevents the individual from establishing valid boundaries between self and external worlds': *Modernity and Self-Identity: Self and Society in the Late Modern Age* (Cambridge: Polity Press, 2006), p. 170.
7. Bethan Benwell, 'Introduction', in *Masculinity and Men's Lifestyle Magazines*, ed. Bethan Benwell (Oxford: Blackwell, 2003), pp. 6–29 (p. 8).
8. Tolson, *The Limits of Masculinity*, p. 48.
9. Segal, *Slow Motion*, p. 255.
10. Anthony Giddens, *Europe in the Global Age* (Cambridge: Polity Press, 2007), p. 137.
11. See Anthony Clare, *On Men: Masculinity in Crisis*, pp. 69, 85 for discussions on the crises of identity some men experience when work no longer defines them.
12. George Monbiot, *How Did We Get into This Mess?* (London: Verso, 2016), p. 10.
13. Liz Jones, review of *Until Our Blood is Dry*, *Planet*, 216 (2014), 157–8 (p. 157).
14. Giddens, *Modernity and Self-Identity: Self and Society in the Late Modern Age*, p. 170.
15. Richard John Evans, review of *Dark Edge*, *New Welsh Review*, 40 (1998), 88–9 (p. 89).
16. Susan Rubin Suleiman, *Authoritarian Fictions: The Ideological Novel as a Literary Genre* (New York: Columbia University Press, 1983), p. 7.
17. Suleiman, *Authoritarian Fictions*, p. 10.
18. Braidotti, *Nomadic Theory*, p. 27.
19. Evans, review of *Dark Edge*, 88.
20. See Roger Horrocks, *Male Myths and Icons; Masculinity in Popular Culture* (London: Palgrave Macmillan, 1995), p. 18.
21. Rutherford, 'Preface', *Masculinity and Men's Lifestyle Magazines*, p. 3.

[22] Rutherford, 'Preface', *Masculinity and Men's Lifestyle Magazines*, p. 2.
[23] Butler, *Gender Trouble*, p. 185.
[24] Giddens, *Modernity and Self-Identity*, p. 172.
[25] Lasch, *The Culture of Narcissism*, p. 202.
[26] Homi K. Bhabha, *The Location of Culture*, p. 29.
[27] Forth, *Masculinity in the Modern West*, p. 220.
[28] Catherine Merriman, review of *Dark Edge*, *Planet*, 131 (1998), 104–5 (p. 105).
[29] Merriman, review of *Dark Edge*, p. 105.
[30] Suleiman, *Authoritarian Fictions*, pp. 22–3.
[31] Braidotti, *Nomadic Theory*, p. 133.
[32] Monbiot, *How Did We Get into This Mess?*, p. 10.
[33] Kit Habianic, 'Getting to Know ... Kit Habianic', interview with Lorraine Mace and Maureen Vincent-Northam, *The Writer's ABC Checklist* (20 August 2014), n.p.
[34] From Idris Davies's *Gwalia Deserta*: 'And we shall remember 1926 until our blood is dry': *Collected Poems of Idris Davies*, p. 30.
[35] Williams, 'The Welsh Industrial Novel', in *Who Speaks for Wales?*, p. 105.
[36] Liz Jones, review of *Until Our Blood is Dry*, 157.
[37] See Freud, 'On Narcissism', The Penguin Freud Library, vol. 11, p. 67.
[38] Giddens, *Modernity and Self-Identity*, p. 171.
[39] Connell, 'a masculinity particularly involved in the maintenance of patriarchy': *Masculinities*, p. 18.
[40] Whitehead, *Men and Masculinities*, p. 94.
[41] Giddens, *Modernity and Self-Identity*, p. 191.
[42] Giddens, *Modernity and Self-Identity*, p. 191.
[43] Dylan Moore, review of *Until Our Blood is Dry*, *Wales Arts Review*, 10 (22 May 2014), n.p.
[44] Middleton, *The Inward Gaze*, p. 152.
[45] Jacques Lacan, *Écrits: A Selection*, trans. Alan Sheridan (London and New York: Routledge, 1989), p. 18.
[46] Gramsci, *Selections from the Prison Notebooks*, p. 266.
[47] Moore, review of *Until Our Blood is Dry*.
[48] M. M. Bakhtin, 'The *Bildungsroman* and Its Significance in the History of Realism (Toward a Historical Typology of the Novel)', in *Speech Genres and Other Late Essays*, trans. Vern W. McGee (Austin: University of Texas Press, 1986), pp. 10–59 (p. 23).
[49] Bakhtin, 'The *Bildungsroman* and Its Significance in the History of Realism', pp. 23–4.
[50] 'Chronotope' is a term coined by Bakhtin for 'the intrinsic connectedness of temporal and spatial relationships that are artistically expressed in literature': M. M. Bakhtin, *The Dialogic Imagination*, ed. Michael Holquist, trans. Caryl Emerson and Michael Holquist (Austin: University of Texas Press, 1998), p. 85.

Notes

51 Kirsti Bohata, *Postcolonialism Revisited* (Cardiff: University of Wales Press, 2004) p. 80.
52 Bhabha, *The Location of Culture*, p. 63.
53 There are no clear references to the American Western in *Dark Edge*, but Edwin's quasi-religious response to landscape bears a remarkable similarity to the hero of Owen Wister's *The Virginian* (1902), and arguably suggests how deeply embedded in the Valleys' imagination were Western images of freedom, yearning and self-transformation. Wister's hero states, for example: 'Often when I have camped here, it has made me want to become the ground, become the water, become the trees, mix with the whole thing. Not know myself from it. Never unmix again': Owen Wister, *The Virginian: A Horseman of the Plains* (New York: Dover Thrift Edition, 2006), p. 267.
54 Bhabha, *The Location of Culture*, p. 28.
55 Bakhtin, 'The *Bildungsroman* and Its Significance in the History of Realism', p. 24.
56 James A. Davies, '"Two Strikes and You're Out": 1926 and 1984 in Welsh Industrial Fiction', in *British Industrial Fictions*, ed. Gustav Klaus and Stephen Knight (Cardiff: University of Wales Press, 2000), p. 146.
57 M. Wynn Thomas and Jane Aaron, 'Pulling You Through the Changes', in *A Guide to Welsh Literature*, vol. VII: *Welsh Writing in English*, ed. M. Wynn Thomas, pp. 278–309 (p. 295).
58 Davies, 'Two Strikes and You're Out', p. 146.
59 Charlotte Williams, 'I going away, I going home', cited by Kirsti Bohata, *Postcolonialism Revisited*, p. 27.
60 Whitehead, *Men and Masculinities*, p. 153.
61 Macherey, *A Theory of Literary Production*, p. 87: 'we investigate the silence, for it is the silence that is doing the speaking.'
62 Giddens, *Modernity and Self-Identity*, p. 176.
63 See Rosalind Gill, 'Power and the Production of Subjects: A Genealogy of the New Man and the New Lad', in *Masculinity and Men's Lifestyle Magazines,* ed. Bethan Benwell (Oxford: Blackwell, 2003), pp. 34–56 (p. 37). John Beynon believes that in the new man, 'elements from both the nurturer and the narcissist strands have been scrambled together' and need to be unscrambled: *Masculinities and Culture* (Buckingham: Open University Press, 2002), p. 99.
64 Gill, 'Power and the Production of Subjects', p. 39.
65 Gill, 'Power and the Production of Subjects', p. 37.
66 Butler, *Gender Trouble*, p. 51.
67 Giddens, *Modernity and Self-Identity*, p. 6.
68 Segal, *Slow Motion*, p. 269.
69 Anthony Clare, *On Men*, p. 135.
70 Iwan is frequently described reading 'his tall pink newspaper'. Given that Scrapper is 'A communist like his dad' (*Until Our Blood*, p. 42), 'pink' here probably identifies it as *The Morning Star*.

71 Whitehead, *Men and Masculinities*, pp.152–3.
72 Middleton, *The Inward Gaze*, p. 121.
73 Beddoe, in 'Images of Welsh Women': 'Wales […] is a land of coalminers, rugby players and male voice choirs', p. 227.
74 Bhabha, *The Location of Culture*, p. 231.
75 Bhabha, *The Location of Culture*, p. 230.
76 Bhabha, *The Location of Culture*, p. 230.
77 See David L. Collinson and Jeff Hearn, '"Breaking the Silence": On Men, Masculinities and Managements', in *Men as Managers, Managers as Men*, ed. Collinson and Hearn, pp. 1–24 (p. 3).
78 Norman Fairclough, *Language and Power* [1989], 3rd edn (Abingdon: Routledge, 2015), p. 184.
79 Ross Poole, 'Modernity, Rationality and "The Masculine"', p. 50.
80 Poole, 'Modernity, Rationality and "The Masculine"', p. 50.
81 Poole, 'Modernity, Rationality and "The Masculine"', p. 54.
82 Poole, 'Modernity, Rationality and "The Masculine"', p. 54.
83 Poole, 'Modernity, Rationality and "The Masculine"', p. 52.
84 Lasch, *The Culture of Narcissism*, p. 222.
85 See Collinson and Hearn, 'Breaking the Silence: On Men, Masculinities and Managements', p. 3.
86 Fairclough, *Language and Power*, p. 78.
87 See Raymond Williams, *Keywords* (London: Fontana, 1990), p. 191.
88 Lentricchia, *Criticism and Social Change*, p. 150.
89 Fairclough, *Language and Power*, p. 113.
90 Alan Sinfield, *Literature, Politics and Culture in Postwar Britain* (Berkeley and Los Angeles: University of California Press, 1989), p. 34.
91 David Howell, '"Where's Ramsay MacKinnock?" Labour Leadership and the Miners', in *Digging Deeper*, pp.181–98 (p. 197). See also James Thomas, '"Taffy was a Welshman, Taffy was a Thief": Anti-Welshness, the Press and Neil Kinnock', *Llafur*, 7/2 (1997), 95–108.
92 Bakhtin, *The Dialogic Imagination*, p. 271.
93 Wendy Holloway, 'Masters and Men in the Transition from Factory Hands to Sentimental Workers', in *Men as Managers, Managers as Men*, ed. David L. Collinson and Jeff Hearn, pp. 25–42 (p. 29).
94 Collinson and Hearn note that 'business suits appear to have a transnational significance': 'Breaking the Silence: On Men, Masculinities and Managements', in *Men and Managers, Managers as Men*, p. 11. In *Until Our Blood is Dry*, they have a cultural significance also. The text's reference to the suits worn by Cross, Henshall and Turnbull links Cross with metropolitan 'power dressers' rather than with his constituents.
95 Wendy Holloway, 'Masters and Men in the Transition from Factory Hands to Sentimental Workers', p. 29.
96 Poole, 'Modernity, Rationality and the "Masculine"', p. 50.

⁹⁷ John Sam Jones, W*elsh Boys Too* (Cardigan: Parthian, 2000). See also: Daryl Leeworthy, *A Little Gay History of Wales* (Cardiff: University of Wales Press, 2019).

⁹⁸ Wynn Thomas and Aaron, 'Pulling You Through the Changes', p. 305.

⁹⁹ Ian M. Harris, *Messages Men Hear: Constructing Masculinities* (London: Taylor and Francis, 1995), p. 1.

¹⁰⁰ Terry Threadgold, 'Introduction', *Feminine/Masculine and Representation*, ed. Terry Threadgold and Anne Cranny-Francis (London: Unwin Hyman, 1990), pp. 1–35 (p. 31).

¹⁰¹ See Victoria Robinson, Alexandra Hall and Jenny Hockey, 'Masculinities, Sexualities and the Limits of Subversion: Being a Man in Hairdressing', *Men and Masculinities*, 14/1 (2011), 31–50. The article notes 'the tenacity of associations between hairdressing, femininity and homosexuality and their "problematic" place in the schemes generated by hegemonic masculinity' (p. 46).

¹⁰² Butler, *Gender Trouble*, p. 140.

¹⁰³ Robinson, Hall and Hockey, 'Subversion Masculinities, Sexualities and the Limits of Being a Man in Hairdressing', p. 38.

¹⁰⁴ Segal, *Slow Motion*, p. 151.

¹⁰⁵ As Tim Edwards, for instance, points out, 'The equation of fashion with the feminine, with the not masculine, with the effeminate, as well as with the homosexual, remains a chain of socially constructed and perpetuated links that are decidedly difficult to overcome': *Men in the Mirror: Men's Fashion, Masculinity and Consumer Society* (London: Cassell, 1997), p. 4.

¹⁰⁶ Kimmel, *The Gendered Society*, p. 237.

¹⁰⁷ See Connell, 'from the point of view of hegemonic masculinity, gayness is easily assimilated to femininity': *Masculinities*, p. 78.

¹⁰⁸ Devaney, 'Mining – a World Apart', p. 157.

¹⁰⁹ Bakhtin, *The Dialogic Imagination*, p. 45.

¹¹⁰ Macherey, *A Theory of Literary Production*, p. 86.

¹¹¹ Macherey, *A Theory of Literary Production*, p. 86.

¹¹² Connell, *Masculinities*, p. 78.

¹¹³ Schoene-Harwood, *Writing Men*, p. 174.

¹¹⁴ Harris, *Messages Men Hear: Constructing Masculinities*, p. 3.

¹¹⁵ Katie Gramich, 'Both In and Out of the Game: Welsh Writers and the British Dimension', in *A Guide to Welsh Literature*: vol. VII, ed. M. Wynn Thomas (Cardiff: University of Wales Press, 2003), p. 255.

¹¹⁶ Threadgold, 'Introduction', in *Feminine/Masculine and Representation*, p. 4.

¹¹⁷ Wynn Thomas and Aaron, 'Pulling You Through the Changes', p. 305.

¹¹⁸ Rosalind Gill, 'Power and the Production of Subjects: A Genealogy of the New Man and the New Lad', p. 39.

[119] Ned Thomas, 'Wales', in *The Oxford Guide to Contemporary World Literature*, ed. John Sturrock (Oxford: Oxford University Press, 1996), pp. 432–46 (p. 444).
[120] MacInnes, *The End of Masculinity*, p. 77.

Conclusion

[1] Beddoe, 'Images of Welsh Women', p. 227.
[2] George Orwell, *The Road to Wigan Pier* [1937] (London: Penguin, 1986), pp. 18–31 (pp. 18, 31).
[3] Orwell, *The Road to Wigan Pier*, p. 18.
[4] Daniel G. Williams, *Wales Unchained: Literature, Politics and Identity in the American Century*, p. 45.
[5] Pascale Casanova, *The World Republic of Letters*, trans. M. B. Devoise (Cambridge MA: Harvard University Press, 2004), p. 175.
[6] Connell, *Masculinities*, p. 77.
[7] Butler, *Gender Trouble*, p. 191.
[8] Macherey, *A Theory of Literary Production*, p. 101.
[9] Macherey, *A Theory of Literary Production*, p. 101.
[10] A term Anthony Giddens has coined to describe 'mechanisms which prise social relations free from the hold of specific locales, re-combining them across wide time-space distances': *Modernity and Self-Identity* (Cambridge: Polity Press, 1991), p. 2.

Bibliography

Primary Texts

Arnold, Matthew, 'Thyrsis', in *The Oxford Book of English Verse 1250–1918*, ed. Sir Arthur Quiller-Couch [1900, new edn 1939] (Oxford: Oxford University Press, repr. 1979).

Berry, Ron, 'A Necessary Kind of Love', unpublished essay. Private collection of Dr Lesley Berry.

——, *Flame and Slag* [1968], Foreword by Leighton Andrews (Cardigan: Parthian, 2012).

——, *So Long, Hector Bebb* [1970] (Cardigan: Parthian, 2006).

Bush, Duncan, *Glass Shot* (London: Martin Secker and Warburg, 1991).

Coombes, Bert, *These Poor Hands: The Autobiography of a Miner Working in South Wales* [1939] (Cardiff: University of Wales Press, 2011).

Defoe, Daniel, *Robinson Crusoe* [1729] (London: Penguin, 2012).

Davies, Tom, *Black Sunlight* (London: Macdonald, 1986).

Davies, Idris, *Collected Poems*, ed. Islwyn Jenkins, 2nd edn (Llandysul: Gomer Press, 1990).

Davies, Rhys, *My Wales* (New York and London: Funk and Wagnalls, 1938).

Dickens, Charles, *Hard Times* [1854], ed. Kate Flint (London: Penguin, 2003).

Evans, Caradoc, *My People* [1915] (Bridgend: Seren, 1987).

Faulkner, William, *As I Lay Dying* [1930] (London: Penguin, 1963).

Gallie, Menna, *Strike for a Kingdom* [1959], ed. Angela V. John (Dinas Powys: (Honno Welsh Women's Classics, 2003 and 2011).

——, *The Small Mine* [1962], ed. Jane Aaron (Dinas Powys: Honno, 2000).

——, *Travels with a Duchess* [1968], ed. Angela V. John (Dinas Powys: Honno, 2011).

Granelli, Roger, *Dark Edge* (Bridgend: Seren, 1997).

Gunn, Thom, 'Sense', in *Collected Poems* (London: Faber and Faber, 1993).

Habianic, Kit, *Until Our Blood is Dry* (Cardigan: Parthian, 2014).

Heinemann, Margot, *The Adventurers* (London: Lawrence and Wishart, 1960).

Hemingway, Ernest, 'Fifty Grand', in *Men Without Women* (London: Jonathan Cape, 1975).

Homer, *The Odyssey*, trans. E. V. Rieu (Harmondsworth: Penguin, 1948).

Jarrett, Nigel, *Miners at the Quarry Pool* (Cardigan: Parthian, 2013).

Jones, Gwyn, *Richard Savage* (London: Victor Gollancz, 1935).
——, *Times Like These* [1936] (London: Victor Gollancz, 1979).
Jones, Jack, *Black Parade* [1935] (Cardigan: Parthian, 2009).
——, *Rhondda Roundabout* [1934] (London: Hamish Hamilton, 1949).
Jones, Jon Sam, *Welsh Boys Too* (Cardigan: Parthian, 2000).
Jones, Lewis, *Cwmardy* [1937] (London: Lawrence and Wishart, 1978).
——, *We Live* [1939] (London: Lawrence and Wishart, 1978).
Llewellyn, Richard, *How Green was My Valley* [1939] (London: Four Square, 1958).
Marvell, Andrew, 'The Picture of Little T. C. in a Prospect of Flowers', in *The Poems of Andrew Marvell*, ed. Hugh MacDonald (London: Routledge and Kegan Paul, 1963).
Meredith, Christopher, *Shifts* (Bridgend: Seren, 1988).
Milton, John, 'L'Allegro', in *John Milton: Poems*, ed. B. A. Wright (London: J. M. Dent, 1962).
Mortimer, John, *Paradise Postponed* (London: Viking, 1985).
Shakespeare, William, *Hamlet*, in *The Arden Shakespeare*, ed. Ann Thompson and Neil Taylor (London: Thomson Learning, 2006).
——, *Much Ado About Nothing*, in *The Arden Shakespeare*, ed. A. R. Humphreys (London: Methuen, 1981).
Sheers, Owen, *The Green Hollow* (London: Faber, 2016).
Sinclair, Upton, *The Jungle* [1906] (London: Penguin, 1965).
Smith, Dai, *Dream On* (Cardigan: Parthian, 2013).
——, *The Crossing* (Cardigan: Parthian, 2020).
Theocritus, *Greek Pastoral Poetry,* trans. Anthony Holden (London: Penguin, 1974).
Thomas, Gwyn, *Sorrow for Thy Sons* (London: Lawrence and Wishart, 1986).
Thomas, R. S., *Selected Poems,* ed. Anthony Thwaite (London: J. M. Dent, 1996).
Trezise, Rachel, *Sixteen Shades of Crazy* (London: Blue Door, 2010).
Virgil, *The Aeneid*, trans. W. F. Jackson Knight (London: Penguin, 1956).
Walsh, Louise, *Black River* (Llanrwst: Gwasg Carreg Gwalch, 2016).
Williams, Raymond, *Loyalties* (London: Chatto and Windus, 1985).
Wister, Owen, *The Virginian: A Horseman of the Plains* [1902] (New York: Dover Thrift, 2006).
Zola, Émile, *Germinal* [1885], trans. Leonard Tancock (London: Penguin, 1954, repr è. 1983).

Archives Consulted

Berry, Ron, Centre for Research into the English Literature and Language of Wales, University of Swansea.
Gallie, Menna, National Library of Wales, Aberystwyth.

Bibliography

Jones, Gwyn, National Library of Wales, Aberystwyth.
Jones, Lewis, South Wales Miners' Library, University of Swansea.

Secondary Texts

Aaron, Jane, 'Foreword', in *The Small Mine* (Dinas Powys: Honno Welsh Women's Classics, 2000).
Adorno, Theodor W., *The Culture Industry* (London: Routledge, 1992).
Alpers, Paul, *What is Pastoral?* (Chicago: University of Chicago Press, 1997).
Althusser, Louis, *Lenin and Philosophy and Other Essays,* trans. Ben Brewster (New York: Monthly Review Press, 1971).
Andrews, Leighton, 'Foreword', in *Flame and Slag* (Cardigan: Parthian, 2012).
Austin, Craig, 'Great Welsh Novels Revisited: *So Long, Hector Bebb*', *Wales Arts Review*, www.walesonline (10 November 2016).
Bachelard, Gaston, *The Poetics of Space* (Boston, MA: Beacon Press, 1969).
Bailly, Lionel, *Lacan* (Oxford: One World, 2012).
Bakhtin, Mikhail M., 'The *Bildungsroman* and Its Significance in the History of Realism (Toward a Historical Typology of the Novel)', in *Speech Genres and Other Late Essays*, trans. Vern W. McGee (Austin: University of Texas Press, 1986), pp. 10–59.
——, *The Dialogic Imagination*, ed. Michael Holquist, trans. Caryl Emerson and Michael Holquist (Austin: University of Texas Press, 1998).
——, *Rabelais and His World,* trans. Hélène Iswolsky (Bloomington: Indiana University Press, 1984).
Barrell, John, *Poetry, Language and Politics* (Manchester: Manchester University Press, 1988).
Barthes, Roland, *Elements of Semiology*, trans. Annette Lavers and Colin Smith (New York: Hill and Wang, 1986).
——, *The Pleasure of the Text*, trans. Richard Miller (New York: Hill and Wang), 1975.
——, *S/Z*, trans. Richard Miller (Oxford: Blackwell, 2002).
Bartra, Roger, *The Artificial Savage: Modern Myths of the Wild Man*, trans. Christopher Follett (Ann Arbor: University of Michigan Press, 1997).
——, *Wild Men in the Looking Glass: The Mythic Origins of European Otherness*, trans. Carl T. Berrisford (Ann Arbor: University of Michigan Press, 1994).
Baudrillard, Jean, 'Simulacra and Simulations', in *Jean Baudrillard: Selected Writings*, ed. Mark Poster (Stanford: Stanford University Press, 1988).
Bayard, Elizabeth, in *Saturday Review*, 16 January 1960 (Menna Gallie Archive), National Library of Wales, Aberystwyth.
Beddoe, Deirdre, 'Images of Welsh Women', in *Wales, The Imagined Nation*, ed. Tony Curtis (Bridgend: Poetry Wales, 1986), pp. 227–37.
Bell, David, *Ardent Propaganda: Miners' Novels and Class Conflict 1929–1939* (Uppsala: Swedish Science Press, 1995).

Belsey, Catherine, *Critical Practice* (London: Methuen, 1980).
Benwell, Bethan, 'Introduction' to *Masculinity and Men's Lifestyle Magazines*, ed. Bethan Benwell (Oxford: Blackwell, 2003), pp. 6–29.
Bernheimer, Richard, *Wild Men in the Middle Ages: A Study in Art, Sentiment and Demonology* (Cambridge, MA: Harvard University Press, 1952).
Beynon, Huw, and Peter McMylor, 'Decisive Power: The New Tory State against the Miners', in *Digging Deeper*, ed. Huw Beynon (London: Verso, 1985), pp. 29–45.
Beynon, John, *Masculinities and Culture* (Buckingham: Open University Press, 2002).
Bhabha, Homi K., *The Location of Culture* (London: Routledge, 1993).
Bianchi, Tony, 'Aztecs in Troedrhiwgwair: recent fictions in Wales', in *Peripheral Visions*, ed. Ian A. Bell (Cardiff: University of Wales Press, 1995), pp. 44–76.
Blevins, Winfred (ed.), *Dictionary of the American West* (Ware: Wordsworth, 1995).
Bly, Robert, *Iron John* (London: Rider, 2001).
Boddy, Kasia, *Boxing: A Cultural History* (London: Reaktion, 2009).
Bodington, Steve, 'The Political Morality of Work', in *The Achilles Heel Reader: Men, Sexual Politics and Socialism*, ed. Victor J. Seidler (London: Routledge, 1991), pp. 176–82.
Bohata, Kirsti, *Postcolonialism Revisited* (Cardiff: University of Wales Press, 2004).
Bolich, G. G., *Cross-dressing in Context* (Raleigh, NC: Psyche's Press, 2008).
Braidotti, Rosi, *Nomadic Subjects: Embodiment and Sexual Difference in Contemporary Feminist Theory*, second edn (New York: Columbia University Press, 2011).
——, 'The Contested Posthumanities', in *Conflicting Humanities,* ed. Rosi Braidotti and Paul Gilroy (London: Bloomsbury, 2016).
Brendon, Piers, *The Decline and Fall of the British Empire 1781–1997* (London: Vintage, 2008).
Brewer, John, *The Pleasures of the Imagination: English Culture in the Eighteenth Century* (London: Routledge, 2013).
Brod, Harry, and Michael Kaufman, *Theorising Masculinities* (London: SAGE, 1994).
Brown, Tony, 'Separate, different, individual', *New Welsh Review*, 48 (2000), 20–2.
Buell, Laurence, *Writing for an Endangered World* (Cambridge, MA: Harvard University Press, 2001).
Bunce, Michael, *The Countryside Ideal: Anglo-American Images of Landscape* (London: Routledge, 1994).
Burdett, Georgia, 'Filling the void: representing disability in contemporary Welsh writing in English during the twentieth century' (unpublished doctoral thesis, University of Swansea, 2015).
Burdett, Georgia, and Sarah Morse (eds), *Fight and Flight: Essays on Ron Berry* (Cardiff: University of Wales Press, 2020).

Burstyn, Varda, *The Rites of Men: Manhood, Politics and the Culture of Sport* (Toronto and London: University of Toronto Press, 1999).

Butler, Judith, *Excitable Speech: A Politics of the Performative* (London: Routledge, 1997).

——, *Gender Trouble: Feminism and the Subversion of Identity* [1990] (Abingdon: Routledge, 2006).

——, 'Performative Acts and Gender Constitution: An Essay in Phenomenology and Feminist Theory', in *Performing Feminisms: Feminist Critical Theory and Theatre*, ed. Sue-Ellen Chase (Baltimore and London: Johns Hopkins University Press, 1990), pp. 270–82.

Byrne, Aidan, 'Constructions of Masculinity in Four 1930s Welsh Novels in English: Lewis Jones's *Cwmardy* and *We Live*, Richard Llewellyn's *How Green Was My Valley*, and Gwyn Thomas's *Sorrow For Thy Sons* (unpublished doctoral thesis, University of Wolverhampton, 2007).

——, '"The Male Shoutings of Men": Masculinity and Fascist Epistemology in *How Green Was My Valley*', in *The International Journal of Welsh Writing in English*, vol. 1, ed. Alyce von Rothkirch (Cardiff: University of Wales Press, 2013), pp. 167–90.

Campbell, Beatrix, *Wigan Pier Revisited: Poverty and Politics in the 80s* (London: Virago, 1984).

Casanova, Pascale, *The World Republic of Letters*, trans. M. B. De Bevoise (Cambridge, MA: Harvard University Press, 2004).

Chatman, Seymour, *Story and Discourse: Narrative Structure in Fiction and Film* (Ithaca and London: Cornell University Press, 1980).

Clare, Anthony, *On Men: Masculinity in Crisis* (London: Chatto and Windus, 2000).

Cobley, Paul, *Narrative* (London: Routledge, 2001).

Collini, Stefan, *Public Moralists: Political Thought and Intellectual Life in Britain 1850–1930* (Oxford: Clarendon Press, 1999).

——, *The Nostalgic Imagination: History in English Criticism* (Oxford: Oxford University Press, 2019).

Collinson, David L., and Jeff Hearn, 'Breaking the Silence: On Men, Masculinities and Managements', in *Men as Managers, Managers as Men*, ed. David L. Collinson and Jeff Hearn (London: SAGE, 1996), pp. 1–24.

Connell, R. W., 'An Iron Man: The Body and Some Contradictions of Hegemonic Masculinity', in *Sport, Men and the Gender Order*, ed. Michael A. Messner and Donald F. Sabo (Champaign, IL: Human Kinetic, 1990), pp. 83–95.

——, *Gender and Power* (Cambridge: Polity Press in association with Blackwell, 1996).

——, *Masculinities* (Cambridge: Polity Press, 2005).

——, *The Men and the Boys* (Cambridge: Polity Press, 2000).

Connell, R. W., and James Messerschmidt, 'Hegemonic Masculinity: Rethinking the Concept', *Gender & Society*, 19 (2005), 829–59.

Courtney-Morgan, Steffan, 'Masculinity and the miners' strike in south Wales 1984–85' (unpublished doctoral thesis, University of Swansea, 2008).
Crang, Mike, *Cultural Geography* (London: Routledge, 1998).
Cullen, Patrick, *Spenser, Marvell and Renaissance Pastoral* (Cambridge, MA: Harvard University Press, 1970).
Cunningham, Valentine, *British Writers of the Thirties* (Oxford: Oxford University Press, 1988).
——, 'The Age of Anxiety and Influence: or, Tradition and the Thirties Talents', in *Rewriting the Thirties: Modernism and After*, ed. Keith Williams and Steven Matthews (London: Addison-Wesley Longman, 1997).
Curtis, Ben, 'The Miner's Lamp', *www.walesonline* (9 May 2013).
Davies, Emma, 'He Was a Queer Lad for his Age', *Welsh Writing in English*, ed. Tony Brown, 8 (2003), 29–45.
——, '"Manufacturing men": literary masculinities in industrial Welsh writing in English' (unpublished MA thesis, University of Swansea, 2001).
Davies, James A., 'Kinds of Relating: Gwyn Thomas (Jack Jones, Lewis Jones, Gwyn Jones) and the Welsh Industrial Experience', *The Anglo-Welsh Review*, 86 (1987), 73–86.
——, '"Two Strikes and You're Out": 1926 and 1984 in Welsh Industrial Fiction', in *British Industrial Fictions*, ed. H. Gustav Klaus and Stephen Knight (Cardiff: University of Wales Press, 2000), pp. 137–47.
Davies, John, *A History of Wales* (London: Penguin, 1993).
Davies, Rebecca, '"Not just supporting but leading": the involvement of the women of the south Wales coalfield in the 1984–85 miners' strike' (unpublished doctoral thesis, University of Glamorgan, 2010).
Dawson, Graham, 'The Blond Bedouin', in *Manful Assertions: Masculinities in Britain since 1800*, ed. Michael Roper and John Tosh (London: Routledge, 1991), pp. 113–44.
Day, Gary, *Class* (London and New York: Routledge, 2001).
de Beauvoir, Simone, *The Second Sex* [1949], trans. H. M. Parchley (London: Vintage, 1997).
de Berg, Henk, *Freud's Theory and Its Use in Literary and Cultural Studies* (Rochester, NY: Camden House, 2003).
DeKoven, Marianne, *Rich and Strange: Gender, History, Modernism* (Princeton: Princeton University Press, 1991).
Devaney, Kevin, 'Mining – A World Apart', in *The Achilles Heel Reader*, ed. Victor J. Seidler (London: Routledge, 1991), pp. 151–60.
Dentith, Simon, 'Tone of Voice in Industrial Writings in the 1930s', in *British Industrial Fictions*, ed. H. Gustav Klaus and Stephen Knight (Cardiff: University of Wales Press, 2000).
Docker, John, *Postmodernism and Popular Culture* (Cambridge: Cambridge University Press, 1994).
Donaldson, Mike, 'What is Hegemonic Masculinity?', *Theory and Society*, Special Issue: *Masculinities,* 22/5 (1993), 643–57.

Eagleton, Terry, *Criticism and Ideology: A Study in Marxist Literary Theory* (London: Verso, 1992).

Easthope, Anthony, *What a Man's Gotta Do: The Masculine Myth in Popular Culture* (London and New York: Routledge, 1992).

Edley, N., and M. Wetherell, *Men in Perspective: Practice, Power and Identity* (Hemel Hempstead: Prentice Hall/Harvester Wheatsheaf, 1995).

Edwards, T., *Men in the Mirror: Men's Fashion, Masculinity and Consumer Society* (London: Cassell, 1997).

Empson, William, *Some Versions of Pastoral* [1935] (London: Chatto and Windus, 1968).

Ettin, Andrew V., *Literature and the Pastoral* (New Haven and London: Yale University Press, 1984).

Evans, Geraint, and Helen Fulton (eds), *The Cambridge History of Welsh Literature* (Cambridge: Cambridge University Press, 2019).

Evans, Richard John, Review of *Dark Edge*, *New Welsh Review*, 40 (1998), 88–9.

Fairclough, Norman, *Language and Power* (Abingdon: Routledge, 2015).

Faludi, Susan, *Stiffed: The Betrayal of the Modern Man* (London: Vintage, 2000).

Farrell, Warren, *The Myth of Male Power* (New York: Berkley, 2001).

Ferrebe, Alice, *Masculinity in Male-Authored Fiction, 1950–2000* (London: Palgrave Macmillan, 2005).

Fiedler, Leslie A., *Love and Death in the American Novel* (London: Penguin, 1984).

Fish, Angela, 'Flight-deck of experience', *New Welsh Review*, 18 (1992), 60–4.

Fish, Stanley, *Is There a Text in This Class?* (Cambridge, MA: Harvard University Press, 1990).

Forth, Christopher E., *Masculinity and the Modern West: Gender, Civilisation and the Body* (Basingstoke: Palgrave Macmillan, 2008).

Fox, Pamela, *Class Fictions* (Durham, NC: Duke University Press, 1994).

Francis, Hywel, Interview with Billy Griffiths, unpublished archive, Swansea Miners' Library, University of Swansea, (1969).

——, 'Foreword', in *Cwmardy* and *We Live* (Cardigan: Parthian, Library of Wales edn, 2006).

Francis, Hywel and Dai Smith, *The Fed* (London: Lawrence and Wishart, 1980).

Freud, Sigmund, 'On Narcissism' and 'Beyond the Pleasure Principle', The Penguin Freud Library, vol. 11, trans. James Strachey, ed. Angela Richards (London: Penguin, 1991).

Fromm, Erich, *Marx's Concept of Man* (New York: Frederick Ungar, 1961).

Frow, John, *Genre* (London: Routledge, 2005).

George, Philip, 'Three Rhondda Working Class Writers', *Llafur*, 3/2 (1981), 5–13.

Giddens, Anthony, *Capitalism and Modern Social Theory: An Anaylsis of the Writings of Marx, Durkheim and Max Weber* (Cambridge: Cambridge University Press, 1987).

——, *Europe in the Global Age* (Cambridge: Polity Press, 2007).

——, *Modernity and Self-Identity: Self and Society in the Late Modern Age* (Cambridge: Polity Press, 2006).
Gidwell, David Ingli, 'Life writing: the Rhondda and Ron Berry' (unpublished doctoral thesis, Cardiff University, 2007).
Gifford, Terry, *Pastoral* (New York and London: Routledge, 1999).
Gill, Rosalind, 'Rethinking Masculinity: Men and their Bodies', *fathom.lse,ac,uk* (12 March 2016).
——, 'Power and the Production of Subjects: A Genealogy of the New Man and the New Lad', in *Masculinity and Men's Lifestyle Magazines*, ed. Bethan Benwell (Oxford: Blackwell, 2003).
Glancy, Mark, *Hollywood and the Americanisation of Britain: From the 1920s to the Present* (London: I. B. Tauris, 2014).
Glover, David, and Cora Kaplan, *Genders* (London: Routledge, 2000).
Gramich, Katie, 'Both In and Out of the Game: Welsh Writers and the British Dimension', in *A Guide to Welsh Literature*, vol VII: *Welsh Writing in English*, ed. M. Wynn Jones (Cardiff: University of Wales Press, 2003), pp. 255–77.
——, 'Cymru or Wales? Explorations in a divided sensibility', in *Studying British Cultures: An Introduction*, ed. Susan Basnett (London and New York: Routledge, 1997), pp. 97–112.
——, 'Mountains and Mirrors', *Planet*, 128 (1998), 70–5.
——, 'Pimps, Punks and Pub Crooners: Anarchy and Anarchism in Contemporary Welsh Fiction', in *To Hell with Culture*, ed. H. Gustav Klaus and Stephen Knight (Cardiff: University of Wales Press, 2005), pp. 178–93.
——, 'The Masquerade of Gender in the Stories of Rhys Davies', in *Decoding the Hare*, ed. Meic Stephens (Cardiff: University of Wales Press, 2001), pp. 204–15.
——, '"Those Blue Remembered Hills": Gender in Twentieth-century Welsh Border Writing by Men', in *Gendering Border Studies*, ed. Jane Aaron, Henrice Altink and Chris Weedon (Cardiff: University of Wales Press, 2010), pp. 142–62.
——, *Twentieth-Century Women's Writing in Wales: Land, Gender, Belonging* (Cardiff: University of Wales Press, 2007).
Gramsci, Antonio, *Selections from the Prison Notebooks*, ed. and trans. Quintin Hoare and Geoffrey Nowell-Smith [1971] (London: Lawrence and Wishart, 2003).
Greenblatt, Stephen, *Renaissance Self-Fashioning* (Chicago and London: University of Chicago Press, 1980).
Griffiths, Ceri, *Literature in the Public Service: Sublime Bureaucracy* (Basingstoke: Palgrave Macmillan, 2003).
Gross, Elizabeth, 'Inscriptions and body-maps: representations and the corporeal', in *Feminine/Masculine Representation*, ed. Terry Threadgold and Anne Cranny-Francis (London: Unwin Hyman, 1990), pp. 62–74.
——, 'The Body of Signification', in *Abjection, Melancholia and Love*, ed. John Fletcher and Andrew Benjamin (London and New York: Routledge, 1990–1), pp. 80–103.

Gutterman, David S., 'Postmodernism and the Interrogation of Masculinity', in *The Masculinities Reader*, ed. Stephen M. Whitehead and Frank J. Barrett (Cambridge: Polity Press, 2006), pp. 56–71.
Habianic Kit, *Wales Online* (22 August 2014).
Hamilton Buckley, Jerome, *Season of Youth: The Bildungsroman from Dickens to Golding* (Cambridge, MA: Harvard University Press, 1974).
Hammond, Paul, *Love between Men in English Literature* (London: Macmillan, 1996).
Harris, Ian M., *Messages Men Hear: Constructing Masculinities* (London: Taylor and Francis, 1995).
Harvey, Karen, *Reading Sex in the Eighteenth Century: Bodies and Gender in English Erotic Culture* (Cambridge: Cambridge University Press, 2004).
Hawthorn, Jeremy, *Unlocking the Text* (London: Edward Arnold, 1987).
Head, Dominic, *The Cambridge Introduction to Modern British Fiction, 1950–2000* (Cambridge: Cambridge University Press, 2002).
Hendon, Steve, 'The Landscape of "Particular Men": Representations of Great War Masculinities: Llewelyn Wyn Griffith and David Jones', in *The International Journal of Welsh Writing in English*, vol 2, ed. Alyce von Rothkirch (Cardiff: University of Wales Press, 2014), pp. 54–82.
Hirsch, Marianne, 'The Novel of Formation as Genre', *Genre*, 12/3 (1979), 293–311.
Hogenkamp, Bert, 'Miners' Cinemas in South Wales in the 1920s and 1930s', *Llafur*, 4/2 (1985), 64–76.
Holden, Anthony, *Greek Pastoral Poetry* (London: Penguin, 1974).
Holderness, Graham, 'Miners and the Novel: from bourgeois to proletarian', in *The British Working-Class Novel in the Twentieth Century,* ed. J. M. Hawthorn (London: Edward Arnold, 1984), pp. 19–35.
Holloway, Wendy, 'Masters and Men in the Transition from Factory Hands to Sentimental Workers', in *Men as Managers, Managers as Men*, ed. David L. Collinson and Jeff Hearn (London: SAGE, 1996), pp. 25–42.
Holman, C. Hugh, and William Harmon, *A Handbook to Literature* (New York: Macmillan, 1992).
Hooker, Jeremy, *Imagining Wales: A View of Modern Welsh Writing in English* (Cardiff: University of Wales Press, 2001).
Hopkins, Chris, *English Fiction in the 1930s: Language, Genre, History* (London: Continuum, 2006).
Horne, John, 'The Age of Nation States and World War', in *Masculinities in Politics and War: Gendering Modern History*, ed. Stefan Dudink, Karen Hornemann and John Tosh (Manchester: Manchester University Press, 2004), pp. 22–39.
Horrocks, Roger, *Male Myths and Icons: Masculinity in Popular Culture* (London: Palgrave Macmillan, 1995).
——, *Masculinity in Crisis* (Basingstoke: Palgrave Macmillan, 1994).

Howell, David, '"Where's Ramsey McKinnock?" Labour Leadership and the Miners', in *Digging Deeper*, ed. Huw Beynon (London: Verso, 1985), pp. 181–98.

Husband, Timothy, *The Wild Man: Medieval Myth and Symbolism* (New York: Metropolitan Museum of Art, 1981).

James, David, and Philip Tew, *New Versions of Pastoral: Post-Romantic, Modern and Contemporary Responses to the Tradition* (Madison, WI: Fairleigh Dickinson University Press, 2009)

Jameson, Frederic, 'Postmodernism and Consumer Society', in *Postmodern Culture*, ed. Hal Foster (London: Pluto, 1985), pp. 111–25.

John, Angela V., 'A Miner Struggle? Women's Protests in Welsh Mining History', *Llafur*, 4/2 (1984), 72–90.

——, 'Introduction', in *Strike for a Kingdom* [1959] (Dinas Powys: Honno Welsh Women's Classics, 2003 and 2011).

—— (ed.), *Our Mothers' Land: Chapters in Welsh Women's History 1830–1939* (Cardiff: University of Wales Press, 1991), pp. 1–16.

——, 'Place, Politics and History: The Life and Novels of Menna Gallie', *Llafur*, 9/3 (2006), 47–57.

——, *Rocking the Boat: Welsh Women Who Championed Equality 1840–1990* (Cardigan: Parthian, 2018).

Jones, Gareth, The *Boxers of Wales: Rhondda* (Cardiff: St David's Press, 2012).

Jones, Glyn, *The Dragon has Two Tongues* (London: J. M. Dent, 1968).

Jones, Gwyn, 'Anglo-Welsh Literature, 1934–1946: A Personal View', *Transactions of the Honourable Society of Cymmrodorion* (London: Issued by the Society, 1987).

——, *Collected Short Stories* (Cardiff: University of Wales Press, 1997).

Jones, Liz, Review of *Until Our Blood is Dry*, *Planet*, 216 (2014), 157–8.

Kimmel, Michael S., 'Masculinity as Homophobia: Fear, Shame and Silence in the Construction of Gender Identity', in *The Masculinities Reader*, ed. Stephen M. Whitehead and Frank J. Barrett (Cambridge: Polity Press, 2006), pp. 266–87.

——, *The Gendered Society* (Oxford and New York: Oxford University Press, 2000).

Kirk, John, *Twentieth Century Writing and the British Working Class* (Cardiff: University of Wales Press, 2003).

Klaus, H. Gustav, 'Socialist Fiction in the 1930s: Some Preliminary Observations', in *The 1930s: A Challenge to Orthodoxy*, ed. John Lucas (Brighton: Harvester, 1978), pp. 13–41.

Knight, Stephen, 'A collective challenge to constraining forces', *New Welsh Review*, 47 (1999), 28–31.

——, *A Hundred Years of Fiction* (Cardiff: University of Wales Press, 2004).

——, '"A New Enormous Music": Industrial Fiction in Wales', in *A Guide to Welsh Literature*, vol. VII: *Welsh Writing in English*, ed. M. Wynn Thomas (Cardiff: University of Wales Press, 2003), pp. 47–90.

——, 'Anarcho-Syndicalism in Welsh Fiction in English', in *To Hell With Culture*, ed. H. Gustav Klaus and Stephen Knight (Cardiff: University of Wales Press, 2005), pp. 51-63.

——, *Crime Fiction, 1800–2000: Detection, Death, Diversity* (Basingstoke: Palgrave Macmillan, 2003).

——, 'How Red Was My Story', *Planet*, 98 (1993), 83–95.

——, 'Industrial Fiction', in *The Cambridge History of Welsh Literature,* ed. Geraint Evans and Helen Fulton (Cambridge: Cambridge University Press, 2019), pp. 388–404.

——, 'The Golden Age', in *The Cambridge Companion to Crime Fiction*, ed. Martin Priestman (Cambridge: Cambridge University Press, 2003), pp. 77–94.

——, '"The Uncertainties and Hesitations that were the Truth": Welsh Industrial Fictions by Women', in *British Industrial Fictions*, ed. H. Gustav Klaus and Stephen Knight (Cardiff: University of Wales Press, 2000), pp. 163–80.

Knights, Ben, *Writing Masculinities* (London: Macmillan, 1999).

Kristeva, Julia, *Powers of Horror: An Essay in Abjection* (New York: Columbia University Press, 1982).

Lacan, Jacques, *Écrits: A Selection*, trans. Alan Sheridan (London and New York: Routledge, 1989).

Lasch, Christopher, *The Culture of Narcissism* (New York and London: W.W. Norton,1991).

Leeworthy, Daryl, *A Little Gay History of Wales* (Cardiff: University of Wales Press, 2019).

——, 'The Full-Time Amateur: Sport in Ron Berry's South Walian Imagination,' in *Fight and Flight*, ed. Georgia Burdett and Sarah Morse (Cardiff: University of Wales Press, 2020), pp. 69–89.

Lentricchia, Frank, *Criticism and Social Change* (Chicago and London: University of Chicago Press, 1983).

Leverenz, David, *Manhood and the American Renaissance* (Ithaca and London: Cornell University Press, 1989).

——, 'The Last Man in America', in *The American Literary History Reader*, ed. Gordon Hutner (Oxford: Oxford University Press, 1995), pp. 262–76.

Light, Julie, 'Manufacturing the Past – The Representation of Mining Communities in History, Literature and Heritage: "Fantasies of a World that Never Was?"', *Llafur*, 8.1 (2000), 19–31.

Linton, Ralph, *The Study of Man* (New York: Appleton-Century-Crofts, 1936).

Lodge, David, *After Bakhtin: Essays on Fiction and Criticism* (London and New York: Routledge, 1990).

Lovering, John, 'The Theory of the Internal Colony', *Planet*, 45/46 (November 1978), 89–96.

Mace, Lorraine, and Maureen Vincent-Norman, 'Getting to Know Kit Habianic', *The Writer's ABC Checklist* (20 August 2014).

Macherey, Pierre, *A Theory of Literary Production* [1966], trans. Geoffrey Wall (London: Routledge and Kegan Paul, 1978).

MacInnes, John, 'The Crisis of Masculinity and the Politics of Identity', in *The Masculinities Reader*, ed. Stephen M. Whitehead and Frank J. Barrett (Cambridge: Polity Press, 2001), pp. 311–29.

——, *The End of Masculinity* (Buckingham: Open University Press, 1998).

Magennis, Caroline, *Sons of Ulster: Masculinities in the Contemporary Northern Ireland Novel* (Dublin: Peter Lang, 2010).

Mallet, Phillip (ed.), *The Victorian Novel and Masculinity* (Basingstoke: Palgrave Macmillan, 2015).

Marinelli, Peter V., *Pastoral* (London: Methuen, 1971).

Marx, Karl, 'Economic and Philosophical Manuscripts', in Erich Fromm, *Marx's Concept of Man* (New York: Frederick Ungar, 1961).

McGill, Michael E., *The McGill Report on Male Intimacy* (New York: Harper and Row, 1985).

Mee, Bob, *Boxing News*, www.boxingonline (22 October 2014).

Merriman, Catherine, Review of *Dark Edge*, *Planet*, 131 (1998), 104–5.

Meyn, Rolf, 'Lewis Jones's *Cwmardy* and *We Live:* Two Welsh Proletarian Novels in Transatlantic Perspective', in *British Industrial Fictions,* ed. H. Gustav Klaus and Stephen Knight (Cardiff: University of Wales Press, 2000), pp. 124–36.

Middleton, Peter, *The Inward Gaze: Masculinity and Subjectivity in Modern Culture* (London and New York: Routledge, 1992).

Mingay, G. E., *English Landed Society in the Eighteenth Century* (London: Routledge and Kegan Paul, 1963).

Monbiot, George, *How Did We Get into This Mess?* (London: Verso, 2016).

Moore, Dylan, Review of *Until Our Blood is Dry*, *Wales Art Review*, 10 (22 May 2014).

Moore, Robert, and Douglas Gillette, *King, Warrior, Magician, Lover: Rediscovering the Archetypes of the Mature Masculinity* (New York: HarperCollins, 1991).

Morgan, David H. J., *Discovering Men* (London and New York: Routledge, 1992).

Morgan, Kenneth O., *Rebirth of a Nation* (Cardiff: University of Wales Press, 2002).

Morse, Sarah, '"Maimed Individuals": The Significance of the Body in *So Long, Hector Bebb* (1970)', in *Mapping the Territory: Critical Approaches to Welsh Fiction in English*, ed. Katie Gramich (Cardigan: Parthian, 2010), pp. 271–87.

——, 'The black pastures: the significance of landscape in the work of Gwyn Thomas and Ron Berry' (unpublished doctoral thesis, University of Swansea, 2010).

Morton, H. V., *In Search of England* (London: Methuen, 1927).

Mulvey, Laura, 'Visual Pleasure and Narrative Cinema' [1975], in *Film Theory and Criticism: Introductory Readings*, ed. Leo Braudy and Marshall Cohen (New York: Oxford University Press, 1999), pp. 833–44.

Nardi, Peter M., 'Seamless Souls: An Introduction to Men's Friendships', in *Men's Friendships*, ed. Peter M. Nardi (London, SAGE, 1992), pp. 1–14.

——, 'Sex, Friendship and Gender Roles Among Gay Men', in *Men's Friendships*, ed. Peter M. Nardi (London, SAGE, 1992), pp. 173–85.

Newman, John Henry, *The Idea of a University Defined and Illustrated: In Nine Discourses Delivered to the Catholics of Dublin* (Project Gutenberg, 2008).

Oates, Joyce Carol, *On Boxing* (London: Bloomsbury, 1987).

O'Leary, Paul, 'Masculine Histories: Gender and the Social History of Modern Wales', *The Welsh History Review*, 22/2 (2004), 252–77.

Orwell, George, *The Road to Wigan Pier* [1937] (London: Penguin, 1986).

Osborne, Huw, *Queer Wales: The History, Culture and Politics of Queer Life in Wales* (Cardiff: University of Wales Press, 2016).

Parker, Mike, *Neighbours from Hell?* (Talybont: Y Lolfa, 2007).

Paxton, Nancy L., *George Eliot and Herbert Spencer: Feminism, Evolutionism and the Reconstruction of Gender* (Princeton: Princeton University Press, 1991).

Petersen, Alan, 'Research on Men and Masculinities: Some Implications of Recent Theory, for Future Work', *Men and Masculinities*, 6 (2003), 54–69.

Pikoulis, John, 'Heroes of Zero Ambition', *New Welsh Review*, 50 (2000), 6–33.

——, 'Lewis Jones', *The Anglo-Welsh Review*, 74 (1983), 62–71.

——, Review of *History is What you Live*, *New Welsh Review*, 41 (1998), 78–9.

——, 'The Wounded Bard', *New Welsh Review*, 26 (1994), 22–39.

——, 'Word-of-mouth cultures cease in cemeteries', *New Welsh Review*, 34 (1996), 9–15.

Plain, Gill, *Twentieth-Century Crime Fiction: Gender, Sexuality and the Body* (Edinburgh: Edinburgh University Press, 2001).

Poole, Ross, 'Modernity, Rationality and "the Masculine"', in *Feminine/Masculine and Representation*, ed. Terry Threadgold and Anne Cranny-Francis (London: Unwin Hyman, 1990), pp. 46–60.

Price, Cecil, *Gwyn Jones* (Cardiff: University of Wales Press, 1976).

Prys-Williams, Barbara, *Twentieth-Century Autobiography: Writing Wales in English* (Cardiff: University of Wales Press, 2004).

Raglan, Lord, *The Hero: A Study in Tradition, Myth and Drama* (London: Methuen, 1936).

Reeser, Todd W., *Masculinities in Theory: An Introduction* (Chichester: Wiley-Blackwell, 2010).

Reilly, Matthew, *Edward Elgar and the Nostalgic Imagination* (Cambridge: Cambridge University Press, 2009).

Renfrew, Alistair, *Towards a New Material Aesthetics: Bakhtin, Genre and the Fates of Literary Theory* (London: Legenda, 2006).

Rimmon-Kenan, Shlomith, *Narrative Fiction: Contemporary Poetics* (London: Routledge, 1994).

Robinson, Sally, *Marked Men: White Masculinity in Crisis* (New York: Columbia University Press, 2000).

Robinson, Victoria, Alexander Hall and Jenny Hockey, 'Masculinities, Sexualities and the Limits of Subversion: Being a Man in Hairdressing', *Men and Masculinities*, 14/1 (2011), 31–50.

Rosen, David, *The Changing Fictions of Masculinity* (Urbana and Chicago: University of Illinois Press, 1993).

Rowland, Susan, *From Agatha Christie to Ruth Rendell* (Basingstoke: Palgrave, 2001).

Rubin, Gayle, 'The Traffic in Women: Notes on the "Political Economy" of Sex', in *Toward an Anthropology of Women*, ed. Rayna R. Reiter (New York and London: Monthly Review Press), 1975, pp. 157–210.

Rutherford, Jonathan, *Forever England: Reflections on Masculinity and Empire* (London: Lawrence and Wishart, 1997).

——, 'Preface' in *Masculinity and Men's Lifestyle Magazines*, ed. Bethan Benwell (Oxford: Blackwell, 2003).

Said, Edward, *Orientalism* (London: Penguin, 1978).

Scaggs, John, *Crime Fiction* (London and New York: Routledge, 2005).

Schoene-Harwood, Berthold, *Writing Men: Literary Masculinities from 'Frankenstein' to the New Man* (Edinburgh: Edinburgh University Press, 1999).

Schwartz, Bill, 'Let Them Eat Coal', in *Digging Deeper*, ed. Huw Beynon (London: Verso, 1985), pp. 47–68.

Sedgwick, Eve Kosofsky, *Between Men: English Literature and Male Homosocial Desire* (New York: Columbia University Press, 1985).

Segal, Lynne, *Slow Motion: Changing Masculinities; Changing Men* (London: Virago, 1990).

Seidler, Victor J., *Man Enough: Embodying Masculinities* (London: SAGE, 1997).

——, 'Rejection, Vulnerability and Friendship', in *Men's Friendships*, ed. Peter M. Nardi (London: SAGE, 1992), pp. 15–34.

——, 'The Sexual Politics of Men's Work', in *The Achilles Heel Reader*, ed. Victor J. Seidler (London: Routledge, 1991), pp. 125–39.

Shaw, Katy, *Mining the Meaning: Cultural Representations of the UK 1984–85 Miners' Strike* (Newcastle upon Tyne: Cambridge Scholars, 2012).

Shorter Oxford English Dictionary [1933], ed. C. T. Onions; third edn, ed. G. W. S Friedrichsen (Oxford: Oxford University Press, 1973, repr. 1974).

Shur, Owen, *Victorian Pastoral: Tennyson, Hardy and the Subversion of Forms* (Columbus: Ohio State University Press, 1989).

Sinfield, Alan, *Literature, Politics and Culture in Postwar Britain* (Berkeley and Los Angeles: University of California Press, 1989).

Smith, David, 'A Novel History', in *Wales: The Imagined Nation: Essays in Cultural and National Identity,* ed. Tony Curtis (Bridgend: Seren, 1991), pp. 129–58.

——,'Author's Notes', *Wales Online* (10 August 2013)

——, 'Focal Heroes: A Welsh Fighting Class', in *Sport and the Working Class in Modern Britain*, ed. Richard Holt (Manchester and New York: Manchester University Press, 1990), pp. 198–217.
——, 'Introduction', in *Cwmardy* (London: Lawrence and Wishart, 1991).
——, *Lewis Jones* (Cardiff: University of Wales Press, 1982).
——, 'Myth and Meaning in the Literature of the South Wales Coalfield – the 1930s', *The Anglo-Welsh Review*, 22/49 (1976), 1–41.
Smith, Emma, *Masculinity in Welsh Writing in English: The Cases of Lewis Jones, Glyn Jones, Gwyn Thomas and Ron Berry* (Saarbrücken: VDM, 2009).
Snee, Carole, 'Working Class Literature or Proletarian Writing?', in *Culture and Crisis in Britain in the 1930s*, ed. Jon Clark, Margot Heinemann and David Margolies (London: Lawrence and Wishart, 1974).
Spender, Dale, *Man Made Language* (London and New York: Routledge, 1980).
Srivastva, Suresh, and Frank J. Barrett, 'The Transforming Nature of Metaphors in Group Development', *Human Relations*, 41/1 (1988), 31–64.
Stallybrass, Peter, and Allon White, *The Politics and Poetics of Transgression* (Ithaca and New York: Cornell University Press, 1986).
Stanhope, Philip Dormer, fourth Earl of Chesterfield, *Lord Chesterfield's Letters*, ed. and intro. David Roberts (Oxford: Oxford University Press, 1992).
Steinberg, Warren, *Masculinity: Identity, Conflict and Transformation* (Boston, MA: Shambala, 1993).
Stephens, Meic, *The Oxford Companion to the Literature of Wales*, compiled and ed. Meic Stephens (Oxford: Oxford University Press, 1986).
Stephens, Raymond, 'The Novelist and Community: Menna Gallie', *Anglo-Welsh Review*, 14/34 (1964–5), 52–63.
Storr, Anthony, *Freud* (Oxford: Oxford University Press, 1989).
Suleiman, Susan Rubin, *Authoritarian Fictions: The Ideological Novel as a Literary Genre* (New York: Columbia University Press, 1983).
Sullivan, Ceri, *Literature in the Public Service: Sublime Bureaucracy* (Basingstoke: Palgrave Macmillan, 2013).
Symons, Julian, *Bloody Murder* (London: Viking, 1985).
Tambling, Jeremy, *Narrative and Ideology* (Milton Keynes: Open University Press, 1991).
Taylor, D. J., Review of David Lodge, *Quite a Good Time to Be Born: A Memoir: 1935–1975*, *Guardian Review*, 17 January 2015, p. 6.
Taylor, Ian, 'The life and works of Ron Berry' (unpublished MA thesis, University of Swansea, 1998).
Threadgold, Terry, 'Introduction', in *Feminine/Masculine and Representation*, ed. Terry Threadgold and Anne Cranny-Francis (London: Unwin Hyman, 1990), pp. 1–35.
Tolson, Andrew, *The Limits of Masculinity* (London: Tavistock, 1977).
Thomas, James, '"Taffy was a Welshman, Taffy was a Thief": Anti-Welshness, the Press and Neil Kinnock', *Llafur*, 7/2 (1997), 95–108.

Thomas, M. Wynn, 'Afterword' in Emyr Humphreys, *A Toy Epic* (Bridgend: Seren, 1989).

———, *Internal Difference: Twentieth-Century Writing in Wales* (Cardiff: University of Wales Press, 1992).

———, 'The Relentlessness of Emyr Humphreys', *New Welsh Review*, 13 (1991), 37–40.

Thomas, M. Wynn, and Jane Aaron, 'Pulling You Through the Changes', in *A Guide to Welsh Literature*, vol VII: *Welsh Writing in English*, ed. M. Wynn Thomas (Cardiff: University of Wales Press, 2003), pp. 278–309.

Thomas, Ned, 'Parallels and Paradigms', in *A Guide to Welsh Literature*, vol. VII: *Welsh Writing in English*, ed. M. Wynn Thomas (Cardiff: University of Wales Press, 2003), pp. 310–26.

———, 'Wales', in *The Oxford Guide to Contemporary World Literature*, ed. John Sturrock (Oxford: Oxford University Press, 1996), pp. 432–46.

Tompkins, Jane, *West of Everything* (Oxford: Oxford University Press, 1992).

Thompson, E. P., *The Making of the English Working Class* [1963] (London: Penguin, 1968).

Tosh, John, 'Domesticity and Manliness', in *Manful Assertions: Masculinities in Britain since 1800*, ed. Michael Roper and John Tosh (London: Routledge, 1991), pp. 44–73.

———, 'Hegemonic Masculinity and the History of Gender', in *Masculinities in Politics and War: Gendering Modern History*, ed. Stefan Dudink, Karen Hagemann and John Tosh (Manchester: Manchester University Press, 2004), pp. 41–62.

———, *Maleness and Masculinities in Nineteenth-Century Britain* (Harlow: Pearson, 2005).

von Rothkirch, Alyce, 'Liberty and the Party Line: Novelising Working-Class History in Lewis Jones's *Cwmardy* and *We Live*', in *Mapping the Territory: Critical Approaches to Welsh Fiction in English,* ed. Katie Gramich (Cardigan: Parthian, 2010), pp. 81–101.

———, 'There's a Change Come over the Valley: Masculinism in Early Twentieth-century Welsh Drama in English', in *Beyond the Difference,* ed. Daniel G. Williams and Alyce von Rothkirch (Cardiff: University of Wales Press, 2004), pp. 71–83.

Ward, Michael R. M., 'The performance of young working-class masculinities in the south Wales Valleys' (unpublished doctoral thesis, Cardiff University, 2013).

Ward, Stephanie, 'The Life and Work of Menna Gallie: Llafur Welsh People's History', *History Workshop Journal,* 63/1 (2007), 369–71.

Watt, Ian, *The Rise of the Novel* (London: Penguin, 1963).

Whitehead, Stephen M., *Men and Masculinities* (Cambridge: Polity Press, 2002).

Whitehead, Stephen M., and Frank J. Barrett, *The Masculinities Reader* (Cambridge: Polity Press, 2006).

Williams, Daniel G., *Black Skin; Blue Books* (Cardiff: University of Wales Press, 2012).
——, *Wales Unchained: Literature, Politics and Identity in the American Century* (Cardiff: University of Wales Press, 2015).
Williams, Gareth, '"The Dramatic Turbulence of Some Irrecoverable Football Game": Sport, Literature and Welsh Identity', in *Sport in the Making of Celtic Cultures*, ed. Grant Jarvie (London: Leicester University Press, 1999), pp. 55–70.
Williams, Gwyn A., *When Was Wales?* (London: Penguin, 1991).
Williams, Raymond, *Communications* (London: Penguin, 1962).
——, *Culture and Society 1780–1950* (London: Penguin, 1982).
——, 'Culture is Ordinary' [1958], in *Resources of Hope: Culture, Democracy, Socialism* (London: Verso, 1989), pp. 3–14.
——, *Keywords* (London: Fontana, 1990).
——, *Marxism and Literature* [1977] (Oxford: Oxford University Press, 2009).
——, *The Country and the City* (Oxford: Oxford University Press, 1973).
——, 'The Social Significance of 1926', *Llafur*, 2/2 (1977), 5–8.
——, 'The Welsh Industrial Novel,' in *Who Speaks for Wales? Nation, Culture, Identity*, ed. Daniel Williams (Cardiff: University of Wales Press, 2003), pp. 95–111.
——, 'Working-Class, Proletarian, Socialist: Problems in Some Welsh Novels', in *The Socialist Novel in Britain*, ed. H. Gustav Klaus (Brighton: Harvester Press, 1982), pp. 110–37.
Wright, Martin, *Wales and Socialism*, (unpublished doctoral thesis, Cardiff University, 2011).
Yallop, Helen, *Age and Identity in Eighteenth-century England* (Abingdon: Routledge, 2013).
Yamamoto, Dorothy, *The Boundaries of the Human in Medieval English Literature* (Oxford: Oxford University Press, 2000).

Index

Aaron, Jane, 73, 136, 148, 153, 159
Aberfan disaster, 11–12
adultery, 81, 92, 104, 122, 150
adulthood, 52, 54, 56, 79, 85–8, 89, 92, 93, 97
Aeneid, 106–7
agency, 9, 16, 17, 26, 51, 56, 67, 83, 87, 101, 129, 134, 142
alienation, 28, 45, 46, 53, 71
alpha males, 19, 124
ambition, 7, 14, 31, 34–8, 52, 125
America, 12, 64, 70, 107, 113, 158
Amiel, Henri-Frédéric, 118
amorality, 18–19, 144
anglicisation, 35, 80, 85, 91, 93, 95, 158
animality, 101, 110, 114–15, 118
anxieties, 7, 17, 60, 61–2, 91, 137, 147
arete, 103–4, 110
Arnold, Matthew, 22–3
As I Lay Dying (Faulkner), 100, 158
Augustanism, 7, 29–32
Austin, Craig, 100, 103
Australia, 64, 109
authenticity, 9, 36–7, 54, 109, 125
authoritarianism, 73, 95, 120, 121, 122, 123–4, 130
autobiography, 47–9, 157
autonomy, 6, 8, 49–50, 57, 64, 72, 87, 91–2, 130

Bakhtin, Mikhail, 10, 50, 84, 134, 136, 147, 151
banter, 23, 26, 27–8, 56, 68
Barrett, Frank J., 59
Barthes, Roland, 75, 76, 90

Bartra, Roger, 115, 116
Beddoe, Deirdre, 1, 142, 156
Bell, David, 45, 50, 51
Benwell, Bethan, 121
Berry, Ron, 9–10, 101, 103, 107, 112, 113; *see also So Long, Hector Bebb*
Beynon, Huw, 120
Bhabha, Homi K., 8, 127, 136, 142
Bildungsroman, 8, 10, 11, 47, 49–52, 55, 57, 72, 87, 88, 93, 120, 134–7, 154
Black River (Walsh), 12
Boddy, Kasia, 101
bodies *see* female body; male body
Bodington, Steve, 45, 49
Boer War, 64, 68–71
Bohata, Kirsti, 135, 159
Bolich, G. G., 84
boxing, 1, 9, 99–111, 117, 118, 158
boyhood, 52, 54, 56, 85–8, 97
Braidotti, Rosi, 1, 6, 8, 124
Brewer, John, 31
Brown, Tony, 35
brutality, 9, 13, 17–18, 19, 31–2, 53, 103, 122, 124–5, 127–8; *see also* violence
Bunce, Michael, 30
Burstyn, Varda, 101, 106
business, 7, 14–15, 32, 34–8, 42
Butler, Judith, 2, 4, 19, 27, 41, 53, 69, 84–5, 124–5, 149, 159
Byrne, Aidan, 45, 54

capitalism
  and autonomy, 6, 8, 49, 130
  in *Cwmardy*, 8, 45–6, 47, 49, 51–2, 64, 65, 72, 83

and individual identity, 6, 8, 45–6, 47, 49, 51, 65, 85, 124–5, 130, 157
industrial capitalism, 2, 4–8, 14, 29, 45–6, 47, 52, 65, 157
and labour, 2, 4, 7, 24, 26, 28, 64, 65, 72, 143–4
laissez-faire capitalism, 18, 29
and masculinity, 1, 2, 5–6, 8, 14, 26, 43, 52, 64, 65, 83, 85
patriarchal capitalism, 1, 2, 3, 5, 11, 33–4, 43, 45–6, 85, 109
and power, 3, 4, 18, 45
in *Times Like These*, 7, 14, 18, 24, 25, 29, 33–4
welfare capitalism, 134
see also neoliberalism
carnival, 27, 84–5
Casanova, Pascale, 158
character, 7, 18–19
charisma, 10, 146, 147
childbirth, 66, 83
childhood experience, 57, 104, 123, 129, 132; *see also* boyhood
child-rearing, 1, 26
chronotopes, 10, 135–6
civilisation, 9, 37, 101, 112, 114–16, 160
Clare, Anthony, 140
closure, 34, 75, 76–8
collaboration, 14, 20–1, 26–7, 31, 42, 43
collective identity, 1, 2, 45, 53, 134, 142, 156
Collini, Stefan, 18, 30, 32
Collinson, David L., 16
colonialism, 7, 22, 68–9, 72, 73, 79, 86, 91, 95, 98, 158; *see also* Empire
comedy, 73, 76, 77–8, 84–5, 93–6
commodification, 45, 51, 71, 92, 124, 125
communality, 5, 7, 14, 20–1, 42, 87, 99, 134
competitiveness, 9, 30, 34, 43, 52, 104, 120
conformity, 4, 5, 43, 45–6, 52, 55, 58, 65, 106

Connell, R. W., 2–3, 48, 62, 95, 99, 109, 130, 159
conservatism, 11, 74–5, 77, 80–1, 87, 133
consumerism, 10, 124, 125, 128
courage, 5, 18, 64, 101
Courtney-Morgan, Steffan, 5–6
cowboys, 113–14, 115, 118
crime fiction *see* whodunnits
Crime Writers' Gold Dagger Award, 73
crisis of masculinity, 99
cross-dressing, 84
Crossing, The (Smith), 12
Cullen, Patrick, 25
cultural hybridity, 7–8, 35–6, 41
Cunningham, Valentine, 64, 67
Cwmardy (Jones)
  alienation, 45, 46, 53, 71
  and autobiography, 47–9
  autonomy, 8, 49–50, 57, 64, 72
  and *Bildungsroman*, 8, 11, 47, 49–51, 52, 55, 57, 72
  capitalism, 8, 45–6, 47, 49, 51–2, 64, 65, 72, 83
  compared with *Times Like These*, 6, 13, 43, 159
  conflicts between inner and outer self, 8, 34, 46–57, 64–72
  critical reception, 45
  economics, 45, 46, 47
  emotion, 45, 46, 48, 50, 51, 53, 56, 58, 62–3, 71, 159
  Empire, 46, 64, 68–71, 72, 83, 158
  gendered tropes, 58, 60–3
  generic hybridity, 47–50
  generic subversion, 8, 11, 52, 57–8, 72
  identity, 45, 46, 47, 49, 53, 64–5, 68–71
  imagination, 44, 46, 53, 56–7, 58–60
  inter-gender relations, 66–7, 122
  male body, 45, 55–6, 64, 69, 72
  narrative structure, 46–7
  narrative voice, 67
  patriarchy, 45–6, 62–3, 66–7, 71–2, 159

political activism, 8, 46, 50, 56
representations of masculinity, 8, 26, 34, 43, 44–72, 83, 95, 122, 134, 158, 159
rural life, 20, 44
self-realisation, 8, 46, 49–50, 57, 64, 66, 71
sensitivity, 48, 49, 51, 52, 56, 58, 68, 159
social class, 45, 46, 50, 54, 58, 64–5, 158
subjectivity, 51, 57–63
violence, 26, 67–8, 122

danger, 1, 55, 103, 117, 152–3
Dark Edge (Granelli)
 and *Bildungsroman*, 10, 121, 134–7, 154
 conflicts between inner and outer self, 34, 41
 consumerism, 124, 125, 128
 critical reception, 124, 128
 identity, 125–6, 134–7, 160
 individualism, 120, 122, 124–5, 128, 134, 142
 inter-gender relations, 21, 122, 123, 124, 126–8, 132, 158
 male body, 124–5, 127–8
 mining culture, 134, 142, 154
 narcissism, 10, 121, 122–8, 154
 nationhood, 134–7
 neoliberalism, 10, 120, 122, 123, 125, 128, 133, 134
 paired narratives, 10, 120–1, 133, 154
 patriarchy, 10, 120–8
 power, 17, 95, 120–8, 154
 representations of masculinity, 10, 17, 34, 41, 95, 120–8, 132–7, 142, 154, 158, 160
 and *roman à thèse*, 10, 124, 128, 132–3, 154
 self-realisation, 125, 134–7
 violence, 121, 122, 124, 126–8, 132
Davies, Emma, 63, 117
Davies, Idris, 80
Davies, James A., 6, 13, 21–2, 24, 34–5, 41, 136, 137

Davies, Rhys, 160
Dawson, Graham, 56
death, 9, 34, 46, 47, 52, 61, 66–8, 83, 90–1, 96–7, 103–5, 117–19, 133
decorum, 21, 24, 27–8, 31
deference, 27
Defoe, Daniel, 115–16
degradation, 7, 45
de-humanisation, 20, 25, 53
DeKoven, Marianne, 62–3
desire, 40, 48, 54, 56, 60
Devaney, Kevin, 55, 150, 152
Dickens, Charles, 93
Docker, John, 11
domestic labour, 1, 2, 131, 138
domestic space, 4, 26, 65–7, 77, 81–2, 90, 92, 93, 99, 125, 127–8, 129, 130, 157
domestic violence, 122, 124, 127–8, 131, 132, 139–40
dominant cultural processes, 7, 14, 34, 42, 159
dominant masculinity, 7, 14–19, 25, 42, 43, 72, 79–80, 81–2, 83, 159
Donoghue, Steve, 109
'Down the Mine' (Orwell), 45, 58, 156
Dream On (Smith), 11, 12
dreams, 61–2
drinking, 31, 67–8, 71, 102; *see also* pubs
duty, 18, 19, 50

Easthope, Anthony, 23
economics, 5–6, 16–17, 25, 45–7, 99, 125, 132, 143–4; *see also* capitalism
efficiency, 143, 146, 148
emergent cultural processes, 7, 14, 42, 159
emergent masculinity, 7, 14–15, 34–41, 42, 159
emotion, 6, 31, 33, 45–8, 50–1, 53, 56, 58, 62–3, 71, 82, 92, 131, 138, 140–2, 159
empathy, 46, 71, 83, 130, 132
Empire, 46, 64, 68–71, 72, 80, 83, 93, 95, 158; *see also* colonialism

entitlement, 122, 126, 129–30
Ettin, Andrew V., 20
Evans, Richard John, 124
exclusion, 1, 2, 91, 104
exploitation, 5, 42, 45, 70, 103, 158

Fairclough, Norman, 39, 143, 145
family, 5, 26, 36, 47, 81, 88–93, 97, 102, 104, 120, 129–32, 137–42, 157
fantasy, 56, 125–6, 158
fascism, 17, 79, 95
Faulkner, William, 100, 158
fear, 17–18, 36, 38, 40, 56, 62, 83–4, 115, 117, 123, 127, 151
female body, 60–2
Female Eunuch, The (Greer), 9, 80–1
feminisation, 4, 31, 60–3, 74, 82–5, 89–92, 149, 150, 160
feminism, 1, 9, 79, 80–1, 99, 158, 160
festivities, 21, 22, 84–5
fighting, 32, 46, 67–8; *see also* boxing; violence
First World War, 30
folk heroes, 64
Forth Christopher E., 101, 104, 109, 110, 112, 127
fragmentation, 9, 41, 47, 51
Francis, Hywel, 48
Freud, Sigmund, 60, 92, 117, 127, 130
Fromm, Erich, 40

Gallie, Menna, 8–9, 79–81; *see also Strike for a Kingdom*
gender definition, 5, 10, 45, 61, 63, 67, 86, 101, 122, 142–3
gender differentiation, 1, 3–4, 73, 75, 85, 106
gender fluidity, 84–5, 88
gender identification, 10, 56
gender roles, 1, 8, 66, 84, 123, 131, 137–41, 148–50
gendered spaces, 1, 4, 5, 26, 48, 65–70, 77, 81–2
gendered tropes, 58, 60–3
generic hybridity, 11, 47–50, 154

generic subversion, 8–9, 11, 52, 57–8, 72, 74–9, 87, 97–8, 160
gentlemanliness, 7, 15, 30–3, 36, 40
Georgian values, 18, 20, 30–2, 37, 40, 42–3
Germinal (Zola), 8, 49–50, 57
Giddens, Anthony, 37, 38, 122, 123, 130, 137–8, 139
Gifford, Terry, 22, 23
Gill, Rosalind, 138, 154
Glover, David, 82, 83
Grahame, Kenneth, 94
Gramich, Katie, 7, 13, 29, 61, 73, 153, 159
Gramsci, Antonio, 2–3, 5, 46, 133
Granelli, Roger, 10; *see also Dark Edge*
Greb, Harry, 107
greed, 18–19
Green Hollow, The (Sheers), 11–12
Greenblatt, Stephen, 63–4, 70
Greer, Germaine, 9, 80–1
Griffiths, Billy, 48
Griffiths, Niall, 100
Gutterman, David S., 86
Gwalia Deserta (Davies), 80
gwerin culture, 5

Habianic, Kit, 10, 129; *see also Until Our Blood is Dry*
hairdressing, 10, 121, 148–9, 154, 155
Hall, Alexandra, 149
Hardy, Oliver, 94
Harris, Ian M., 148, 152
Hearn, Jeff, 16
hegemonic masculinity, 3–4, 29–30, 50, 67–71, 74, 83, 92, 101, 109, 111, 115, 130, 143–6, 152, 157, 159; *see also* normative masculinity
hegemony, 2–4, 14, 16, 17–18, 25, 32, 42, 123, 127, 133, 160
Hemingway, Ernest, 108
heroism, 2, 53, 58, 64, 68, 74, 83, 101, 103–9, 112, 129, 148, 156, 160
heterosexuality, 60, 69, 79–80, 148, 150, 151–3

Index

hierarchical power systems, 2–4, 14, 19, 32, 70, 73–4, 85, 86, 94–6, 157
history, 11–12, 47, 49, 94, 135–6, 137, 157
Hockey, Jenny, 149
Holloway, Wendy, 147
*hombre*s, 70, 124
home, 4, 26, 32, 65–7, 71, 90, 92, 93, 99, 115, 125, 127–8, 129, 130, 157
homogeneity, 1, 2, 45, 142, 156
homosexuality, 10, 121–2, 148–55
homosociality, 5, 14, 20–1, 23–8, 55–6, 150
Hopkins, Chris, 20
Horne, John, 96
How Green Was My Valley (Llewellyn), 20
Howell, David, 146
hubris, 103–4, 110
humanism, 8, 45–6, 48, 55, 72
humiliation, 7, 17–18, 55, 126–7, 144
hunting, 54–5, 113, 115–18
hybrid identities, 7–8, 35–6, 41, 95, 134, 136, 137, 158
hyper-masculinity, 93, 99, 101, 103, 109, 112, 116, 118–19, 122
hypertrophy, 9, 101, 125

identity
  and capitalism, 6, 8, 45–6, 47, 49, 51, 65, 85, 124–5, 130, 157
  collective identity, 1, 2, 45, 53, 134, 142, 156
  crises of, 154
  in *Cwmardy*, 45–7, 49, 53, 64–5, 68–71, 158
  in *Dark Edge*, 125–6, 134–7, 160
  gendered identities, 3, 4, 16, 84, 85, 89, 157
  hybrid identities, 7–8, 35–6, 41, 95, 134, 136, 137, 158
  and labour, 10, 26, 46
  national identity, 11, 135–7
  in *Strike for a Kingdom*, 92, 95, 158
  in *Times Like These*, 7–8, 15, 16, 26–7, 33, 35–41, 42–3, 136, 159

  in *Until Our Blood is Dry*, 142–4, 154, 160
Idylls (Theocritus), 26, 28
illegitimacy, 47, 104
imagination, 44, 46, 53, 56–7, 58–60
imperialism *see* colonialism; Empire
incest, 82, 97
individualism, 120, 122, 124–5, 128, 134, 142
indolence, 25–6
industrial fiction, 6, 8, 10, 11, 13, 29, 41, 121, 137, 148, 158, 159
industrial relations, 3, 4, 10, 17, 31, 42, 96, 120, 129; *see also* strikes
instinct, 9, 114, 116–17
instrumental rationality, 143–5, 147–8
intellect, 9, 27, 114, 116–17, 133–4, 142
inter-gender relations
  in *Cwmardy*, 66–7, 122
  in *Dark Edge*, 21, 122, 123, 124, 126–8, 132, 158
  in *So Long, Hector Bebb*, 9–10, 9, 102, 110–12
  in *Strike for a Kingdom*, 21, 77–8, 81–2, 122, 137, 158
  in *Times Like These*, 21, 26, 33, 38–40, 122, 137
  in *Until Our Blood is Dry*, 21, 120–3, 130–2, 137–42, 150, 152, 158
  see also adultery; intimacy; marriage; sexuality
intergenerational relations, 26–7
internalisation, 4, 5, 51, 68
intimacy, 6, 33, 66, 90, 112, 131, 139, 141–2
isolation, 9, 80, 86, 103, 123

Jarrett, Nigel, 11
John, Angela V., 73, 82
Jones, Gareth, 101
Jones, Glyn, 6
Jones, Gwyn, 6–8, 13, 15, 29–30, 36, 159; *see also* Richard Savage; *Times Like These*
Jones, John Sam, 148

Jones, Lewis, 6, 8, 13, 47–9, 58, 67, 72; *see also Cwmardy*; 'Pit Cage, The'; *We Live*
Jones, Liz, 123, 129
journalism, 12, 143, 144, 146–7
juvenalisation, 74, 76, 86–8, 160
juxtaposition, 7, 20, 24, 25, 32–3, 40, 54

Kaplan, Cora, 82, 83
Keats, John, 78, 135
Kimmel, Michael, 20, 92, 150
Knight, Stephen, 6, 13, 22, 29, 35, 47, 64, 73, 74, 86, 97, 159
Knights, Ben, 33, 56, 60

labour
  and alienation, 28, 45
  and capitalism, 2, 4, 7, 24, 26, 28, 64, 72, 143–4
  dangerous labour, 1, 55
  domestic labour, 1, 2, 131, 138
  and exploitation, 42, 45, 70, 103, 158
  and gender definition, 10, 122, 148–52, 155
  and identity, 10, 26, 46
  and management, 10, 14, 15–20, 29, 34, 121, 130, 142–8, 154–5
  mechanisation of, 28, 45, 71
  physical labour, 1, 20, 27
  as site of masculinity, 5, 53–4, 57, 85–6, 150, 151–3
  unemployment, 33, 74, 99, 160
  see also industrial relations; mining; strikes; trade unions
Lacan, Jacques, 54, 56, 132
laissez-faire capitalism, 18, 29
landscape, 10, 20, 25–6, 44, 57, 115–16, 134, 135–6
Lasch, Christopher, 121, 126, 144
Laurel, Stan, 94
Leeworthy, Daryl, 100, 103
leisure, 25, 26, 32, 71
Lentricchia, Frank, 90, 145
Leverenz, David, 17
lisible reading, 75, 76, 93
Llewellyn, Richard, 20

McHill, Michael E., 66
Macherey, Pierre, 15, 41, 46–7, 65, 88, 137, 144, 151–2, 159
machismo, 1, 5, 43, 67–8, 126, 142, 144, 150
MacInnes, John, 155
McMylor, Peter, 120
magnanimity, 32–3, 34
Malamud, Bernard, 107
male body, 5, 8, 23–5, 27, 45, 55–6, 64, 69, 72, 100–2, 106, 109–10, 124–5, 127–8, 156–7
male-voice choirs, 1, 2, 77, 156
management, 10, 14, 15–20, 29, 34, 121, 130, 142–8, 154–5
manual dexterity, 20, 26, 27, 64, 101
Marinelli, Peter V., 21, 23
market economy, 16, 125, 143, 144
marriage, 10, 26, 33, 66, 75, 77–8, 81–2, 99, 102, 111–12, 120–4, 127–8, 130–2, 137–42, 150; *see also* inter-gender relations
Marvell, Andrew, 22
Marx, Karl, 77
Marxism, 2–3, 8, 28, 76
masculinisation, 4, 61, 118, 152
masochism, 17–18
matriarchy, 88, 89–92
mechanisation, 28, 45, 71
'men of character', 7, 18–19
Meredith, Christopher, 11, 137
Merriman, Catherine, 128
metaphor, 59, 106, 133
Meyn, Rolf, 47, 49, 57
Middleton, Peter, 51–2, 56, 59, 67, 132, 141
migration, 153, 158
military service, 46, 55–6, 64, 68–71; *see also* soldiers; warfare
Milton, John, 22, 26
Miners at the Quarry Pool (Jarrett), 11
miners' strike (1984–5), 10, 96, 120–55, 160
mining
  Aberfan disaster, 11–12
  decline and disappearance of, 10, 99, 160

and heroism, 2, 45, 53, 58, 64, 74, 148
mechanisation of, 28, 45, 71
mining culture, 4, 8–9, 134, 142, 150, 151–4
physical and dangerous nature of, 1, 55, 152–3
as site of masculinity, 53–4, 57, 64, 82, 150, 151–3, 156
strikes, 4, 8, 10, 15, 17–18, 26, 73, 74, 79, 96, 120–55, 160
see also labour
Monbiot, George, 123, 124
Monmouthshire, 7, 36
Moore, Dylan, 131, 133
Morse, Sarah, 103, 111
Mortimer, John, 37–8
mountains, 44, 50, 54, 57, 59, 60–2, 70
myth, 9, 22, 23, 24, 102, 103–9, 112, 113, 115, 119, 156, 158, 160
mythic realism, 104, 112

narcissism, 10, 95, 121, 122–32, 138, 143, 144, 154
narrative structures, 9, 46–7, 100, 120–1, 133, 154
narrative voices, 9, 24, 38, 40, 67, 75, 77, 84–9, 91, 100, 137, 151, 158
nationhood, 16–17, 134–7, 142
Natural, The (Malamud), 107
neoliberalism, 10, 120, 122, 123, 125, 128, 133, 134, 142–8
'new men', 121, 138, 140
normative masculinity, 2, 6, 49, 52–8, 82–4, 89, 92–3, 121, 134, 150; *see also* hegemonic masculinity
nostalgia, 30, 65, 136
nurturing, 4, 6, 67, 82–3, 84

Oates, Joyce Carol, 103, 106, 111
Orwell, George, 45, 58, 156
otherness, 46, 68–9, 79–80, 85, 91, 92, 96, 101, 112, 115, 160
Oxford Companion to the Literature of Wales, 42

pain, 67–8, 109–10
paired narratives, 10, 120–1, 133, 154
Paradise Postponed (Mortimer), 37–8
parody, 41, 76, 84
passivity, 6, 9, 46, 49–50, 51, 54, 60, 82, 83, 89
pastoral, 7, 14, 20–26, 28–9, 42–3, 112, 158; *see also* rural life
patriarchy
in *Cwmardy*, 45–6, 62–3, 66–7, 71–2, 159
in *Dark Edge*, 10, 120–8
patriarchal capitalism, 1, 2, 3, 5, 11, 33–4, 43, 45–6, 85, 109
and politics, 3, 120–5, 128, 143–8, 154–5
and power, 1, 2–4, 16–19, 29, 73, 78, 81–2, 83–4, 97, 120–32, 150, 157
in *So Long, Hector Bebb*, 99, 103, 106, 109
in *Strike for a Kingdom*, 8, 73, 75–6, 78, 79, 81–5, 88, 92–3, 97, 137
in *Times Like These*, 7, 14–21, 26, 29, 33–4, 41, 42–3
in *Until Our Blood is Dry*, 10, 120–3, 129–33, 148–9, 150
performativity, 4, 7, 20, 32, 37–41, 48, 54, 84–5, 135, 146, 150, 152, 159
physical labour, 1, 20, 27
physical strength, 1, 5, 26, 27, 52, 64, 110, 117, 156
Pikoulis, John, 48, 49, 51, 52, 100
'Pit Cage, The' (Jones), 72
Plain, Gill, 73, 75, 77, 88, 93, 94
poetry, 22–3, 29, 77, 78, 90, 92, 135
police, 10, 17, 70, 73–4, 76, 83–4, 91–7, 120, 122–4, 126–8, 146, 154
politeness, 14, 15, 17, 30–4, 36–7, 101
political activism, 8, 46, 50, 56, 146, 158
political discourse, 19, 143–8, 154–5
Poole, Ross, 143, 144, 147–8

Pope, Alexander, 29
Porter, Dennis, 77
post-industrial decline, 1, 10, 11, 99, 136
postmodernism, 11
power
  and colonialism, 68–9, 73, 79, 86
  in *Dark Edge*, 17, 95, 120–8, 154
  and discourse, 19, 143–8, 154–5
  and gendered identities, 3, 4
  hierarchical systems of, 2–4, 14, 19, 32, 70, 73–4, 85, 86, 94–6, 157
  institutional power, 93, 94–7, 124, 126, 127
  and knowledge, 154, 157
  and masculinity, 1, 3–4, 6, 10, 14, 16–19, 32, 54–5, 74, 80, 120–32, 143–8, 150, 154, 157
  and narcissism, 10, 121, 122–32, 143, 144, 154
  and patriarchy, 1, 2–4, 16–19, 29, 73, 78, 81–2, 83–4, 97, 120–32, 150, 157
  and politics, 120–5, 128, 143–8, 154–5
  power struggles, 10, 120–2, 130
  powerlessness, 76, 86, 129, 130, 131
  in *Strike for a Kingdom*, 73–4, 78, 81–2, 83–4, 93, 94–7
  in *Times Like These*, 14, 16–19, 29, 32, 95
  in *Until Our Blood is Dry*, 95, 120–3, 129–32, 143–8, 150, 154–5
  and violence, 3, 94, 95–6, 122, 124, 126–8, 131–2
pragmatism, 16, 17, 105, 106, 119
predation, 18, 110, 111, 113
primitiveness, 9, 101, 112, 114–16, 160
public space, 1, 5, 26, 48, 65, 67–70, 127, 129, 134
pubs, 46, 67, 71, 77, 82, 105; *see also* drinking

Raglan, Fitzroy, 104, 105
rationality, 3, 18, 48, 52, 59, 62, 143–5, 147–8
'real men', 1, 156
realism, 10, 58, 102, 104, 108, 124, 128, 129, 158
Reeser, Todd W., 88
religion, 19, 21, 81
religious iconography, 105–6
residual cultural processes, 7, 14, 28–9, 30, 33, 34, 42, 106, 159
residual masculinity, 7, 14, 20–34, 42–3, 159
respect, 10, 24, 28, 29, 105, 121, 138
Richard Savage (Jones), 29–30
Richards, Alun, 160
Rimmon-Kenan, Shlomith, 101
rites of passage, 79, 85–6, 87, 88, 89, 93, 97
ritual, 7, 27, 88, 103
Robinson, Victoria, 149
Robinson Crusoe (Defoe), 115–16
roman à clef, 47
roman à thèse, 10, 58, 124, 128, 132–3, 154
romantic fiction, 76
Rowland, Susan, 83
Rubin, Gayle, 8, 85, 89
rugby, 1, 2, 21, 27, 30, 38, 156
rural life, 5, 11, 20, 44; *see also* pastoral
Rutherford, Jonathan, 87, 125

sadism, 17–18, 111–12, 128, 144
Savage, Richard, 29–30
Scaggs, John, 75, 76
Schoene-Harwood, Berthold, 19, 55, 152
scriptible reading, 75, 90, 94
Segal, Lynne, 99, 122, 139, 149
self-improvement, 30, 35–8, 40, 102
self-knowledge, 49–50, 57
self-made men, 35–40
self-realisation, 8, 46, 49–50, 57, 64, 66, 71, 109, 115, 125, 134–7, 144

Index

sensitivity, 48, 49, 51, 52, 56, 58, 68, 91, 138, 159
sentiment, 18, 30–1, 33, 37, 117; *see also* emotion
sexuality, 33, 51, 55, 60, 63, 69, 81, 92, 110–12, 117
shadow masculinity, 7, 41
Shakespeare, William, 92, 94
Shaw, Katy, 11
Sheers, Owen, 11–12
Shifts (Meredith), 11, 137
Smith, Dai, 11, 12, 13, 100, 113, 159
Smith, David, 64, 72
Smith, Emma, 50, 116
Snee, Carole, 44, 46, 58, 64
So Long, Hector Bebb (Berry)
 civilisation, 9, 101, 112, 114–15, 160
 cowboys, 113–14, 115, 118
 critical reception, 100
 draft versions, 9, 100, 102, 105–6, 108
 heroism, 101, 103–9, 112, 160
 hyper masculinity, 99, 101, 103, 109, 112, 116, 118–19
 inter-gender relations, 9–10, 9, 102, 110–12
 male body, 100, 101–2, 106, 109–10
 myth, 9, 102, 103–9, 112, 113, 115, 119, 158, 160
 narrative fragmentation, 9, 100
 narrative voices, 100, 158
 patriarchy, 99, 103, 106, 109
 primitiveness, 9, 101, 112, 114–15, 160
 re-issue of, 100
 representations of masculinity, 9–10, 99–119, 158, 160
 as response to feminism, 9, 99
 tragedy, 9, 102, 103, 110, 112, 118, 119
 violence, 99, 101–2, 105, 106–7, 109, 116–18
 wild men, 9, 113, 114–18

sociability, 31–2
social class, 7–8, 15, 30, 33, 35–9, 45, 46, 50, 54, 58, 64–5, 73–6, 91, 156, 158
social Darwinism, 18–19
social realism, 102, 129, 158
socialism, 9, 146
soldiers, 1, 46, 64, 68–71, 96, 106; *see also* military service; warfare; warrior culture
solitude, 54, 56, 66, 80, 112–13, 136
South Africa, 68–9
Spencer, Herbert, 18–19
sporting fiction, 9, 11, 100, 107–8, 158
Srivastva, Suresh, 59
steel industry, 11
stereotypes, 64, 77, 78, 80, 85, 89, 149
strength *see* physical strength
Strike for a Kingdom (Gallie)
 adultery, 81, 92, 122
 adulthood, 79, 85–8, 89, 92, 93, 97
 boyhood, 85–8, 97
 colonisation, 73, 79, 86, 91, 95, 98, 158
 comedy, 73, 76, 77–8, 84–5, 93–6
 conflicts between inner and outer self, 34, 92–3
 critical reception, 73, 97
 family, 81, 88–93, 97
 feminisation, 74, 82–5, 89–92, 160
 gender fluidity, 84–5, 88
 generic subversion, 8–9, 11, 74–9, 87, 97–8, 160
 identity, 2, 95, 158
 inter-gender relations, 21, 77–8, 81–2, 122, 137, 158
 juvenalisation, 74, 76, 86–8, 160
 narrative voice, 9, 75, 77, 84–9, 91
 nationhood, 17
 patriarchy, 8, 73, 75–6, 78, 79, 81–5, 88, 92–3, 97, 137
 power, 73–4, 78, 81–2, 83–4, 93, 94–7
 representations of masculinity, 8–9, 17, 34, 73–98, 122, 134, 137, 158, 159–60

runner-up for Crime Writers' Gold
  Dagger Award, 73
shared characteristics of men,
  women and children, 8, 82–8, 97
social class, 73, 74–6, 91
violence, 83, 94, 95–6
as a whodunnit, 8–9, 11, 73–9,
  93–8, 160
strikes, 4, 8, 10, 15, 17–18, 26, 73,
  74, 79, 96, 120–55, 160
subalternity, 80, 86, 130, 155
subjectivity, 4, 51, 57–63, 132, 136,
  151
subordination, 4, 35, 66, 69, 71, 80,
  130, 143, 157
Suleiman, Susan Rubin, 49, 50–1, 57,
  124, 128
Symons, Julian, 74
sympathy, 74, 83

Tarzan, 115, 116, 117, 118
Thatcher, Margaret, 120, 125, 128
Theocritus, 26, 28
Thomas, D. A., 12
Thomas, Gwyn, 160
Thomas, M. Wynn, 5, 11, 94, 136,
  148, 153, 159
Thomas, Ned, 154
Thomas, R. S., 45
Thomson, James, 29
Threadgold, Terry, 148, 153
Times Like These (Jones)
  ambition, 7, 14, 31, 34–8
  business, 7, 14–15, 32, 34–8, 42
  capitalism, 7, 14, 18, 24, 25, 29,
    33–4
  collaboration, 14, 20–1, 26–7, 31,
    42, 43
  communality, 7, 14, 20–1, 42
  compared with *Cwmardy*, 6, 13,
    43, 159
  conflicts between inner and outer
    self, 34, 37–41
  critical reception, 6, 13–14, 21–2,
    41–2, 159
  dominant masculinity, 7, 14–19,
    25, 42, 43, 159
  economics, 16–17, 25

  emergent masculinity, 7, 14–15,
    34–41, 42, 159
  homosociality, 14, 20–1, 23–8
  identity, 7–8, 15, 16, 26–7, 33,
    35–41, 42–3, 136
  inter-gender relations, 21, 26, 33,
    38–40, 122, 137
  intergenerational relations, 26–7
  juxtapositions, 7, 20, 24, 25, 32–3,
    40
  male body, 23–5, 27
  narrative voice, 24, 38, 40
  nationhood, 16–17, 136
  pastoral, 7, 14, 20–6, 28–9, 42–3,
    158
  patriarchy, 7, 14–21, 26, 29, 33–4,
    41, 42–3
  politeness, 14, 15, 17, 30–4, 36–7
  power, 14, 16–19, 29, 32, 95
  representations of masculinity,
    6–8, 13–43, 95, 122, 137,
    140–1, 158, 159
  residual masculinity, 7, 14, 20–34,
    42–3, 159
  social class, 7–8, 15, 30, 33, 35–9,
    158
Times Literary Supplement, 97,
  100
Tolson, Andrew, 52, 122
Tompkins, Jane, 44–5, 70, 114, 115
Tonypandy, 96
Tosh, John, 5, 68, 69
trade unions, 18, 47, 74, 133, 134–5,
  146, 147
tragedy, 9, 102, 103, 110, 112, 118,
  119, 129, 132, 158–9
trauma, 11, 46, 53, 56, 136, 137

unemployment, 33, 74, 99, 160
Until Our Blood is Dry (Habianic)
  critical reception, 131, 133
  family, 120, 129–32, 137–42
  homosexuality, 10, 121–2, 148–55
  gender roles, 131, 137–41, 148–50
  identity, 142–4, 154, 160
  individualism, 120, 122
  inter-gender relations, 21, 120–3,
    130–2, 137–42, 150, 152, 158

Index

management, 10, 121, 130, 142–8, 154–5
mining culture, 150, 151–4
narcissism, 10, 121, 122–3, 129–32, 143, 144, 154
narrative voice, 137, 151
nationhood, 17, 142
neoliberalism, 10, 120, 122, 142, 143–8
paired narratives, 10, 120–1, 133, 154
patriarchy, 10, 120–3, 129–33, 148–9, 150
power, 95, 120–3, 129–32, 143–8, 150, 154–5
representations of masculinity, 10, 17, 95, 120–3, 129–33, 137–55, 158–9, 160
tragedy, 129, 132, 158–9
violence, 96, 121, 122, 131–2, 138–9, 145

Victorian values, 7, 18–19, 30–1
violence
  in *Cwmardy*, 26, 67–8, 122
  in *Dark Edge*, 121, 122, 124, 126–8, 132
  domestic violence, 122, 124, 127–8, 131, 132, 139–40
  and industrial relations, 3, 17, 26, 31, 83, 94, 95–6, 124, 127–8, 145
  lawful and unlawful violence, 101–2
  and masculinity, 55, 67–8, 83, 99, 101–2, 106–7, 109, 116–18, 121–2, 124, 126–8, 131–2
  police violence, 83, 94, 95–6, 124, 127–8
  and power, 3, 94, 95–6, 122, 124, 126–8, 131–2
  in *So Long, Hector Bebb*, 99, 101–2, 105, 106–7, 109, 116–18
  in *Strike for a Kingdom*, 83, 94, 95–6
  in *Until Our Blood is Dry*, 96, 121, 122, 131–2, 138–9, 145
  warrior culture, 104, 106–7, 109
  see also brutality; fighting; warfare

Walsh, Louise, 12
warfare, 17, 64, 68–71, 101, 106; *see also* military service; soldiers
warrior culture, 104, 106–7, 109
water, 23–4, 60, 62–3
Watt, Ian, 103
We Live (Jones), 8, 47
welfare capitalism, 134
Welsh Boys Too (Jones), 148
Welsh language, 11, 80, 93, 136
Whitehead, Stephen, 2, 3–4, 130, 137, 140
whodunnits, 8–9, 11, 73–9, 93–8, 160
wild men, 9, 113, 114–18
wilderness, 112–14
Williams, Daniel G., 100
Williams, Raymond, 6–7, 14, 34, 35, 39, 42, 45, 129, 145, 159
Wills, Harry, 107
work *see* labour

Yallop, Helen, 29–30
Yamamoto, Dorothy, 101, 114, 115

Zola, Émile, 8, 49–50, 57